Cricket and Race

'I have always been more than a little suspicious of those who have attempted over issues like the infamous Basil D'Oliveira affair in 1970, to disguise the link between cricket, politics and race. Jack Williams' book should put an end to this hypocritical nonsense once and for all. The author reminds us that Lord Rosebery made the connection very early on in his observations about the Empire and that cricketers from Duleepsinhji to Constantine to Worrell were aware of it.

Reading again the account of how the 1970 South African tour was forcibly cancelled and the entirely bogus, though in a few exceptional cases, well-intentioned views of those who supported the tour, reminded me of how far we have come. This book is brilliantly researched and must be read by all who really love the game.'
Sir Trevor McDonald OBE

'Very little has been published on cricket and racism . . . this book is a brave and intelligent attempt to fill the gap . . . An eye-opening treatise that deserves to be in every cricket library . . . I am glad that I read it.'
Christopher Ondaatje, *Times Higher Education Supplement*

'Jack Williams writes from within the world of cricket and cricketers, and from a deep commitment to racial justice. His research has been exhaustive. He quotes fairly those with whom he disagrees. I welcome the challenge that *Cricket and Race* presents to all of us to question racist attitudes that we may still harbour at every level from Club Cricket to Test Cricket.'
David Sheppard, Rt Rev Lord Sheppard of Liverpool

Cricket and Race

Jack Williams

BERG

Oxford • New York

First published in 2001 by
Berg
Editorial offices:
150 Cowley Road, Oxford, OX4 1JJ, UK
838 Broadway, Third Floor, New York, NY 10003-4812, USA

Berg is an imprint of Oxford International Publishers Ltd.

Library of Congress Cataloging-in-Publication Data
A catalogue record for this book is available from the Library of Congress.

British Library Cataloguing-in-Publication Data
A catalogue record for this book is available from the British Library.

ISBN 1 85973 304 2 (Cloth)
1 85973 309 3 (Paper)

Typeset by JS Typesetting, Wellingborough, Northants.
Printed in the United Kingdom by Biddles Ltd, Guildford and King's Lynn.

Contents

Acknowledgements

I wish to thank the many people without whose help this book could not have been written. Roger Knight allowed me to consult the minutes of the MCC Committee and Janet Fisher of the ECB granted me access to a wide range of materials that the ECB has inherited from the Cricket Council. I am grateful to the staffs of so many libraries but must mention in particular Stephen Green and Glenys Williams who were always most welcoming and helpful when I was researching at Lord's. Very special thanks are due to Don Ambrose who let me borrow so many items from his wonderful collection of cricket books and also for pointing out to me matters that would otherwise have escaped my attention. The Inter-library Loans Unit of the John Moores University acquired materials from the most unlikely sources. The Reverend Malcolm Lorimer let me use the library of Lancashire CCC and I learned much from talking to him about his encounters with racism during his ministry in Moss Side. I owe much to those whom I interviewed and as some of them made comments that could offend others, I have felt it better not always to name them. My biggest debt all is to my wife Pat for her unfailing encouragement and patience. I must emphasize that those who have helped me are not responsible for the argument and conclusions of the book. These are entirely my responsibility.

List of Abbreviations

ADA	Anti-Demonstration Association
ANC	African National Congress
CCC	County Cricket Club
ECB	England and Wales Cricket Board
FIFA	Fédération Internationale de Football Association
ICC	From 1909 to 1965 Imperial Cricket Conference; from 1965 to 1989 International Cricket Conference; from 1989 International Cricket Council
IOC	International Olympic Committee
MCC	Marylebone Cricket Club
SAACB	South African African Cricket Board
SACA	South African Cricket Association
SACB	South African Cricket Board
SACBOC	South African Cricket Board of Control
SACOS	South African Council on Sport
SACU	South African Cricket Union
SANROC	South African Non-racial Olympic Committee
SASA	South African Sports Association
STST	Stop the Seventy Tour
TCCB	Test and County Cricket Board
UCBSA	United Cricket Board of South Africa

Introduction

Race was at the heart of cricket throughout the twentieth century. In the late Victorian period and for at least the first half of the twentieth century, cricket was taken to encapsulate the essence of England and had a key role in how the English, particularly the economically privileged, imagined their national identity, but this was very much a white identity. Cricket was intertwined with the Empire. Test cricket was played only between England and colonies or former colonies. As cricket was believed to express a distinctively English morality and as apologists for the Empire stressed the moral obligation to extend the benefits of British rule, the nature of cricket as an imperial game meant that cricket and imperialism became mutually supporting ideologies. But the Empire was also based on assumptions of white supremacy. The Liberal Prime Minister Lord Rosebery, an enthusiast for empire, asked 'What *is* Empire but the predominance of race?'[1] The associations of cricket with the Empire meant that it was helping to sustain a racist political system.

In the last third of the twentieth century, cricket became embroiled in the tensions surrounding Britain's adjustment to the retreat from empire, which have coincided with the strains of becoming part of the European Union and economic dislocation stemming from the erosion of Britain's manufacturing base. As a major sport of white South Africans, cricket was intimately involved in debates about how far an international sporting boycott should have been used to overturn the racism of apartheid. Migration to Britain from the Caribbean, India and Pakistan and the emergence of immigration as a subject of political controversy meant test matches in England became opportunities for racist abuse from whites but also opportunities for African-Caribbeans and Asians to express their distinctive cultural identities. Racism figured in criticisms of West Indian fast bowling in test cricket and in accusations that Pakistani teams were habitual cheats. From the 1970s recreational cricket was the one sport played extensively by males from the three major ethnic groups in England – Asians, African-Caribbeans and whites – and whilst there were instances of racial prejudice in recreational cricket, club cricket also had the potential to promote ethnic contact and understanding.

1. Malik, K. (1996), *The Meaning of Race: Race, History and Culture in Western Society,* London: Macmillan, p. 115.

This book explores racism in cricket in England. It considers the forms and intensity of racism in cricket and assesses how far cricket has encouraged ethnic tolerance and co-operation. It does not contend that examining racism in cricket is the key to unlocking the complexities of ethnic relations in twentieth-century England. Inequalities in income, employment, housing, education and the criminal justice system may be more important barometers of ethnic relations, but it is being argued that given the depth of interest in cricket among those of African-Caribbean and South Asian descent, a study of cricket and racism can add a valuable dimension to understanding of the social and cultural context surrounding racial assumptions in England. Responses to the selection of players of African-Caribbean and Asian descent for England are relevant to debates about the inclusive and exclusive nature of English national identity in the last quarter of the twentieth century and about how far Englishness is still seen as a white identity. An appraisal of ethnic relations in cricket can reveal much about the capacity of sports in general to weaken ethnic prejudices and help to evaluate whether contemporary England, a multi-cultural society, is or has realistic possibilities of becoming, one characterized by ethnic tolerance and harmony. It can also register how far leisure interests have led to the cultural assimilation of those with ancestral roots in the Caribbean and South Asia.

This book concentrates on the twentieth century, although the chapter that looks at the period before the First World War includes material from the 1880s and 1890s. One reason for looking at the whole century is that ethnic identities are now seen to be historically derived. The images people have of themselves are created from narratives about their histories, about how they have seen themselves and others in the past. A further justification for looking at all of the twentieth century is that the social and political pressures surrounding racialized identities in Britain during the last third of the twentieth century can be seen as a result of imperialism, a socio-political phenomenon that reached its climax in the late nineteenth and early twentieth centuries. Britain's multi-ethnic population is very largely a result of imperialism: 'they are here because we were there'. The ethnic tensions of the late twentieth-century Britain are part of the imperial legacy, made more intense by the difficulties that many whites have in adjusting to Britain's decline as a world power. At the beginning of the twentieth century Britain had the world's largest empire. By the end of the twentieth century Britain was no longer an economic or political superpower but merely another member of the European Union.

Race and Racism

In the nineteenth and early twentieth centuries, most whites in the Western world seem to have accepted race as a scientific fact. It was believed that on the basis of skin pigmentation in particular, but also other physical characteristics such as the shape of the cranium and facial features, humanity could be divided into distinct groups or races. Crude applications of Darwin's theories of natural selection, technological achievement and the study of social institutions buttressed beliefs that physical characteristics, and especially skin colour, were measurable and signified differences in mental abilities from which races could be placed in an hierarchy reflecting innate and largely unchanging intellectual capacity and attainment. Invariably it was those with white skins who were regarded as the superior race and placed at the top of a typology of races. The darker the skin pigmentation, the more primitive and naturally inferior a race was considered to be. There was scientific debate about polygenesis, about whether different human races had evolved from separate species.

In the 1990s differing levels of achievement in certain areas of social activity between populations with origins in different parts of the world have been attributed to differences in genetic endowment. *Taboo: Why Black Athletes Dominate Sports and Why We Are Afraid to Talk about It* by Entine,[2] for instance, has argued that the success of black athletes in sprint races can be explained by genetic factors that give them a natural advantage over other populations in such events. Most biologists and anthropologists, however, appear to have discarded race as a scientific concept. To emphasize that the term has no scientific basis some insist on placing quotation marks around the word race. Whilst skin pigmentation and facial features differ between those originating in different parts of the world, it is now recognized that these may vary immensely even between siblings and cannot be measured with precision.

Social analysts have also helped to challenge the scientific status of race. The notion of race has always been part of the wider issue of identity, of how one group defines itself by how it imagines it differs from others.[3] Among social scientists the issue of identity has come to focus on identity as a form of social consciousness. Woodward has argued that identities are 'produced, consumed and regulated within culture – creating meanings through symbolic systems of representation about the identity positions which we might adopt.'[4] The impact of postmodernism and poststructuralism on the study of identity as the product of discursive processes has been accompanied by a recognition that identities are not essentialist or fixed and unchanging, but are fluid and contingent, changing as the historical pressures and cultural assumptions that shape them change. Identities have also come to seen as multi-layered, with individuals subscribing to a range of identities and feeling certain identities more strongly in some social situations than in others. The rise of

2. Entine, J. (1999), *Taboo: Why Black Athletes Dominate Sports and Why We Are Afraid to Talk about It*, New York: Public Affairs.

3. For summaries of historical and recent contributions to debates about the nature of race and racism, see Bulmer, M. and Solomos, J. (eds) (1999), *Racism*, Oxford: Oxford University Press.

4. Woodward, K. (ed.) (1997), *Identity and Difference*, London: Sage, p. 2.

feminism has emphasized how the social experience and social consciousness of the two sexes from the same ethnic group can differ so much. The variability and contingency of identity have undermined confidence in the concept of race as a valid method for dividing and categorizing humanity.

Race has always been very much an ideology of power. Assumptions surrounding physical differences have been used to formalize, and to justify, the organization of social relationships, which exclude certain groups from political influence and economic resources. Foucault has shown how defining or labelling a group can be instruments of control, and assigning people to a particular race can be seen as a form of labelling. In the eighteenth century, for instance, designating Africans with black skins as a distinctive race lacking the capacity for finer feelings was used to excuse the Atlantic slave trade and slave plantation labour. Edward Said in his studies of Orientalism has argued that white discourses invented the notion of the East and determined how those from the East should have been treated. At the global level the gulf between the rich and poor, between what is frequently termed the North and the South, is one very largely of colour, of white affluence and black poverty. In late twentieth-century Britain there has been much speculation about the death of class, usually implying that traditional perceptions of class involving a sense of conflict between capital and labour have been eroded. Yet this alleged disappearance of the traditional white working class has also been accompanied by claims for the existence of an economically and socially disadvantaged underclass which is very largely a black underclass. Arguing that the underclass is politically powerless is to claim that blacks are politically powerless. In contemporary Britain it can be argued that the tiny number of senior politicians and civil servants, judges, police officers and directors of large companies who are not white registers the political and economic power of whites and shows that ethnicity can be equated with class power.[5] But assumptions of racial identity have also been hostile to the formation of class consciousness. Racial consciousness can be a cause of division within classes and create senses of race solidarity that transcend class boundaries. Impressionistic evidence suggests that in British towns with large numbers of inhabitants with African-Caribbean and Asian origins, there is a sense of racial solidarity among whites regardless of differences in levels of income and lifestyle, and that whites who call themselves working class often believe that they have more in common with middle- and upper-class whites than with those from the working class who are not white.

5. For discussion of the connections between race and class in late twentieth-century Britain, see Cohen, P. and Bains, H.S. (eds) (1988), *Multi-Racist Britain,* London: Macmillan, part I; Gilroy, P. (1987), *'There Ain't No Black in the Union Jack: The Cultural Politics of Race and Nation,* London: Hutchinson, chapter 1. Mason, D. (1995), *Race and Ethnicity in Modern Britain,* Oxford: Oxford University Press, examines the connections between ethnicity, economic deprivation and social inequality.

Race may have lost much of its credibility as a scientific concept, but the phrase is still very much alive in everyday discourse and suggests that many with white skins in Britain still believe that physical differences, rather than culture and history, are the cause of differences in behaviour and outlook. Skin colour is taken to represent the 'otherness' of those who are not white and many whites seem to believe that being born in Britain does not make British those with Asian or African-Caribbean ancestral roots. Although racial discrimination has been made illegal, there is much to suggest that those who are not white feel excluded from certain cultural spaces on account of their skin colour and they have a strong sense of being marginalized in contemporary Britain. Stereotyping on the basis of colour is common in everyday discourse. Within cricket Indian batsmen have often been stereotyped as naturally 'wristy' and West Indians as naturally exuberant stroke players. Whilst achievement in sport for an ethnic group may be a source of pride, the assumption that its members are genetically equipped for certain sports, such as the strong presence of those of African-Caribbean descent in sprinting and boxing, can easily lead to the belief that they are ill-equipped to succeed in other cultural spaces. Everyday discourse suggests that many whites still believe that the monopolizing of positions with the greatest levels of economic and political power in Britain by whites reflects a natural aptitude for such posts.

The terms 'racism' and 'racialism' are usually taken to imply at least a belief that different races exist and that different races have differing characteristics and capabilities, but more often, and for the purposes of this book, they include assumptions that one or some races are superior to others and that imagined racial differences justify the exercise of social and political power by one group over others and the exclusion of some groups from certain cultural spaces. Racists can be defined as those who accept the existence of race but the term 'racist' is often used to describe those who practise racist discrimination. It has been argued that individuals may be unaware that their attitudes and behaviour are racist, with the result that some may see behaviour as racially offensive even where no offence was intended and where conscientious efforts have been made to avoid being racist. Moreover regarding race and racism as cultural constructs means that definitions, and awareness, of what constitutes racially offensive behaviour change over time. Anecdotal evidence suggests that sensitivity to racial prejudice was much stronger at the end than the beginning of the twentieth century and few are now prepared to admit in public to believing in an hierarchy of races or to profess that racial discrimination is acceptable or desirable. In the 1990s, especially following the MacPherson report into the Stephen Lawrence affair, the term 'institutional racism' entered everyday political discourse, though the precise meaning of this expression is rarely made clear. Often it is used to suggest, and particularly with regard to the police, that the culture of those working within an institution fosters racist assumptions, but it is also taken to mean that the structure of an institution encourages racist views. One aim of this book is to examine whether cricket should be seen as an example of institutional racism. Belief in an hierarchy of races and the exercise of racial prejudice are not restricted to whites, but in twentieth-century Britain, racism has usually been an expression of white supremacy. Those who have suffered from racism have not usually been white.

Although race has become discredited by most biologists and anthropologists as a means of categorizing humanity, skin coloration and facial characteristics do differ among humanity, and for historical reasons, groups with a particular skin colour have often shared the same culture. In the last two or three decades the terms 'ethnicity' and 'ethnic group' have been used to describe those with a common culture and but often these terms are employed as what are thought to be politically correct, and less offensive, euphemisms for 'race' and 'racial origin'. Officialdom in the UK now asks people to state to which ethnic group they belong and not what race. Ethnic and racial prejudice have much in common, though while many if not all would probably argue that racism involves animosity to those of a different skin colour, discrimination against the Irish in Britain and 'ethnic cleansing' in the Balkans during the 1990s showed how virulent ethnic hatreds could exist between those with the same skin colour. Racism is always a form of ethnic animosity, but ethnic animosities are not always racist. The links between racism and ethnicity have given rise in the last two decades to what has been described as 'new racism'. This attitude tends to regard culture and ethnicity as unchanging and assumes that the cultures of various ethnic groups are so different as to be incompatible. It represents a belief that there is a British culture and identity and that those from other ethnic groups threaten what is imagined to be the traditional British way of life and values.

Discussion of racism in cricket, as with any form of cultural expression, has to consider the terminology for describing those from different ethnic groups, a matter calling for great care as some words have been regarded as insulting at one time but acceptable at another. Between the wars whites tended to believe that the term 'Negro' was a respectful method for referring to those of African descent whereas 'black' was thought especially abusive. By the 1970s the word 'Negro' was seen as a reflection of white supremacy and conferring a spurious scientific status to the notion of race. The rise of political liberation movements among those of African descent in America since the 1960s has meant that in the United States and Britain 'black' has become accepted as an inoffensive method for describing those of African descent, though some may feel that the word ought to be used as an adjective rather than a noun. In the last two decades some have used 'black' to describe all of those in Britain who are not white, including all of those with ancestral roots in different parts of Asia. In this book, however, 'black' is used to describe only those of African descent, those who would formerly have been called Negroes. Those with ancestral roots in Bangladesh, India, Pakistan and Sri Lanka are described as 'Asians' rather than 'black' even though some of them do not object to being called black. The reason for not calling them black is that the involvement of Asians and those of African-Caribbean descent with cricket in England has varied so much, though of course both groups have experienced prejudice in cricket from whites. It would be more accurate to describe Asians as South Asians but as the words 'Asian' and 'South Asian' have come to be used more or less interchangeably in contemporary Britain, the word 'Asian' seems no less appropriate than 'South Asian'. Whilst many of those with ancestral roots in Asia do not appear to find the term 'Asian' offensive, some argue that 'British Muslims', 'British Hindus' or 'British Sikhs' would be more appropriate descriptions for them. Using the term 'Asian' is not meant to impose on those with ancestral roots in what is often called the sub-continent a common cultural identity which overlooks the heterogeneity of their religions, languages, histories and political affiliations, nor is it meant to imply that they are not committed to Britain. Use in this book of the terms 'coloured' and 'non-white' is not intended to suggest that whiteness is the standard against which all skin colours should be judged but as what it is hoped is an inoffensive way of referring to those who are not white.

Victims of racism, of course, are those with the deepest appreciation of its nature and the ethno-centricity of all cultures means that no one can comprehend in its entirety the culture of another group. This prompts the question whether a white male, born and raised in England, can write with sympathy and understanding about racism in cricket or any other cultural form. I have no easy answer to this question. Aspects of black and Asian experience have been and will remain impenetrable to me, though it can also be argued that British African-Caribbeans and British Asians cannot understand all of each other's culture or that of British whites. Paradoxically the view that only those who belong to a culture can understand it provides the major justification for an English white undertaking a study of racism in English cricket. As racism in cricket in England has been perpetrated usually by whites, a white may well have the truest insights into the white mindset that has produced instances of racism in cricket. It is also possible that whites have spoken to me with a greater openness than they would have done to a black or Asian researcher, though black or Asian researchers may have provoked more revealing responses when talking to their ethnic groups. Because cultures change over time, historians have always had to bear in mind the problems associated with studying other cultures. The past has been described another country. It could equally be described as another culture. All historians have to accept, or rather should accept, that they may be able to develop at best only an impartial understanding of the culture of a group from the past.

Racism and Sport

Much has been written in the past three decades about racism in Britain. Mostly this literature has been concerned with discrimination against blacks and Asians in schooling, employment, the criminal justice system and housing, and a growing number of studies have examined gender and racism. Far less has been written about ethnic minorities and sport, which is surprising, especially as sport and racism are both so very much concerned with the body and because the voluntary nature of leisure activities such as sports can provide interesting insights into how those from different ethnic groups relate to each other. Reasons for the varying levels of involvement with sport among women from ethnic minorities have been analysed by Carrington, Chivers, Williams, Lyons, Verma and Darby,[6] though Werbner and Fleming are among the far smaller number of researchers who have considered how sport has fashioned male identities among the ethnic minorities.[7] Belief in white supremacy as a justification for empire means that studies of how sport helped to sustain imperialism are relevant to the issue of sport and racism, but racism has not usually been the main theme of these. Mangan has discussed the connections between the games ethos and imperialist ideology in the Victorian public schools has shown how this was diffused throughout the Empire and fostered a sense of political identity between Britain and white colonists.[8] The debates in the 1970s and 1980s about how far British sport ought to have been used as a tactic in the campaigns against the apartheid regime in South Africa have been examined in detail. The extent of apartheid in South African sport and the beginnings of the South African Non-Racial Olympic Committee were assessed by Archer and Bouillon.[9] Jarvie analysed the relationship of apartheid with class in South Africa and examined resistance both inside and outside South Africa, including that in Britain, to apartheid in sport in the mid 1980s.[10] Writing after the collapse of apartheid, Nauright and Booth have examined how segregation shaped sport in South Africa and have assessed how far sport in South Africa became multi-national in the 1990s.[11] To date, however, no monograph has considered the attitudes within a particular British sport towards apartheid.

6. Carrington, B., Chivers, T. and Williams,T. (1987), 'Gender, leisure and sport: a case-study of young people of South Asian descent', *Leisure Studies,* 6; Dixey, R. (1982), 'Asian Women and Sport: the Bradford Experience', *British Journal of Physical Education,* 13 (4); Lyons, A. (1988), *Asian Women and Sport,* London: Sports Council; Verma, G. and Darby, D. (1994), *Winners and Losers: Ethnic Minorities in Sport and Recreation,* London: Falmer.

7. Werbner, P. (1996), '"Our Blood is Green": Cricket, Identity and Social Empowerment among British Pakistanis,', in MacClancy, J. (ed.), *Sport, Identity and Ethnicity,* Oxford: Berg; Fleming, S. (1991), 'Sport, schooling and Asian male youth culture', in Jarvie, G. (ed.), *Sport, Racism and Ethnicity,* London: Falmer; Fleming, S. (1995), *"Home and Away": Sport, and South Asian Male Youth,* Aldershot: Ashgate.

8. Mangan, J.A. (1998), *The Games Ethic and Imperialism: Aspects of the Diffusion of an Ideal,* London: Cass.

9. Archer, R. and Bouillon, A. (1982), *The South African Game: Sport and Racism,* London: Zed.

10. Jarvie, G. (1985), *Class, Race and Sport in South Africa's Political Economy,* London: Routledge & Kegan Paul.

11. Nauright, J. (1997), *Sport, Culture and Identities in South Africa,* London: Leicester University Press; Booth, D. (1998), *The Race Game: Sport and Politics in South Africa,* London: Cass.

Studies of ethnicity and sport have tended to concentrate on sport and national, and regionalised, identities rather than on racism in sport. With regard to the British Isles, *Fields of Praise* by Smith and Williams examines how rugby union helped to fashion Welsh national identity whilst the collection of essays edited by Jarvie examined the forms of Scottish identity expressed through sport. Both books discussed how far national consciousness in these countries was shaped by a sense of not being English.[12] The capacity of sport to foster sectarian animosities in Ireland has been analysed by Sugden and Bairner, a theme also considered in relation to football in Ireland by Cronin and by Murray in Scotland.[13] *Sport, Identity and Ethnicity,* edited by MacClancy, and *Sporting Nationalisms,* edited by Cronin and Mayall, contain case studies from Britain, continental Europe, North America, Asia and Australia which explore the connections between sport, ethnic and regional identities and the assimilation of immigrant groups.[14] No monograph has yet considered how far sports in general have expressed and shaped notions of Englishness, though Williams' *Cricket and England* discusses why cricket was so often seen as a symbol of Englishness between the wars and Holt has shown that from the late nineteenth century until the middle of the twentieth century batsmen were thought to personify such supposedly English qualities as loyalty, reserve and respectability.[15] How far sports focused North of England identities are considered in *Sport and Identity in the North of England,* edited by Hill and Williams, and in Collins' study of rugby league, *Rugby's Great Split.*[16] Russell has discussed the values associated with cricket in Yorkshire and how these expressed a Yorkshire identity that drew much strength from animosity to the South of England.[17] The collection of essays edited by Jarvie, *Sport, Racism and Ethnicity,* discusses the connections between, sport, racism and ethnic identities

12. Smith, D. and Williams, G. (1980), *Fields of Praise: The Official History of the Welsh Rugby Union 1881–1981,* Cardiff: University of Wales Press; Jarvie, G. and Walker, G. (eds) (1994), *Scottish Sport in the Making of the Nation: Ninety Minute Patriots?,* Leicester: Leicester University Press.

13. Sugden, J. and Bairner, A. (1993), *Sport, Sectarianism and Society in a Divided Ireland,* Leicester: Leicester University Press; Murray, B (1985), *The Old Firm: Sectarianism, Sport and Society in Scotland,* Edinburgh: Donald; Cronin, M (1999), *Sport and Nationalism in Ireland: Gaelic Games, Soccer and Irish Identity since 1884,* Dublin: Four Courts.

14. MacClancy, *Sport, Identity and Ethnicity*; Cronin, M. and Mayall, D. (eds) (1998), *Sporting Nationalisms: Identity, Ethnicity, Immigration and Assimilation,* London: Cass.

15. Williams, J. (1999), *Cricket and England: A Cultural and Social History of the Inter-war Years,* London: Cass; Holt, R. (1996), 'Cricket and Englishness: The Batsman as Hero', *International Journal of the History of Sport,* 13 (1).

16. Hill, J. and Williams, J. (eds) (1996), *Sport and Identity in the North of England,* Keele: Keele University Press; Collins, T. (1998), *Rugby's Great Split: Class, Culture and the Origins of Rugby League Football,* London: Cass.

17. Russell, D. (1996), 'Sport and Identity: The Case of Yorkshire County Cricket Club, 1890–1939', *20 Century British History,* 7 (2).

and through examples from inside and outside Britain shows how racism in sport has to be studied in the context of the power relationships of a society.[18]

Sociological analyses of racism in sport, often drawing on evidence from North America, have tended to argue that the strong black presence in some sports such as boxing and sprinting is the result of socio-economic and cultural factors that have caused other ethnic groups to withdraw from them and have led blacks to concentrate on them. Such views refute the contention that blacks have tended to dominate the higher levels of these sports because their bodies are genetically better equipped for them. Cashmore has examined black sporting heroes and has assessed their contribution to the highest levels of sporting competition in Britain.[19] So far no work has drawn together the scattered pieces of research on the black experience in British soccer, a sport with a very high number of black professional players but where the black presence in coaching and management is disproportionately small. The extensive literature on football hooliganism refers to racist abuse among many white football supporters and the autobiographies of prominent black footballers have mentioned their encounters with racism in football. The responses to Arthur Wharton, the first prominent black footballer in Britain, and why he was so quickly forgotten after his playing days, have been linked by Vasili to the ideology of white supremacy that sustained imperialism in the late Victorian and Edwardian periods, whilst Russell in his *Football and The English: A Social History of Association Football in England, 1863–1995* touches on football as an expression of Englishness and the black contribution to football though his main emphasis is on how football has reflected social and economic change in England.[20] Collins has shown how exclusion from the mainstream of sport in Britain and its meritocratic ethos helped rugby league to have a stronger black presence than most other sports.[21] Little has been written about the history of coloured performers in British track and field or in professional boxing, a sport with a very high number of coloured fighters but which, by insisting until 1948 that only whites could compete for British championships, was possibly the only sport in Britain with a formalized colour bar.

Studies of race and ethnicity in cricket are surprisingly few, especially when one considers that cricket was probably the first team ball game in which whites played against coloureds and that cricket was so intertwined with imperialist ideology.

18. Jarvie, *Sport, Racism and Ethnicity.*

19. Cashmore, E. (1982), *Black Sportsmen,* London: Routledge & Kegan Paul.

20. Vasili, P. (1998), *The First Black Footballer: Arthur Wharton 1865–1930: An Absence of Memory,* London: Cass; Russell, D. (1997), *Football and The English: A Social History of Association Football in England, 1863–1995,* Preston: Carnegie.

21. Collins, T.,'Racial Minorities in a Marginalised Sport: Race, Discrimination and Integration in British Rugby League Football', in Cronin and Mayall, *Sporting Nationalisms.*

C.L.R. James' *Beyond A Boundary* has been acclaimed as a classic of cricket literature. When published in 1963, James' book was probably the first major text in English to explore what sport reveals about the values underlying political life and to demonstrate that the insights which sport provides into how groups relate to each other can register the degree of social cohesion and animosity within a society. An African-Caribbean born and raised in Trinidad, James showed how cricket reflected the nuances of the relationships between blacks, whites and those of mixed descent in the Caribbean. He explained how cricket was used to inculcate among the black population those values associated with cricket by the white public school elite of England but, by boosting black confidence, were central in the struggles for decolonization and political emancipation. In the late 1950s James had a decisive role in the campaign for Frank Worrell to be appointed as the first black captain of the West Indian side for a whole series. Worrell's appointment has been seen as a cause and a reflection of the moves towards greater political assertiveness among blacks in the Caribbean. *Beyond a Boundary* has stimulated other scholars, such as Beckles, Stoddart and Sandiford, to investigate the significance of cricket in Caribbean culture and to assess the connections of cricket with black political activism, an issue also discussed with the perceptions of a professional politician by Michael Manley, the former prime minister of Jamaica, in his immensely detailed *A History of West Indies Cricket.*[22]

Mihir Bose has examined how cricket, a sport of the British colonisers, became an expression of Indian nationalism. He shows how the game was taken up by first the Parsees, then the Hindus and Muslims in the nineteenth and early twentieth centuries and assesses the quality of the leadership for cricket in India provided by the princes. Bose explains how cricket has been a symbol of Indian nationalism since the granting of independence, it has also expressed and reinforced regional and religious divisions within India.[23] *Players, Patrons and the Crowd* by Cashman analyses why cricket has such mass following in India. Whilst cricket is often said to be a national passion in Pakistan and of such importance that politicians have frequently interfered with its administration, no satisfactory history of cricket in Pakistan has been written, or at least written in English, although Cashman has produced exploratory forays into how the rivalries between Lahore and Karachi

22. See for instance Beckles, H. McD. (ed.) (1994), *An Area of Conquest: Popular Democracy and West Indies Cricket Supremacy,* Kingston: Ian Randle; Beckles, H. McD. (1998), *The Development of West Indies Cricket, Volume 1 The Age of Nationalism; Volume 2 The Age of Globalism,* London: Pluto; Beckles, H. McD. and Stoddart, B. (eds) (1995), *Liberation Cricket: West Indies Cricket Culture,* Manchester: Manchester University Press; Manley, M. (1988), *A History of West Indies Cricket,* London: Guild.

23. Bose, M. (1990), *A History of Indian Cricket,* London: Deutsch; Bose, M. (1986), *A Maidan View: The Magic of Indian Cricket,* London: Allen & Unwin.

have shaped Pakistan cricket.[24] In the 1970s Odendaal's collection of essays, *Cricket in Isolation,* examined in detail the range of opinion in South Africa to racial discrimination in cricket and analysed the attitudes of the boards of control in the other test match countries to apartheid in South African cricket up to that time, whilst Merrett and Nauright have made a perceptive but unfortunately only an outline survey of the ethnic dimension to cricket in South Africa and in particular as a expression of white political and social discrimination.[25] Bruce Murray's history of the political context of cricket under apartheid in South Africa is eagerly awaited. Whimpress has discussed how aboriginals were introduced to cricket in nineteenth-century Australia and his analysis of why leading aboriginal cricketers were not selected for the Australian national side, whilst pointing out the role of discrimination, shows that other factors, such as questionable actions by fast bowlers and the misfortune to be playing when the emphasis was on spin bowling, were involved.[26] Tatz's *Obstacle Race* examines how the relative absence of aborigines from first-class cricket in Australia had parallels in other major Australian sports.[27]

Little has been published on racism and cricket in England. Sandiford has examined the connections between cricket and imperialism in the Victorian period whilst Williams has considered how the nature of cricket as an imperial sport and belief in cricket as a symbol of English moral worth were mutually supporting.[28] Mulvaney's *Cricket Walkabout* is a detailed study of the playing exploits and reception in England of the Australian aboriginal cricket tour of 1868.[29] Birley's social history of English cricket[30] also assesses cricket's role as an imperial sport and discusses the problems raised for the English cricket establishment by the international sports boycott of South Africa, but in a work spanning several centuries, his treatment of this issue is inevitably brief. *Anyone but England* by Marqusee, whose American Jewish background has added to his awareness of the peculiarities of English society,

24. Cashman, R. (1994), 'The Paradox of Pakistani Cricket: Some Initial Reflections', *Sports Historian,* 14 (May); Cashman, R. (1998), 'The Subcontinent' in Stoddart, B. and Sandiford, K.A.P. (eds), *The Imperial Game: Cricket, Culture and Society,* Manchester; Manchester University Press.

25. Odendaal, A. (ed.) (1997), *Cricket in Isolation: The Politics of Race and Cricket in South Africa,* Cape Town: Odendaal; Merrett, C. and Nauright, J., 'South Africa' in Stoddart and Sandiford, *Imperial Game.*

26. Whimpress, B. (1999), *Passport to Nowhere: Aborigines in Australian Cricket,* Sydney: Walla Walla.

27. Tatz, C. (1996), *Obstacle Race: Aborigines in Sport,* Sydney: University of New South Wales Press.

28. Sandiford, K.A.P. (1994), *Cricket and the Victorians,* Aldershot: Scolar, 1994; Williams, J., *Cricket and England* .

29. Mulvaney, D.J. (1967), *Cricket Walkabout: The Australian Aboriginal Cricketers on Tour 1867–8,* London: Melbourne University Press.

30. Birley, D. (1999), *A Social History of English Cricket,* London: Aurum.

shows how the cricket establishment and the cricket press in the late twentieth century found it difficult to adjust to the post-imperial epoch and could be seen as a metaphor for how the white English have struggled to come to terms with the contemporary world. He discusses the lack of enthusiasm in English cricket for the sporting boycott of South Africa and the resentments provoked by West Indian and Pakistani success in test matches against England.[31] Hill has discussed responses to West Indian and Asian cricketers in league cricket before the Second World War and biographies of coloured cricketers such as Ranjitsinhji and Learie Constantine have looked at how their careers in England were shaped by racial attitudes, although the main emphasis in such works is on playing achievements.[32] Only localized studies have been made of the contribution to recreational cricket by ethnic minorities in the late twentieth century.[33] Searle has discussed discrimination against ethnic minorities, particularly by the Yorkshire county club,[34] but the issue of how far other county clubs have neglected local African-Caribbean and Asian cricketers has not been studied in detail.

This book is intended to fill the gap in the historiography of English cricket that has surrounded racism. By analysing the nature of racial exclusion in cricket and the attitudes to racial identities embedded in cricket discourses over the past hundred years, it assesses what cricket reveals about how far Englishness has been regarded as a quality of whites and about what progress England has made to becoming a multi-cultural society where differing ethnic backgrounds are granted equal tolerance and respect. Hopefully it will confirm C.L. R. James' dictum that the study of cricket can reveal so much about the world beyond the boundary.

31. Marqusee, M. (1994), *Anyone but England: Cricket and the National Malaise,* London: Verso.

32. Hill, J. (1994), 'Reading the Stars: A Post-modernist Approach to Sports History', *Sports Historian,* 14 (May); Hill, J. (1994), 'Cricket and the Imperial Connection: Overseas Players in Lancashire in the Inter-war Years', in Bale, J. and Maguire, J. (eds), *The Global Sports Arena: Athletic Talent Migration in an Interdependent World,* London: Cass; Ross, A. (1983), *Ranji: Prince of Cricketers,* London: Collins; Wilde, S. (1990), *Ranji: A Genius Rich and Strange,* London: Kingswood; Howat, G. (1975), *Learie Constantine,* London: Allen and Unwin.

33. McDonald, I. and Ugra, S. (1998), *Anyone for Cricket? Equal Opportunities and Changing Cricket Cultures in Essex and East London,* London: Roehampton Institute and The Centre for New Ethnicities Research, University of East London and McDonald, I. And Ugra, S. (1999), ' "It's Just Not Cricket!" Ethnicity, Division and Imagining the Other in English Cricket', in Cohen, P. (ed.), *New Ethnicities, Old Racisms?* London, Zed; Long, J., Nesti, M., Carrington, B. and Gilson, N. (1997), *Crossing the Boundary: A Study of the Nature and Extent of Racism in Local League Cricket,* Leeds: Leeds Metropolitan University; Williams, J. (1994), 'South Asians and Cricket in Bolton', *Sports Historian,* 14 (May); Williams, J. (2000), 'Asians, Cricket and Ethnic Relations in Northern England', *Sporting Traditions,* 16 (2).

34. Searle, C. (1990), 'Race before Wicket: Cricket, Empire and the White Rose', *Race & Class,* 31 (3); Searle, C. (1993), 'Cricket and the Mirror of Racism', *Race & Class,* 34 (3).

−1−

Cricket, Race and Empire before 1914

Cricket and English Moral Worth

Cricket in the Victorian and Edwardian periods had a key role in how the white English perceived themselves and in how they imagined that the world viewed them. They saw cricket as an expression of their moral worth. Cricket was thought to have higher standards of sportsmanship than other sports. Cricket discourse emphasized that playing cricket encouraged moral qualities such as selflessness, putting the interests of the team before one's enjoyment, accepting the decisions of umpires and captains without complaint, observing the spirit rather than the letter of its laws, all qualities that were seen as resonating with Christian ethics. The interest in cricket of so many clerics reinforced assumptions that the sportsmanship of cricket expressed Christian morality.

The moral worth of cricket was also related to the supposed antiquity of cricket and the historicist element in English culture, which saw tradition as a source of moral authority. The veneration accorded to institutions and practices such as parliamentary government, the monarchy, the armed services, the universities of Oxford and Cambridge and the older public schools owed much to beliefs about their origins in a distant past. The attempts of cricket historians to show that cricket had been played in medieval England were largely self-delusion, but there was no doubt that cricket had been played in an organized manner at an earlier date than other team ball sports. By the early eighteenth century cricket was firmly established in southeast England. A match with a team purportedly representing the best cricketers of a county had been played as early as 1709. The oldest written rules dated from 1744, the year when interest in the game had reached such a level that spectators paid for admission to a match in London.[1] The need that Victorians felt to invent tradition helps to explain why such importance was attached to the long history of cricket.

Assumptions about the supremely English nature of cricket and of the morality of cricket were linked with perceptions of cricket as essentially a sport of the English countryside. Cricket had originated in the rural villages of the Sussex Weald and

---

1. Wynne-Thomas, P. (1997), *The History of Cricket: From the Weald to the World,* London: Stationery Office, pp. 14, 29.

the adjoining parts of Surrey and Kent. Victorian and Edwardian cricket writers often claimed that village cricket was the purest forms of cricket. Even today cricket is often presented as a sport played on a village green fringed with trees with the spire of the Anglican church and the village inn as indispensable features of the scene.[2] Such adulation of village cricket can be related to the English pastoral tradition, which idealized the rustic as the repository of traditional English moral values and found expression in the revival of folk song and dance, pastoral painting and poetry, the garden village movement and perhaps even the flight to suburbia and the cult of gardening. Those from both ends of the political spectrum demonised the town as morally and physically decayed, the site of sordid money grubbing.[3]

So much moral importance was also accorded to cricket because of its associations with the Empire. Cricket was not played only in the Empire, but before 1914 test cricket was played only by England, Australia and South Africa. Though it remained strong in Pennsylvania, cricket in America declined after the Civil War with the expansion of baseball. In the 1880s and 1890s teams of American cricketers had played against English counties, but by the Edwardian period American touring teams played against amateur teams of English counties. Cricket played in Denmark, Holland and Germany attracted little attention in England. *Cricket,* the leading cricket magazine, appeared weekly in summer and monthly in winter from 1882 until 1913. Most of its pages were devoted to cricket in England but it also gave the score cards of matches played in Australia, the West Indies, India, Ceylon and South Africa and made a special point of mentioning cricket being played in other parts of the Empire. It showed little interest in American cricket and generally ignored matches played in continental Europe except when these were organized by Britons living overseas.

The sportsmanship of cricket and the nature of cricket as a sport of the Empire helped to persuade the white English that they could be trusted to exercise authority over other races in a reasonable and selfless manner. This was seen especially in the value system of the late Victorian and Edwardian public schools. A major aim of the public schools was to provide their students with the moral qualities necessary to administer the Empire. The games cult, to which cricket was central, was seen as essential for producing the character needed by imperial administrators. J.E.C. Welldon, educated at Eton, had been headmaster of Harrow from 1885 until 1898

2. For a fuller discussion of cricket as a representation of English pastoralism, see Bale, J. (1994), 'Cricket Landscapes and English Eternalism', Paper presented at the Eastern Historical Geography Association, Codrington College, Barbados.

3. The values surrounding English pastoralism are discussed further in Boyes, G. (1993), *The Imagined Village: Culture, Ideology and the English Folk Revival,* Manchester: Manchester University Press and in Howkins, A. (1986), 'The Discovery of Rural England', in Colls, R. and Dodds, P. (eds), *Englishness: Politics and Culture 1880–1920,* Beckenham: Croom Helm.

and Bishop of Calcutta from 1898 until 1902. In 1906 he explained that the purpose of a public school education was to impress upon boys 'the dignity of learning, but the yet higher dignity of character'. 'Learning', he continued, 'however excellent in itself, does not afford much necessary scope for such virtues as promptitude, resource, honour, co-operation, and unselfishness; but these are the soul of English games.' The qualities associated with games, he claimed, had produced 'a characteristic of the British race – the power of government; for it is a quality which the race has exhibited in relation to subject peoples at many periods of English history in the many regions of the world where the flag of England flies.'[4]

It is not difficult to make a strong case for seeing imperial expansion as driven by economic motives, but during the late-Victorian and Edwardian heyday of empire, white English apologists for empire, who tended to use the terms English and British interchangeably, emphasized that the Empire was an exercise in morality, that Britain was responding to a moral obligation to extend the benefits of British civilization. In 1896 a writer in the *North American Review* claimed that the British Empire had brought 'civilization, the Christian religion, order, justice' and that 'England has always treated a conquered race with justice, and what under her law is the law for the white man is the law for his black, red and yellow brother.'[5] In 1897 the Colonial Secretary Joseph Chamberlain said that 'this great Empire of ours, powerful as it is, is nothing to what it will become in the course of ages when it will be in permanence a guarantee for the peace and civilisation of the world.'[6] John Lawson Walton, an imperialist Liberal MP, argued in 1899 that for 'subject races . . . no greater boon can be given them in their inevitable struggle with an invading civilisation than the strong and humane authority of British rule.'[7]

Belief in the ethical quality of the Empire was based on assumptions of racial superiority, of the white English race having a natural moral capacity that made it uniquely fitted for the exercise of imperial power. Chamberlain in 1895 said 'the British race is the greatest of governing races that the world has ever seen'.[8] For Lawson Walton the 'basis of Imperialism is race . . . Its genius will find scope in developing and, as duty or legitimate interest demands, in extending its possessions.'[9]

4. Welldon, J.E.C. (1906), 'The Training of an English Gentleman in the Public Schools', *Nineteenth Century*, (September), pp. 403, 406, 410.

5. Wells, D. (1896), 'Great Britain and the United States: Their True Relations', *North American Review*, CCCCLXII (April), p. 403.

6. Garvin, J.L. (1934), *The Life of Joseph Chamberlain, Volume 3, 1895–1900*, London: Macmillan, p. 186.

7. Lawson Walton, J. (1899), 'Imperialism', *Contemporary Review*, lxxv, p. 307–8.

8. Garvin, *Chamberlain*, p. 27.

9. Lawson Walton, 'Imperialism', p. 307.

Even critics of imperialism agreed with assumptions of white English racial superiority. In 1900 the classical scholar Gilbert Murray, for instance, wrote that 'There is in this world an hierarchy of races . . . nations which eat more, claim more, and get higher wages, will direct and rule the others, and the lower work of the world will tend in the long run to be done by other breeds of men. This much we of the ruling colour will no doubt accept as obvious.'[10] Even such a trenchant critic of imperialism as J.A. Hobson in his book *Imperialism: A Study* wrote of 'backward' races and 'inferior' races and did not always put these words in quotation marks. He claimed that the 'Englishman believes that he is a more excellent type than any other man; he believes that he is better able to assimilate special virtues that others may have; he believes that this character gives him a right to rule which no other can possess.'[11]

The assumptions of white English moral superiority surrounding the justifications for empire easily slipped into contempt for those who were not white. Cecil Headlam, an Oxford graduate and writer, wrote in 1903 that soon a white Englishman in India would 'cease to be surprised at the resemblance of human beings to monkeys, when you see them altruistically picking at each other's heads, and otherwise behaving like their cousins in the Zoo. The smell of an alien race, of burning cow-dung and burning Hindu no longer offends your nostrils.' He added that as a white man in India you 'learn that you must be very careful how you hit a man in India. Nearly every native suffers from an enlarged spleen, and any blow to the body is likely to prove fatal . . . It is best to carry a cane and administer rebuke therewith upon the calves or shins, which are tender and not usually mortal.' He added that 'all servants in India are thieves'.[12] By being so very much a sport of the Empire, cricket was intimately bound up with notions of white supremacy.

Cricket and Race in Victorian and Edwardian England

Cricket in England had no colour bar equivalent to that of baseball in the United States. Non-white cricketers were rare in Victorian and Edwardian England, but white cricketers did play with and against coloured cricketers in England and teams of white English cricketers that toured overseas played against coloured players. In 1868 the Australian Aboriginal cricketers, the first party of overseas cricketers to tour England, and the Parsee touring teams of 1886 and 1888, played against socially

10. Murray, G., (1900), 'The Exploitation of the Inferior Races in Ancient and Modern Times', in Murray, G., Hirst, F.W. and Hammond, J.L., *Liberalism and the Empire: Three Essays,* London: Johnson, p. 156.

11. Hobson, J.A. (1905), *Imperialism: A Study,* London: Allen & Unwin, p. 159.

12. Headlam, C. (1903), *Ten Thousand Miles through India & Burma: An Account of the Oxford University Authentics' Cricket Tour,* London: Dent, pp. 93–4.

prestigious teams of white cricketers. The West Indian touring teams of 1900 and 1906, which had black as well as white players, played against English county sides, as did the All-India team in 1911 which included Parsee, Hindu and Muslim players.

British whites stationed in the colonies and permanent settlers tended to form cricket clubs exclusively for white players who played against other white teams but mixed-race teams and matches between white and non-white teams were played. In India the Bombay and Poona Gymkhana clubs, two of the strongest sides in India, had only white players but in 1892 the Bombay Gymkhana began playing against the Bombay Parsees and in 1907 a triangular tournament was introduced in Bombay between the Gymkhana, the Parsees and the Hindus.[13] The Maharaja of Patiala frequently raised teams for which whites and Indians played. He engaged as coaches Henderson, an English professional cricketer, who had coached the Parsee cricketers on their tour of England in 1888, and the English county professionals William Brockwell and Jack Hearne were employed as coaches by the Maharaja of Patiala.[14] In the West Indies whites and non-whites played together in sides representing the different islands. Parties of English cricketers who had mostly played first-class cricket if only occasionally toured India in 1889, 1892 and 1903 and the West Indies in 1895 and 1896–97. In the West Indies they played against some mixed-race teams and in India against white, mixed-race and wholly Asian teams. Reports in *Cricket* of matches outside Britain between mixed-race teams and matches between Indian and white teams in India were more common in the Edwardian period than in the 1880s, though this could have owed more to the growth of cricket playing by Indians than to a softening of racist attitudes among whites.

No cricket club for those who were not white seems to have been formed in England before the First World War, but this could have been because the numbers of non-whites were so low. Evidence about the responses of non-whites who may have tried to join cricket clubs or whether they were reluctant to do so because of fears about discrimination is scarce. Ahsan ul Hak, a Muslim born in the Punjab, played for the socially prestigious Hampstead club while studying in London to be a barrister. A tiny number of non-whites played first-class cricket. The most famous was Ranjitsinhji, one of the super stars of late Victorian and Edwardian cricket. The South African test cricketer C.B. Llewellyn, who may have been coloured, played more than 300 times for Hampshire. Ahsan ul Hak played for the MCC and in three matches for Middlesex in 1902. Mehallasha Pavri, who had been the most successful bowler on the Parsee tour of England in 1888, played one match for Middlesex as an amateur in 1895. C.A. Ollivierre, a black cricketer who played for the West Indian tourists in 1900, stayed in England and played 110 matches for Derbyshire as an

---

13. Vasant Raiji (1986), *India's Hambledon Men,* Bombay: Tyeby, pp. 52–3.
14. *Cricket,* 27 April, 18 May 1899.

amateur between 1901 and 1907. He was probably the first African-Caribbean to play county cricket. T. Holsinger, an ethnic Sri Lankan born in Colombo, was the professional for Lindum CC in Lincoln and played for the Lincolnshire county team in 1907 and 1908. Mehta, who had played for the Parsees, was probably the first non-white cricketer to be a professional with a county club when he joined Lancashire in 1903 though he never played for its first or second elevens.[15] In 1904 *Cricket* listed 40 cricketers in India who had played first-class cricket in England, but only two had what seemed to be Indian names.[16] Ranjitsinhji was the only Oxbridge cricket blue between 1880 and 1914 with an obviously Asian name.

Condescension pervaded much of the writing by English whites about the cricket played by other races and reflected assumptions of white moral and physical superiority. In 1894 *Cricket* made a special point of reprinting an article from *The Bombay Gazette* which alleged that when the Bombay Parsees first took up cricket, they had 'a rather inadequate conception of the ethics of cricket – if everything was fair in love and war, why should it not be so in cricket as well?' In one match a leading Parsee batsman had batted several times by disguising himself. By 1894, the article maintained, Parsee cricketers had 'now acquired from their European masters and models, the moral instincts of the true sportsman. They freely acknowledge their debt to Englishmen from whom they have learnt their national game.'[17] Ranjitsinhji's emphasis in an interview that 'it is not at all the fact that the Indian is too lazy to play the game' suggests that this was a widely held view in England, though he added that 'Constitutionally' the Indian cricketer 'may not be so energetic as the Englishman.'[18] In 1906 Lord Harris, who had been Governor of Bombay from 1890 until 1895, claimed that 'Indians have a good eye and rather long arms, but do not possess the patience and resolution of the Anglo-Saxon. They are very easily excited.'[19] In 1910 Sir George Clarke, Governor of Madras, when distributing prizes at Rajkumar College, the boarding school for Indian boys which Ranjitsinhji had attended, said that 'In India one sees the effects of an early relapse into sedentary habits which inevitably lead to premature old age. Hard work which so many Englishmen are able to perform in India is largely due to the natural habit of keeping up sports and exercises for as long as possible.'[20] Even the great cricketing achievements of Ranjitsinhji do not seem to have dented these beliefs in the natural athletic superiority of whites over Indians.

15. I am grateful to Mr Don Ambrose for providing me with details of Holsinger.
16. *Cricket,* 24 November 1904.
17. *Cricket,* 20 September 1894.
18. *Cricket,* 18 July 1895.
19. *Cricket,* 29 November 1906.
20. *Cricket,* 31 March 1910.

Ridicule infused some comments on Asian cricketers. A white in Bombay could remember 'no more amusing experience than when I first saw the Hindus play. The wicket-keeper in particular was quite the funniest picture I have ever seen at cricket . . . Just fancy, as the only addition to complete the costume, a pair of gloves and leg guards, with nothing but bare feet as continuations!'[21] A report in *Cricket* on a match played by R.S. Lucas' team touring the West Indies in 1895 mentioned that 'The blacks here are a keen enough crowd, but naturally not so well versed in the intricacies of the game. A black man caused some amusement by accompanying each . . . batsman on his way to and from the wicket with musical honours of the weirdest description, produce by a sort of clarinet. There were really three blacks in the S. Kitts XI.'[22] The extensive coverage of public schools cricket and of matches between socially exclusive clubs in the South of England in particular suggests that many readers of *Cricket* would have been belonged to the economically and socially privileged. The printing in *Cricket* of comments which belittled coloured cricketers suggests that its readers were unlikely to have been offended by them. The cartoonist A.E. Morton drew what would now appear to be grossly racist caricatures of the black players on the West Indian tour of England in 1906.[23]

Some of the tiny number of non-white cricketers who played county cricket before 1914 encountered racist hostility. C.B. Llewellyn was born at Pietermaritzburg, Natal, in 1876. He was an attacking left-hand batsman and slow to medium bowler. He claimed to have been the first to bowl the 'chinaman'. Use of the term 'chinaman' to describe a left-handed bowler's googly, a highly unorthodox form of bowling intended to disguise the direction in which the ball would spin, can be seen as expressing an assumption that the Chinese were highly deceptive and very different from the white English. Llewellyn played first for South Africa in a test match against England at Johannesburg in 1895 and again in 1899 and in 1902–3 played in all three of South Africa's test matches against Australia. From 1899 until 1910 he played in England as a professional with Hampshire, performing the double of scoring more than 1,000 runs and taking 100 wickets in five seasons. He played again for South Africa on the tour of Australia in 1910–11 and in 1912 when the Triangular Tournament was held in England. In 1902 he was included in the 14 players from which the England team to play against Australia at Edgbaston was to be chosen but was not selected to play. In 1911 he became the professional for Accrington in the Lancashire League and continued to play as a league professional until the 1930s. Llewellyn and his family always maintained that he was white,[24] but his complexion was so dark

21. *Cricket,* 1 June 1885.
22. *Cricket,* 28 March 1895.
23. For examples of these, see Wolstenholme, G. (1992), *The West Indian Tour of England 1906,* published privately by the author, pp. 13, 22.
24. *Cricketer International,* March 1976.

that many suspected that he was coloured. There has been speculation that he may have been the first coloured cricketer to play test cricket for South Africa and some who knew him in the Bolton area in the 1930s have said that in the 1980s he would have been taken for an Asian. Though Llewellyn may have been of white descent, he encountered prejudice on account of his skin colour. It is thought that he decided to play county cricket in England because of his irritation over the racist sneers that other South African test cricketers, in particular the Transvaal batsman Jimmy Sinclair, made about his colour and their suggestions that he was not white. His obituary in *Wisden* mentions that he left Hampshire because of dispute about pay and when he played for Radcliffe CC as a professional from 1926 until 1932 Llewellyn was an tenacious negotiator over terms[25] but there is also a belief that his departure from Hampshire occurred in part because of his being refused accommodation in hotels and boarding houses when the team was playing away matches and racist comments from other players.[26] Llewellyn's daughter, on the other hand, claimed in 1976 that her father had never referred to any ostracism and that he left county cricket because, with four daughters, he needed the money offered in league cricket.[27]

At least one white professional had reservations about Charles Ollivierre playing for Derbyshire. In 1931 the cricket writer E.H.D. Sewell, the son of an Indian Army officer and who played county cricket as an amateur and as a professional, wrote of Charles Ollivierre as 'this coal-black batsman' and that the Derbyshire and England professional Bill Storer 'believed in England for the English and was not enamoured of importations, especially of the ebony hue.'[28] Whilst the careers of Llewellyn and Ollivierrre show that racism existed in English cricket, it is also possible that their cricketing achievements may well have created goodwill towards non-whites among the white supporters of the Hampshire and Derbyshire county teams. No reports of hostile crowd responses to Llewellyn or Ollivierre have been found.

Responses to Ranjitsinhji

Ranjitsinhji was the most notable coloured cricketer in England before the First World and was one of the biggest stars of English sport in the late-Victorian and Edwardian periods. His playing skills are usually regarded as one of the great glories of the late Victorian and Edwardian Golden Age of English cricket, the historian

---

25. For details of Llewellyn's negotiations over pay, see Williams, J.A. (1992), 'Cricket and Society in Bolton between the Wars', Lancaster University Ph.D. thesis, chapter 3.

26. *Cricketer International,* February 1976, p. 23.

27. *Cricketer International,* March 1976, p. 29.

28. Sewell, E.H.D. (1931), *Cricket Up-to-date,* London: Murray, pp. 247–8.

Eric Midwinter describing him as 'perhaps the most enduring emblem of that luxurious cricket before the carnage of the First World War.'[29] Although Ranjitsinhji's first-class cricket was all but over by 1907, his fame as a major figure of English cricket survives. A biography of him by Alan Ross was published in 1983 and another by Simon Wilde in 1990.[30] Born at Sarodar, India, in 1872 Kumar Shri Ranjitsinhji always called himself an Indian prince and was one of several claiming to be the legitimate heir to the ruler of Nawanagar in north-west India. In 1907 he became the Maharaja Jam Sahib of Nawanagar. He learned to play cricket at Rajkumar College in India. He began studying at Cambridge in 1889 and played for the University in 1893 and 1894 but without great success. He started playing county cricket for Sussex in 1895. Between 1895 and 1904 he was the leading batsman in English cricket and never lower than fifth in the national averages. In 1899 he became the first batsman to score 3,000 runs in an English season and in 1900 again scored more than 3,000 runs. He scored over 2,000 runs in 1896, 1901 and 1904. His batting average was over eighty-seven in 1900 and over seventy-four in 1904. He was not only a great compiler of runs but he scored with apparent ease and in a style quite unlike the English tradition of batting. Gifted with a very quick eye and amazing co-ordination, he played the ball very late and exploited to the full opportunities to score on the leg side when English coaching methods emphasized off-side strokes. He was credited with having devised a new stroke, the leg glance. In 1896 he became only the second player to score a hundred for England in his first test match. In test series against Australia his batting average was 78.33 in 1896, 50.78 in 1897-98 and 46.33 in 1899, though in his four test match innings against Australia in 1902 he scored only 19 runs. Many critics considered him the best bat since Grace.

Ranjitsinhji was immensely popular in England. Crowds flocked to see him bat. As early as 1895 the difficulties of pronouncing his name had led the cricketing public to nickname him not only 'Ranji' but 'Ramsgate Jimmy' and 'Gin, rum and whiskey', which led a writer in *Cricket* to claim that 'under the familiarity lies a deep respect which widens into affection.'[31] In 1896 and 1897 there was talk of him standing for parliament as a Liberal. He became a close friend of leading white English amateur cricketers such as C.B. Fry and A.C. MacLaren. Biographies of Ranjitsinhji do not show that white English county cricketers objected to playing with or against him. W.G. Grace invited Ranjitsinhji to play for his London County Cricket Club, which played against other county sides though it was not in the county championship. Most of the prominent England amateurs were prepared to play

29. *Cricketer International,* September 1996, p. 35.

30. Ross, A. (1983), *Ranji: Prince of Cricketers,* London: Collins; Wilde, S. (1990), *Ranji: A Genius Rich and Strange,* London: Kingswood.

31. *Cricket,* 18 July 1895.

under him as captain on a tour of North America in 1899. Never captain of England, Ranjitsinhji was the captain of Sussex from 1899 until 1903 and received the great honour of captaining the Gentlemen and the MCC in first-class matches. The basis of Ranjitsinhji's appeal was his ability as a batsman and particularly the exciting style of his batsmanship, but he also possessed great personal charm. His engaging manner led W.G. Grace to write that 'Among cricketers "Ranji" is exceedingly popular, his open-hearted generosity and geniality having captured all their hearts.'[32]

Ranjitsinhji's popularity survived revelations about unappealing aspects to his character. In his thoroughly researched and judicious appraisal of Ranjitsinhji's character and achievements,[33] Simon Wilde has shown that he exaggerated the strength of his claims to the gadi of Nawanagar and that the extravagance of his lifestyle meant that he often failed to repay debts. His poor form in the test matches of 1902 may have been due in part to worries that he could have been declared bankrupt. In 1908 the Liberal MP Horatio Bottomley attacked Ranjitsinhji for failing to pay debts to tradespeople and small businesses in Sussex and in 1909 questions were asked about this in the House of Commons. Against the background of these allegations a farewell dinner was arranged for Ranjitsinhji at the Cambridge Guild-hall shortly before his departure to India to take up the gadi of Nawanagar. Such cricketing and public dignitaries as Viscount Clifden, Lord Dalmeny, W.G. Grace, Arthur Priestley MP, the writer Conan Doyle, A.C. MacLaren, C.B. Fry, Henry Leveson Gower, G.J.V. Weigall plus seven professional cricketers were present although the apologies received for not being present from Lord Harris, Lord Curzon, Lord Alverstone, Lord Hawke, the Honourable Alfred Lyttelton MP, Sir Spencer Ponsonby-Fane and the Master of Trinity College could have been related to unease over Ranjitsinhji's financial affairs.[34]

There were instances of hostility towards him. He was not immediately selected for the Cambridge University side, probably because the Hon. F.S. Jackson, the side's captain and later to be a Conservative MP and Governor of Bengal, had reservations about his unorthodox batting technique. It has been suggested that after playing cricket in India in 1892–3, Jackson became more appreciative of Indian cricketers.[35] In 1896, though in magnificent batting form, Ranjitsinhji was not selected for the first test against Australia at Lord's, because, it was alleged, Lord Harris had persuaded the MCC that as the test match was a representative game between England and Australia, Ranjitsinhji should not have been selected because he had not been born

32. Grace, W.G. (1980 reprint of the 1899 edition), *'W.G.' Cricketing Reminiscences & Personal Recollections*, London: Hambledon, p. 371.

33. Wilde, *Ranji*.

34. *Cricket*, 29 October 1908.

35. Wilde, *Ranji*, p. 41.

in England.[36] There may have been an element of racialism in Harris' attitude because he himself had been born in Trinidad but had played for and captained England. The committees of the clubs on which test matches were played selected England teams in the mid 1890s and the Lancashire committee chose Ranjitsinhji to play for England in the next test, which was played at Old Trafford. Ranjitsinhji's scores of 62 and 154 not out probably explain why it was scarcely ever suggested again that he should be not be selected for England, although after his selection for The Oval test match, *The Field* commented that 'The MCC had ruled that a gentleman born in India, of a long line of distinguished Indian ancestry, could not be an Englishman by any ingenuity of reasoning, however good a cricketer he might be. Lancashire and Surrey, however, ruled that he is an Englishman.'[37] Racist attitudes may explain why there was no sustained press campaign for Ranjitsinhji, who played as an amateur, to captain England. On the other hand, Ranjitsinhji's popularity shows that there were limits to the hostility in England to those who were not white.

Some asserted that Ranjitsinhji's cricketing abilities resulted from his contact with white English influences. In the 1920s Ranjitsinhji discouraged requests for his nephew Duleepsinhji to play in India, saying that 'Duleep and I are English cricketers.'[38] W.G. Grace argued that whilst the foundation of Ranjitsinhji's cricket had been laid in India, 'he perfected himself in England . . . it was on Parker's Piece at Cambridge that he acquired the different strokes, unerring judgment and faultless style which made him famous.'[39] In 1899 a writer for *Cricket* felt that it was right for Ranjitsinhji to have declined the captaincy of an Indian cricket tour to England proposed for 1900 because the standard of Indian cricket was so low that he would reaped nothing but 'ridicule and chagrin in his attempt to establish in England the claim of India to cricket honours'. Ranjitsinhji, the writer continued, was 'not an Indian cricketer. His education in the game had been purely English . . . In India he was a comparative failure, and all his sympathies are English. His nationality from a cricketer's point of view is a pure accident.'[40] Beliefs that exposure to white English influences were responsible for developing Ranjitsinhji's cricketing skills can be interpreted as expressions of white supremacism.

The exciting style of Ranjitsinhji's cricket was not the sole cause of his popularity in England. His appeal owed much to his claims that he was a prince. Simon Wilde has shown that when Ranjitsinhji began attracting public attention in the 1890s he stressed and often exaggerated his princely status in order to strengthen his claim to succeed the Maharaja of Nawanagar. In interviews he made a point of mentioning

---

36. *Field,* 18 July 1896.
37. *Field,* 15 August 1896.
38. de Mello, A. (1959), *Portrait of Indian Sport,* London: Macmillan, p. 16.
39. Grace, *'W.G.' Cricketing Reminiscences,* p. 369.
40. *Cricket,* 27 April 1899.

that Kumar Shri were not forenames but indicated his princely status. The title pages of the books he wrote – *The Jubilee Book of Cricket* (published 1897), *With Stoddart's Team in* Australia (published 1898) and *Cricket Guide and How to Play It* (published 1906) – all referred to him as Prince Ranjitsinhji. The frequent references to his being a prince in newspapers and cricket books show almost an obsession with his status as a prince. When Francis Thompson, the poet and literary critic, entitled his review of *The Jubilee Book of Cricket*, 'A Prince of India on the Prince of Games',[41] he was merely reflecting a general trend. The first biography of Ranjitsinhji, that of P.C. Standing, was issued in 1903 and entitled *Ranjitsinhji Prince of Cricket.*[42] Concern with his princely status can be related to an English reverence for the monarchy and for the aristocracy, socio-political institutions which can be seen as the apex of the class structure. The treatment of the black members of the West Indian touring parties in 1900 and 1906 also show that in England preoccupation with class and status could override racial differences. The distinction in cricket between amateurs and professionals was very much one of class. Amateurs, some of whom were shamateurs, belonged to the upper and middle classes. Professionals usually had working-class origins. Most of the black West Indian tourists were amateurs. On both tours the sporting press followed the convention of addressing them on scorecards as 'Mr' or with their initials before their surnames whereas professionals were referred to by only their surnames or had their initials printed after their names. Observance of this convention with black players suggests that the maintenance of class distinctions was felt at least as strongly as a need to assert racial distinctions.

Ranjitsinhji's popularity showed that race, and especially assumptions that differences in skin colour implied different physical capabilities, were important to whites in England. Much of Ranjitsinhji's appeal stemmed from what whites in England imagined was his 'otherness'. Descriptions of Ranjitsinhji frequently stressed the exotic, the unEnglish, element in his batting and appearance. His skill was attributed to the supposed characteristics of his race. In 1913 the journalist A.G. Gardiner wrote that 'Here was what the late Lord Salisbury would have called "a black man" playing cricket for all the world as if he were a white man. Then they realised that he did not play it as a white man, but as an artist of another and superior strain' and that Ranjitsinhji 'combines an Oriental calm with an Oriental swiftness – the stillness of the panther with the suddenness of its spring.'[43] In 1896 a leading article in *The Daily Telegraph* described 'Wrists supple and tough as a creeper of the Indian jungle, and dark eyes which see every twist and turn of the bounding ball, Ranjitsinhji

41. Thompson, F. (1927), 'A Prince of India on the Prince of Games' re-printed in *Essays of To-day and Yesterday: Francis Thompson,* London: Harrap, p. 70.

42. Standing, P.C. (1903), *Ranjitsinhji Prince of Cricket,* Bristol: Arrowsmith.

43. Gardiner, A.G. (1913), *Pillars of Society,* London: Nisbet, pp. 296–8.

has adopted cricket and turned it into an Oriental poem of action.'[44] Grace attributed Ranjitsinhji's popularity to two sources – 'his extraordinary skill as a batsman and his nationality.'[45]

Ranjitsinhji's style of batting with its stress on leg side play was thought to be foreign to the traditional method of English batting, which emphasized off-side strokes. Looking back on cricket in the Edwardian period Neville Cardus wrote that Ranjitsinhji 'not only demonstrated the leg glance; he also expressed the genius of his race.' In Cardus' memory, Ranjitsinhji's cricket 'was of his own country; when he batted a strange light was seen for the first time on English fields, a light out of the East. It was a lovely magic.' Whilst it must be remembered that Cardus was a master of inventing what he felt others ought to have said, he claimed that Ted Wainwright, the Yorkshire and England professional, had said that 'Ranji, he never made a Christian stroke in his life.'[46] Simon Wilde has shown that in 1897 it was said to C.B. Fry that Ranjitsinhji 'Yes, he can play, but he must have a lot of Satan in him.' In 1899 R.H. Lyttelton, the cricket writer educated at Eton and Cambridge and one of six brothers who played first-class cricket, argued that 'The English public is a curious one, and one of its peculiarities is a readiness to deify a cricketer all the more because he is of a different colour. They would have admired Ranjitsinhji as a white batsman, but they worship him because he is black.'[47] Ranjitsinhji himself attributed his cricketing skills to his race. He is supposed to have said that his eyesight was the basis of his batting, which was 'just a gift of my race . . . The message from eye to the brain, and from thence to the muscles, is flashed with a rapidity that has no equal amongst Englishmen.'[48]

Ranjitsinhji, Race and the Empire

Cricket enthusiasts argued that cricket fostered emotional loyalties between Britain and whites who settled in the colonies. An editorial in *The Field* declared in 1896 that 'the value of international matches at various games between England and her colonies . . . will be found to equal, if not surpass, as a factor in the manufacture of goodwill, any treaty, commercial or political, that ever was drawn up . . . our inter-change visits for carrying friendly war into another's country by means of bat and ball do eminent service in keeping alive the kindredship of blood.'[49] At a dinner

44. Wild, R. (1934), *The Biography of Colonel His Highness Shri Sir Ranjitsinhji Vibhaji, Maharaja Jam Sheb of Nawanagar, G.C.S.I., G.B.E., K.C.I.E.,* London: Rich & Cowan, p. 37.

45. Grace, *'W.G.' Cricketing Reminiscences,* p. 368.

46. Cardus, N., (1948 reprint of the 1934 edition), *Good Days,* pp. 30, 61.

47. Wilde, *Ranji,* p. 134.

48. Wilde, *Ranji,* p. 135.

49. *Field,* 27 June 1896.

given to the West Indian touring party by the West Indian Club in 1900 at the Grand Hotel, at which the black members of the team were present, Lord Selborne, the Under-Secretary of State for the Colonies, said that 'it would be impossible to exaggerate the importance to our Imperial unity which our Imperial sports might play . . . he would be a foolish man who denied that cricket, and our taste, as a race for sport, had had a real influence in harmonising and consolidating the different parts of the Empire.'[50]

Playing cricket was also believed to encourage non-whites to accept the white English qualities of sportsmanship and fair play, which in turn would convince them of the beneficence of British rule. 'After looking at the natives playing, both Hindoo and Parsee,' a writer in *Cricket* commented in 1885, 'I was drawn to the conclusion that they came nearer to us in sympathy and feeling through that game than through anything else.'[51] Lord Harris praised all of the West Indian tourists in 1900 for having 'played the game in a thoroughly sportsmanlike spirit – in a way which we in England who hold the game in very great respect, wish to see it played.'[52] After touring India with the Oxford University Authentic team in 1903, Cecil Headlam wrote that the history of British colonization was 'First the hunter, the missionary and the merchant, next the soldier and the politician, and then the cricketer . . . And of these civilising influences the last may, perhaps, be said to do the least harm . . . cricket unites, as in India, the rulers and the ruled. It also provides a moral training, an education in pluck, and nerve, and self-restraint, far more valuable to the character of the ordinary native than the mere learning by heart of a play of Shakespeare.'[53] In 1909 *Cricket* felt it sufficiently important to print an article from the *Madras Times* which claimed that the advantages of the proposed All-India tour of England would be 'great, for, besides the impetus which it will give to Indian cricket, it is surely desirable that English and Indian gentlemen should have as many opportunities of meeting each other on the field of sport, where racial feeling exists in the most excellent *esprit de corps*.'[54]

Much attention was focused on Parsee cricketers who accepted the traditions of cricket's sportsmanship and professed their loyalty to Britain. A writer in *Cricket Chat* claimed of the 1886 Parsee tour that 'Anything which can tend to promote an assimilation of tastes and habits between the English and native subjects of our Empress-Queen cannot fail to conduce the solidity of the British Empire.' For the

50. *The Times*, 14 August 1900.
51. *Cricket*, 11 June 1885.
52. *The Times*, 14 August 1914.
53. Headlam, *Ten Thousand Miles*, pp. 168–9.
54. *Cricket*, 28 October 1909.

same writer, the Parsee adoption of cricket indicated that they were 'the most intelligent as well as the most loyal of the races scattered over our Indian possessions.'[55] Two years later an article in *Cricket* about the second Parsee tour pointed out that 'Politically, as well as from the standpoint of cricket alone, the importance of this identification of the native races of our Indian Empire with our own customs cannot be overrated. Everything which begets sympathy between the component parts of the Imperial regime cannot fail to be of use in strengthening the ties between the governors and the governed, and if for this reason alone this interchange of visits between cricketers of the Old Country and the outlying parts of the British Empire cannot fail to be productive of good.'[56]

Scyld Berry has argued that the reception of the Parsee touring side in 1886 can be related to concern, and especially among Conservatives, about the challenge being posed to British rule in India by the rise of the Indian National Congress. In 1886, the year when Gladstone had proposed Home Rule for Ireland, Dadabhai Naoroji, a Parsee, had stood unsuccessfully as a Liberal candidate at the 1886 general election for Holborn, but was elected in 1892 for Central Finsbury. He was the second president of the Indian National Congress and because of the connections he saw between demands for home rule in Ireland and India, the Irish Nationalists offered him a safe seat in Ireland. Though Naoroji was a Parsee, the Parsee community was among the loyal of the religious communities to British rule and Berry sees the enthusiastic reception of the Parsee touring teams as part of a programme of 'loyalization', as an attempt to ensure that Parsees would continue to support British rule.[57] Matches were arranged against socially prestigious clubs. The team was received at Cumberland Lodge by HRH Prince and Princess Christian and given a dinner in their honour at Lord's by the MCC. D.H. Patel, captain of the side, in his farewell address, declared that 'we Parsees are among the most loyal subjects of the Queen of England and Empress of India . . . the Parsees are unanimous in favour of British rule, for they consider it best, not only for themselves, but for all the different communities of India.'[58] In 1906 J.M. Framjee Patel, a leading patron of Parsee cricket in India, was made an honorary member of the MCC and of Surrey CCC. In 1906 in an interview, probably with C.W. Alcock, the secretary of Surrey CCC, and which was printed on the front page of *Cricket,* he said that Indian cricket 'was the child of progress of the friendly embrace of the East and the West . . . Let cricket be one of the many links to unite the citizens of the greatest Empire the

---

55. Quoted in Raiji, *India's Hambledon Men,* p. 18.

56. *Cricket,* 23 August 1888.

57. Berry, S. (1982), *Cricket Wallah: With England in India 1981–2,* London: Hodder & Stoughton, pp. 21–3.

58. *Cricket,* 19 August 1886.

world has ever seen. Let the providential alliance of Ind and Britain be cemented with the lasting and enduring ties of one peace-loving King-emperor, one beautiful language, one victorious flag and last but not least, one grand Imperial game.' Such comments were very much what the white British wanted to hear, to be told that the non-whites recognized the beneficence of British rule. Patel did, however, point out that the white British did not always respond favourably to Indian requests to be accepted as full citizens of the Empire. 'Educated Indians' he mentioned, 'were quite alive to their Imperial destiny and yearn to share with their white fellow-subjects the rights and privileges of their great imperial heritage along with its burden.'[59]

Ranjitsinhji's popularity can be linked to his professions of loyalty to the Empire. He was never an open supporter of the Congress Party, but in the longer term he may unconsciously have stimulated Indian demands for independence. Mihir Bose has shown that Ranjitsinhji's 'strong romantic image . . . of an Indian conquering the English cricket field . . . played an important part in fostering Indian pride and self-respect'[60] which in turn helped to stimulate support for political independence from Britain. In public he praised the Empire and the benefits which it had brought to India, though he may have hoped that declarations of loyalty to the Empire could persuade the British Government to support his claims to be the heir to the gadi of Nawanagar. In 1908 at the farewell dinner organized for him at the Guildhall in Cambridge, held after he had been confirmed as the Maharaja of Nawanagar, he declared his belief in 'the full honesty and purpose of the British Government in India. There was not a service in the wide world which did its duty in a foreign land with a greater sense of justice than the military and civil servants of India.' He added that he was embarking on a new career with 'this one ideal – to do my duty to my country and my people, to uphold the honour of my house and race, to maintain the unity of our common Empire, and to show unswerving loyalty to the person of my Sovereign.' In the same speech, he also stressed that none could match the loyalty to the King-Emperor of the native Indian princes and that the British ought to give them more assistance in maintaining their authority, a theme which he was to stress many times.[61] In the 1920s when support for Indian independence was growing, Ranjitsinhji said 'I was brought up among the English and have a great affection for them, but I am an Indian at heart, and would not hesitate to advocate the withdrawal of the English from India if I thought it wise. I do not think so, however, and I hope that the firm partnership between King-Emperor and the princes will continue indefinitely.'[62] In 1930 he said at farewell dinner for the Australian

59. *Cricket,* 14 June 1906.
60. Bose, M. (1990), *A History of Indian Cricket,* London: Deutsch, p. 43.
61. *Cricket,* 29 October 1908.
62. Quoted by Ross, *Ranji,* p. 212.

touring team to England that 'The Princes of India have been very old members of Great Britain's teams; and both on easy wickets and difficult wickets they have tried their best to play with a straight bat for the Empire.'[63] He saw cricket as amongst the greatest benefits of British rule in India. In 1910 he told the members of the Young Cricketers CC at Poona that 'Cricket is one of the great boons the Government and English people have presented to us, and let us make the best of it . . . It is because this game brings forth the best virtues of a man that it is worth playing.'[64] There is no way of knowing for certain how Ranjitsinhji would have been regarded had he spoken out frequently against the Empire, but it seems likely that he done so, he would not have been viewed as such a great cricketing hero.

Whilst the British Empire was based on racist assumptions of white supremacy, perceptions of the Empire as a moral obligation were fortified by beliefs that within the Empire all were equal before the law and that those of all colours and creeds could come to accept the Empire as a moral trust in which whites were exercising power for the good of the subject peoples. Such views, no doubt, contained more than a trace of self-delusion and perhaps of hypocrisy, and were based on the assumption, in itself an expression of white supremacy, that those other than the white British would come to realize the wisdom of accepting British values and customs. Ranjitsinhji himself took the view that those of all races could feel that they belonged to the Empire. Whilst it can be argued that as a maharaja, Ranjitsinhji may have been aware that the survival of the Indian principalities with their semi-autonomous powers in India relied on co-operation with the Raj, he spoke often of 'our' Empire, stressed the loyalty of the princes to British rule and complained that too often British governments had not been prepared to treat them as loyal partners. At the dinner organized for him just before he left for Nawanagar in 1908, he said 'I think that the British Empire should treat all British subjects alike' and protested that Indians were not allowed to settle in Australia, Canada and South Africa.[65] The source of Ranjitsinhji's popularity with many British whites was that for them he demonstrated the success of British imperialism. He showed that those were not white could absorb through contacts with whites the values that underlay British civilization and come to realize that the Empire was founded on a disinterested concern among British whites for the welfare of the subject peoples of the Empire. In 1899 T.F. Dale pointed out the 'lordly scorn of our fellow-countrymen for the ways of those whose misfortune it is not only to be born of another nation, but that nation a dark-skinned one' but argued that in India sports played between whites and Indians were 'the real solvent of race distinctions . . . and that in giving our native fellow-subjects our

63. Wild, *The Biography of . . . Ranjitsinhji*, p. 286.
64. *Cricket*, 27 October 1910.
65. Ross, *Ranji*, p. 153.

love for our manly outdoor recreations, we insensibly draw closer to them and they to us'. By excelling at cricket, a sport so close to white perceptions of England and of the moral value of Englishness, and by accepting its code of sportsmanship and the social relationships of cricket, Ranjitsinhji was living proof of how those who were not white could assimilate white English values. He helped to convince the British that those who been colonised would come to accept the qualities and customs underlying British imperialism. In Dale's view there was 'no better example of the fusion of East and West in a single personality' than in Ranjitsinhji.[66] A.G. Gardiner wrote in the *Daily News* that Ranjitsinhji, 'through his genius for the English game, he has familiarised the English people with the idea of the Indian as a man of like affections with ourselves, and with capacities beyond ours in directions supposed to be peculiarly our own.'[67]

Ranjitsinhji, the Parsee cricketers and the African-Caribbeans who toured England helped to persuade whites before the First World War that people of colour could be trusted, not necessarily trusted to govern themselves but trusted to acquiesce with, and support, white rule in the Empire and even become apologists for the imperialist ideal. Ranjitsinhji was living proof of how those who were not white could come to recognize the Empire as an expression of white moral worth. But the acceptance of the morality of Empire by those such as Ranjitsinhji did not imply that the white English were abandoning their assumptions of white English superiority or were recognizing other cultures to be of equal worth. It was far from a recognition that white rule over the Empire would be relinquished. A tone of self-regard pervaded much cricket discourse. It was implied that non-white cricketers who practised the English tradition of sportsmanship were to be congratulated for having the good sense to recognize the superiority of the example that the white English had set them. Acceptance of white English cricket mores by those who were not white was seen as proof of white English moral excellence.

66. Dale, T.F., (1899), 'Polo and Politics', *Blackwoods Magazine,* 165, (June), pp. 1033–6.
67. Ross, *Ranji,* p. 158.

–2–

Cricket and Racism between the Wars

The presence of non-whites in English cricket became a little stronger between the wars. Test match status was granted to the West Indies and India. The West Indies played their first test match against England at Lord's in 1928 and had further test tours to England in 1933 and 1939. In the winters of 1929–30 and 1934–5 England played four match test series in the West Indies. India played one test match against England in England in 1932 and three in 1936 and in 1933–4 England played three test matches against India in India. Neither the West Indies nor India were accorded five match series in England which suggests they were not considered to present much of a challenge to England. The sporting press between the wars did not consider test series against the West Indies, India or New Zealand equivalent to matches against Australia. In January 1930 England teams played two test matches at the same time – one against New Zealand and the other against the West Indies. India did not win a test match against England between the wars and whilst the West Indies did not win a test match in England until 1950, the West Indies won one of the 1929–30 tests and by winning two tests to England's one in 1934–5 took the series, but this did not provoke great concern in England, probably because the England touring party had not included all of England's leading players.

Very few who were not white played county cricket between the wars. Two Asian princes – Kumar Shri Duleepsinhji, a nephew of Ranjitsinhji, and Iftikhar Ali Khan, the Nawab of Pataudi – played for England between the wars. Both had privileged backgrounds and played first-class cricket as amateurs. Duleepsinhji was educated at Cheltenham College and Cambridge University where he gained a cricket blue. From 1924 until 1932 he played for Sussex and was the captain in 1931 and 1932. He played for England in 12 test matches. In the 1950s he was the Indian High Commissioner to Australia. Pataudi was an Oxford cricket blue and between 1932 and 1938 played for Worcestershire. He played three times for England between 1932 and 1934. In 1946 he captained India against England. Ranjitsinhji, Duleepsinhji and Pataudi each scored a century in their first test matches against Australia. In 1929 Duleepsinhji did not play against South Africa after the first test. Duleepsinhji believed that he was not selected for the Gentlemen and Players match, to be held just before the third test, because 'people of great influence' had told the England selectors that he must not be chosen and that if he had scored a century, public opinion would have forced his recall to the England team. The South African captain told Duleepsinhji that none of the South African tour management or players objected to playing against him, but Duleepsinhji was informed by the English cricket authorities that 'some South African politicians . . . could not face the risk of century being scored against their team by a coloured man.'[1] Mihir Bose in his history of Indian cricket has claimed that A.W. Carr, a former England captain and the captain of Nottinghamshire, and Pelham Warner, another former England captain, cricket journalist and England selector, did not think that Duleepsinhji should have played for England.[2] The sporting press in England made little reference to Duleepsinhji's omission from the England team. Only two other non-white cricketers received Oxbridge blues between the wars – de Saram from Ceylon who also played for Minor Counties cricket for Hertfordshire and Jahangir Khan who played four times for India. Neither played for a first-class county team. Dr. C.H. Gunasekara from Ceylon played thirty-nine times for Middlesex between 1919 and 1921 and Hardit Singh Malik played a handful of matches for Sussex just before and after the First World War. No African-Caribbean played county cricket regularly between the wars. No coloured cricketer seems to have played county cricket as a professional between the wars.

Racial prejudice can be found in English cricket between the wars, but it does not seem to have been so very strong and was perhaps less marked than in other areas of life. The African-Caribbean cricketer Learie Constantine first played cricket in England with the West Indian touring party that played against county sides in 1923. In his book *Colour Bar,* published in 1954, which showed that he was acutely aware of racial discrimination and which catalogued instances of racial insults and exploitation, he recalled that playing cricket in four continents, he had

> come across some colour prejudice now and then. There have been "incidents", mostly hushed up by us all. There have been some rivalries and vendettas that owed a lot of their sharpness and quite a bit of their fun to colour. For in sport we found it possible at times to have fun even when really out for blood . . . Sportsmen mostly have big hearts and are quick to be kind, slow to be cruel. Perhaps there is just a tinge of extra sharpness when in direct competition with a man of another colour, but the sport can be all the better and keener for that. On the whole I have no complaints.[3]

Few English whites commented in public that Duleepsinhji and Pataudi should not have been selected for England and few condemned the appointment of Duleepsinhji as captain of Sussex. No prominent figure from cricket or politics argued

---

1. Constantine, L. (1946), *Cricket in the Sun,* London: Stanley Paul, p. 90.
2. Bose, M. (1990), *A History of Indian Cricket,* London: Deutsch, p. 64. See also *Wisden Cricket Monthly,* January 1996, p. 8.
3. Constantine, L. (1954), *Colour Bar,* London: Stanley Paul, p. 193.

between the wars that England should not be playing cricket against non-whites and no first-class cricketer appears to have made a public statement that he did not wish to play against the Indians or West Indians because of their colour. Some whites, of course, may not have wanted cricket to be played against non-whites, but choosing to keep their comments to themselves or the non-reporting of such views suggests a reluctance to publicize racist views. The restricted press comment about Duleepsinhji being dropped from the England team because of South African objections to playing against a non-white cricketer may have meant that the cricket establishment in England was afraid of a public condemnation of such co-operation with a racist request. When reservations were expressed about playing test matches against India or the West Indies, they usually stressed the lack of playing strength required for test cricket. In 1933, after England had defeated the West Indians at Lord's by an innings and 27 runs, Neville Cardus wrote that 'English cricket ought always to be strong enough to find a second eleven good enough to beat the aspirants from the West Indies' and that 'the time has come to ask the MCC to put an end to Test matches that are not Test matches.'[4]

Much press reporting of the West Indian tours concentrated on the playing details of matches, of how batsmen scored runs and of how bowlers took wickets with only occasional reference to skin colour. Indeed it is often impossible from press reports to establish which players were black. In 1928 the *Daily Herald* referred occasionally to Learie Constantine as 'the dusky terror', 'the fastest of the three coloured cyclones' and 'this dark-skinned Jessop' but its reporting in 1939 did not make such comments. In cricket books and newspapers the playing failures of the black West Indians were often attributed to their temperaments which were seen as a result of their race. H.J. Henley, a cricket correspondent for the *Daily Mail,* wrote in 1928 that 'several of the West Indies team seem to become intoxicated by the exuberance of their own brilliancy . . . None the less, these batsmen must continue to play that is in their blood. They cannot change their temperament.'[5] In his *Playing for England! My Test-cricket Story,* Jack Hobbs in 1931 wrote of the West Indian tourists of 1928 with great affection, and especially of Joe Small, who had 'a smile that was all over his face.' For Hobbs the 'chief characteristic' of West Indian cricketers was 'I speak of temperament this time – very high up in the air one minute, very down in the mouth the next. They were just big boys. Which explains why they bowled fast and could not play slow bowling. All boys want to bowl fast.'[6]

Cardus described West Indian cricketers in similar terms. In 1930 he wrote that the 'erratic quality of West Indian cricket is surely true to racial type. At one moment

---

4. *Manchester Guardian,* 14, 15 August 1933.
5. *Daily Mail,* 21 July 1928.
6. Hobbs, J. (1931), *Playing for England! My Test-cricket Story,* London: Gollancz, p. 140.

these players are eager, confident, and quite masterful; then as circumstances go against them you can see them losing heart. Routine has not yet given them a cloak to cover emotions which live on the surface.' He drew an interesting comparison between West Indian cricket and jazz, the musical form created by blacks. 'The West Indians' he wrote 'in truth, are jazz cricketers. That is to say, they give us a vivid sense of that improvisatory and far from formal energy which is the essence of jazz.'[7] In 1934 when discussing the appeal of the black Trinidadian cricketer Learie Constantine, Cardus claimed that Constantine's 'originality is a vital and full expression of the West Indian temperament . . . When we see Constantine bat or bowl or field, we know at once that he is not an English player, not an Australian player, not a South African player; we know that his cuts and drives, his whirling fast balls, his leaping and clutching . . . are racial; we know they are the consequences of impulses born in the blood, heated by the sun, and influenced by an environment and a way of life much more natural than ours – impulses not common to the psychology of the over-civilised quarters of the world.'[8] Sir Home Gordon commented that George Headley, the black West Indian batsman, did 'not suffer from the mercurial temperament which appears to permit his companions seldom to play an uphill game.'[9] Another writer commented in 1933 that 'These West Indians are lovably sensitive to the course of events. When they take a wicket, they shake hands and smile and show their white teeth; when catch is missed they indulge in gestures of intensest dismay, and they seem always about to drop a catch not because they are not clever fieldsmen but because they expect their hands to be in a dozen different places at the same time.'[10]

Comments such as those of Hobbs and Cardus are not permeated with malevolence to black West Indians and show admiration for their cricketing abilities, but they reek with a sense of white condescension and an assumption that race, as expressed through skin colour, explains differences in behaviour between whites and blacks. C.L.R. James, the black Marxist African-Caribbean writer, had a very different perspective on how West Indians played cricket. In 1932, James, a friend of Constantine, came to Britain and lived in Nelson, the North Lancashire cotton town where Constantine was employed as a professional in the Lancashire League. After reading a match report written by James, Cardus arranged for James to become a cricket correspondent for the *Manchester Guardian*. James objected to descriptions of George Headley as a black batsman. His view was that Headley was a very great

7. Cardus, N. (1930), *Cricket,* London: Longman Green, pp. 137–8. For a further discussion of how Constantine can be seen as a representative of the jazz age in cricket, see Hill, J. (1994), 'Reading the Stars: A Post-modernist Approach to Sports History', *Sports Historian,* 14 (May).

8. Cardus, N. (1948 reprint of the 1934 edition), *Good Days,* London: Hart-Davis, p. 31.

9. Gordon, H. (1939), *Background of Cricket,* London: Barker, p. 105.

10. Constantine, L. (1946), *Cricket in the Sun,* London: S. Paul, 1946, p. 57.

batsman and his skin colour was irrelevant to this, that cricketing ability was not an expression of ethnicity. The African-Caribbean test cricketer Learie Constantine saw the view that black West Indian cricketers were temperamentally unsuited for test cricket as racist prejudice. In his book *Cricket and I*, published in 1933, he wrote that the charge of black West Indian players being temperamental was 'unfounded' and that he 'had not noticed any excess of temperament on the part of the darker members of the side.' He thought that boxing, where 'temperament would prove fatal', proved that black men were not temperamental. Whilst conceding that 'Tears have not infrequently been shed' by black West Indians, Constantine pointed out that this was also done by English, South African and Australian players and proportionately more often.[11]

Constantine did see race as a reason for the underperformance of West Indian sides in test cricket. In *Cricket and I* he argued that 'the trouble as far as colour is concerned goes deeper . . . and lies rather with the composition of the West Indian team itself.' He thought that even West Indian selectors did not realize the difficulties raised by having a multi-racial team. In his view disunity among players had undermined the effectiveness of some West Indian teams. By emphasizing the multi-racial nature of West Indian teams and by mentioning that 'much more depends on the leadership, which must itself be above pettiness, sympathetic, and yet be strong and command respect from all the team', Constantine seemed to be criticising the practice, which was to last until 1960, of the West Indian teams having white captains.[12] As this book was published in England in the expectation presumably of being sold in England, the restrained tone of Constantine's criticism of white captaincy may mean that it was not expected that the English cricket public would not respond favourably to calls for a black captain, although it also possible that Constantine may have suspected that more forthright comments could have reduced his prospects of being selected for future West Indian teams. In 1939 the cricket writer Sir Home Gordon mentioned that when G.C. Grant had captained the West Indies 'to some English eyes the familiarity he permitted from some of his coal-black professionals appeared rather strange', which suggests that some in England might have resented more forthright criticisms from a black player of white captains.[13]

After the Second World War Constantine attacked the appointment of white captains in less equivocal terms. In *Cricket in the Sun*, published in 1946, he declared that West Indian teams, having coloured players, should have a coloured captain. He wrote that 'It is not only what *I* mean – every coloured player who has turned out in an international side has been conscious of it, and it rots the heart of our

11. Constantine, L.N. (1933), *Cricket and I*, London: Allan, pp. 170–1.
12. Constantine, *Cricket and I*, pp. 172–3.
13. Gordon, *Background of Cricket*, p. 105.

cricket, and always will until it is changed.' Choosing an incompetent white captain, an 'atmosphere of servitude is fostered, and we know it well.' For Constantine, always having the West Indian captained by a white was equivalent to insisting that Australia always had to be captained by an Englishman. Constantine claimed that on the tour of England in 1933 'insufficient confidence in captaincy' had caused the West Indian team to underperform.[14] In the 1950 issue of the *Daily Worker Cricket Handbook,* Constantine argued that West Indies cricket would 'never honestly show what it can do until this colour bar is removed . . . the colour question affects every player's chances of selection, and above all it causes some strange choices of captain for touring sides . . . better players have made place for worse ones with white or near-white skins.'[15] After abandoning in 1960 the practice of having a white captain the West Indies became a far more powerful force in test cricket.

Between the wars, cricket writers in England rarely touched on the subject of colour and West Indian captaincy. The disappointing record of West Indian test teams was hardly ever blamed on having white captains. Even in 1957, the last time a West Indian touring party in England had a white captain, there were no sustained comments from the cricket press in England about whether the West Indian team would have been strengthened by having a coloured captain, although Clyde Walcott, an African-Caribbean, was vice-captain of the side, and John Goddard, the white captain, scored only 112 runs in eight test innings and took only two wickets for 128 runs. In the final test of the 1934–5 series against England at Kingston, Jamaica, little comment was made in England about Constantine taking over the captaincy of the West Indies side when the white captain G.C. Grant was injured. The West Indies won the match and so took the series. The appointment of George Headley as captain of the West Indies side, which included white players, against England for the first test at Barbados of the 1947–8 England tour of the West Indies did not stimulate debate in England about whether it had been anomalous for West Indian sides to be captained by whites.

Evidence about how players and spectators in first-class cricket reacted to black and Asian cricketers between the wars is scarce. Nothing has been found to show whether Sussex professionals had reservations about Duleepsinhji becoming their captain, but most professional cricketers knew their place and would not have expected to be consulted about the appointment of a county captain. The fate of Cecil Parkin, who criticized Arthur Gilligan's captaincy of the England team in a newspaper article, showed how overt criticism of cricket authority could damage

---

14. Constantine, *Cricket in the Sun,* p. 62.

15. Thomas, A.A. (ed.) (n.d.), *Daily Worker Cricket Handbook 1950,* London: People's Press Printing Society, pp. 10–11.

employment and playing prospects.[16] Around 1934, members of the Lancashire committee approached Constantine about playing for the county as he had gained a residential qualification for Lancashire whilst playing league cricket at Nelson. Constantine was eager to play county cricket and had the support of T.A. Higson, a chairman and treasurer of Lancashire, but the proposal was killed before it reached the full committee, because, in Constantine's words, 'certain influential people on the Lancashire Board could not tolerate my colour.'[17] Later in the 1930s a further proposal for Constantine to play for Lancashire as a professional may well have been abandoned because of opposition from the club's professionals. In 1975 the Lancashire and England professional Len Hopwood recalled the thought of 'a coloured chap playing for Lancashire was ludicrous . . . We Lancastrians were clannish in those less-enlightened days.' The reaction in the dressing room was 'electric', with the players wanting 'none of Constantine. We would refuse to play.' Hopwood mentioned that they had nothing against Constantine personally who was very popular with them, but 'the thought of a black man taking the place of a white man in our side was anathema. It was a simple as that.'[18] Such an assertion can be taken as evidence of deep-seated racial prejudice among white county cricketers in England, especially as there seemed to have been no similar protest from Lancashire players when the white Australian fast bowler Ted McDonald joined the county staff in 1924 after playing for Nelson in the Lancashire League.

In 1940, when black West Indian workers were brought to Britain to alleviate labour shortages in industry, Constantine was appointed the welfare officer for north-west England by the Ministry of Labour, which perhaps reflected a hope that his standing with blacks and whites would have meant that he was especially fitted to defuse possible incidents of racial friction. But Constantine himself was also the victim of racial prejudice during the war. In 1943 when he was playing in a cricket match at Lord's, he was refused accommodation at the Imperial Hotel in Russell Square. It is thought that the presence at the hotel of 200 white American officers may have influenced the attitude of the hotel but one black man had already written to the Colonial Office about discrimination by London hoteliers. He mentioned that if 'I walk in perhaps twelve millionaires walk out.' The manageress of the Imperial Hotel had was reported to have said 'We are not going to have these niggers in our hotel. He can stop the night, but if he does not go tomorrow morning his luggage

---

16. For a discussion of Parkin's career and abandonment of county cricket in 1926, see Foot, D. (1985), *Cricket's Unholy Trinity*, London: S. Paul.

17. Constantine, *Cricket in the Sun*, p. 90. In his *Colour Bar*, p. 26, Constantine wrote 'there was some unpleasant disagreement because of my colour – some comments came to me – and I was finally rejected.'

18. Bearshaw, B. (1990), *From the Stretford End: The Official History of Lancashire County Cricket Club*, London: Partridge, 1990, p. 271.

will be put outside and his door locked.' When Constantine's superior at the Ministry of Labour was called to the hotel and pointed out that Constantine was a British subject and a civil servant, the hotel manageress replied 'he is a nigger . . . We won't have niggers in this hotel.'[19] As Constantine had already paid a deposit for his room, he sued the Imperial Hotel for breach of contract and was awarded damages of £5.[20] He stressed that he was a British subject and could see no reason why Americans, who were aliens, should been given preference over him.[21] Perhaps because of the limited size of newspapers during the war, the press merely reported the details of the trial and made no comments to indicate what the English cricket world thought of Constantine's treatment at the Imperial Hotel, but Constantine received hundreds of letters of congratulation when he won the court case. In 1954 Constantine wrote of the Imperial Hotel episode that he 'could multiply these stories of personal slights indefinitely' which were 'an unpleasant part of daily life in Britain for anyone of colour.'[22] As so many whites recall Constantine as a naturally friendly man with an engaging personality, it is possible that other black cricketers of his generation may have met even more hostility. The extent of the respect accorded to Constantine was shown in 1945 when he was invited to captain the Dominions team in a match against an England XI, a match regarded as virtually a test match, even though all the other Dominion players were white. From 1962 until 1964 Constantine was the High Commissioner for Trinidad and Tobago and made a life peer in 1969.

Cricket and anti-Semitism

Much of the celebration of cricket as a totem of Englishness was intertwined with the pastoral tradition. Georgina Boyes and Alun Howkins have shown how in the early twentieth century those from the political left and the political right regarded the town as morally and physically corrupt, contaminated by an amoral and sordid pursuit of wealth. Howkins has argued that anti-Semitism was a powerful strand of this antagonism towards the town, with the town being thought the natural habitat of unEnglish money-grubbing Jews.[23] How far anti-Semitism was extended to cricket is not immediately clear. The difficulties of defining Jewishness and the tiny

19. *Daily Mirror,* 20 June 1944.

20. Rich, P.B. (1986), *Race and Empire in British Politics,* Cambridge: Cambridge University Press, pp. 161, 250–1; Fryer, P. (1984), *Staying Power: The History of Black People in Britain,* London: Pluto, pp. 364–7.

21. *Manchester Guardian,* 20 June 1944.

22. Constantine, *Colour Bar,* p. 138.

23. Boyes, G. (1993), *The Imagined Village: Culture, Ideology and the English Folk Revival,* Manchester: Manchester University Press; Howkins, A. (1986),'The Discovery of Rural England' in Colls, R. and Dodds, P. (eds), *Englishness: Politics and Culture 1880–1920,* Beckenham: Croom Helm.

number of those calling themselves Jews who have played county cricket complicate the task of gauging the extent of anti-Semitism in first-class cricket. Percy Fender was thought to be Jewish and captained Surrey from 1921 until 1931, which can be interpreted as evidence that anti-Semitism was not strong in county cricket. On the other hand, Fender was known as a highly imaginative captain and Surrey's failure to win the county championship under his captaincy is usually attributed to the county's weak bowling and hardly ever to the nature of his captaincy. He is believed to have suggested to Douglas Jardine, who succeeded him as captain of Surrey, that bodyline bowling could undermine Bradman's batting. Fender was never invited to captain England which has been blamed in part on prejudice against his supposed Jewish origins, though Fender denied that he was Jewish and was reported to have said that it would not have told against him had he been Jewish.[24] It is possible that critical comments about Australian umpires in the newspaper reports which he sent to England whilst a member of the MCC party touring Australia in 1920–1 may have counted against him. The brothers M.D. and B.H. Lyon were Jewish. They had attended Rugby. M.D. was awarded a cricket blue at Cambridge and B.H. at Oxford. M.D. was considered one of the best cricketers of his generation not to have been selected for England. B.H. was captain of Gloucestershire from 1929 until 1934 and though an astute tactician was never considered among the front runners for the England captaincy. Lord Rothschild, educated at Harrow and Cambridge, played ten matches for Northamptonshire between 1929 and 1931. Aaron Cohen, educated at Cheltenham, played in three matches for Oxford University in 1934 but was not selected for the 'varsity' match.

As nothing other than names and sometimes occupations for committee members of county clubs can be established, it is impossible to be certain about the role of Jews in cricket club administration. A sample of several hundred committee members from various inter-war years and for different counties does not suggest a strong Jewish presence in county cricket administration. Whilst surnames are at best only the crudest guide to Jewish origins, few committee members had what could be described as 'obviously' Jewish names, but it is difficult to decide whether this resulted from prejudice against, or a lack of interest in cricket among Jews. Quash-Cohen was the mainstay of the Manchester CC, in effect the Lancashire CCC third eleven, for much of the 1930s. The poet Siegfried Sassoon was a Jew with a high public profile who was also an enthusiastic club cricketer. Anti-Semitism was strong in some English sports. Golf clubs were often suspected of being reluctant to admit Jews, but this has rarely been said about club cricket. The culture of Orthodox Jews may have made it difficult for them to become involved with cricket. Mr M. Gordon, secretary of Belmont CC, a predominantly Jewish club in London, has suggested

24. *Cricketer International,* October 1991, p. 44; Streeton, R. (1981), *P.G.H. Fender: A Biography,* London: Faber & Faber, p. 20.

that, in general, Jewish culture in Britain has celebrated the cerebral rather than the physical which could explain why, in relation to their numbers, the Jewish presence in the arts, the professions and academia throughout the twentieth century has been disproportionately strong and that in sports relatively weak.[25] Between the wars most recreational cricket was played on Saturdays, the Jewish Sabbath. In 1939 over 1,400 cricket clubs, mainly from the counties of Essex, Kent, Middlesex and Surrey were affiliated to the Club Cricket Conference. Only one, the Maccabi Association, was clearly a Jewish club. In the 1990s this was only Jewish cricket club in the London area that had been formed before the Second World War. Mr Sam Bulka who has been associated with cricket in the London since 1948 believes that around thirty Jewish teams now play regularly in London.[26]

Responses to Sir Julien Cahn also raise suspicions about anti-Semitism in English cricket. Having built up a furniture business inherited from his father, Cahn was one of the major patrons of English cricket between the wars. He laid out a cricket ground at West Bridgford and engaged professional county to players to appear for his eleven, some of whose matches were accorded first-class status. He organized and captained tours to Jamaica, North America, Argentina, Ceylon and New Zealand. He was twice the president of Nottinghamshire CCC and paid for new stands and a winter practice shed. He represented Leicestershire on the Advisory County Cricket Committee, the body that superintended county cricket. In 1934 he gave £1,000 to Leicestershire CCC and in 1935, after Nottinghamshire had lost hundreds members over what had thought to be insufficient support for the county's players involved with bodyline, paid the subscriptions of 800 new members.[27] He employed the New Zealand test cricketer C.S. Dempster as the manager of his furniture whilst he qualified to play for Leicestershire and afterwards so that he could captain Leicestershire as an amateur.[28] Cahn was president of the City of Nottingham Conservative Society and the master of three foxhound hunts, including the Woodland-Pytchley. Philip Snow, the colonial administrator and cricket enthusiast, alleges that Cahn received a baronetcy in 1934 for having 'paid off' Maundy Gregory who had arranged titles to be conferred on some contributors to the Conservative Party's funds. Snow also believes that Cahn patronized cricket 'to gild further his image as the complete English gentleman in the way that he had managed to become a master of foxhounds and live in a baronial hall.'[29]

25. Interview with Mr. M. Gordon, secretary of Belmont CC, 22 May 2000.

26. Interview with Mr. Sam Bulka, secretary of the Maccabi Association CC, 22 May 2000.

27. *[Bolton Evening News] Buff,* 24 February 1934, 6 February 1937.

28. Lambert, D. (1992), *The History of Leicestershire County Cricket Club,* London: Christopher Helm, p. 120.

29. Snow, P. (1997), *The Years of Hope, Colonial Administration in the South Seas and Cricket,* London: Radcliffe, p. 72.

A great cricket enthusiast, Cahn's playing ability was limited and recollections of his cricket sometimes have a rather sniggering tone and show that he did not quite appreciate cricket's code of sportsmanship. Much mirth has been directed at his experiments with inflatable batting pads. Snow recalls that when George Gunn, a former England player and one of Cahn's employees, was the umpire, he would never give Cahn out LBW even though Cahn's 'sole movement was to put his leg in front of the wicket.' Gunn advised the umpire of the visiting side to do likewise if the club wished to have further fixtures against Cahn's side and to enjoy the 'magnificent hospitality' and 'the wine with which the visitors were plied.' Despite his financial support for cricket, Snow mentions that 'Cahn was *persona non grata* with many – including the hierarchy of MCC which unforgivably never elected him to membership – in the all too unpleasant attitude of that era towards those who might not have the requisite ancestry.'[30] Snow may not have been referring to Cahn's Jewish origins and it is possible that many may have felt that Cahn was not quite a gentleman, but given the scale of his support for county cricket, it seems possible that anti-Semitic prejudice could have been a major reason why he was not elected a member of the MCC.

Coloured Players and League Cricket

Non-white cricketers had a great impact on league cricket between the wars. Clubs from the most prestigious leagues were usually allowed to play one professional and many of the strongest clubs engaged as professionals players with experience of county and sometimes test cricket. No non-white cricketer was employed as a professional by a club from the Lancashire League or the Central Lancashire League, the leading leagues in Lancashire, before the First World War, though in 1879, before the establishment of league cricket, Nelson hired Francis Creuze who has been thought to have played as Dick o'Dicks on the Australian Aborigine tour of England in 1868, but he seems more likely to have been a Portuguese who had decided to take the name Dick o' Dicks.[31] C.B. Llewellyn, often thought to be coloured, was the professional for Accrington CC from 1911 until 1915. Learie Constantine, the professional for Nelson from 1929 until 1937, was the first black West Indian professional in the Lancashire League. In 1938 he became the professional for Rochdale in the Central Lancashire League. Other black West Indians who played in the Lancashire League were Edwin St Hill for Lowerhouse from 1931 to 1933, E.A. Martindale

---

30. Snow, *Years of Hope,* pp. 73, 76.

31. *Nelson Cricket Club (at Seedhill) 1878–1978 Centenary Brochure,* (n.p., n.d.), p. 13. I am grateful to Mr Don Ambrose for information about Creuze's Portuguese origins.

for Burnley from 1936 to 1938 and George Headley for Haslingden from 1934 to 1938. In 1933 Francis, the West Indian fast bowler was the professional for Radcliffe in the Bolton League whose professional between 1926 and 1932 had been C.B. Llewellyn. In the late 1930s two Indian test players became professionals in the Lancashire League – Amar Singh for Colne from 1935 to 1938 and for Burnley in 1939 and Lala Armanath for Nelson in 1938 and 1939.

The limited opportunities for West Indian cricketers to be paid for playing cricket in the Caribbean added to the attractions of being a league professional in England. Precise details of the contracts of league professionals are hard to find as club officials often felt that their negotiating position with prospective professionals would be stronger if the sums they had paid to others were not public knowledge. It is most unlikely, however, that any professional would have been paid more than Constantine. Gerald Howat believes that in his first two years at Nelson Constantine's earnings, including collections for outstanding performances, were around £1,200. In 1936 he received a benefit of £500 in addition to his wage as a professional. In 1934 another league club was reputed to have offered him £1,100 to play for one season. In 1938 when Rochdale paid him £800 for playing for 20 weeks and to which collections could be added, he believed that he was the highest paid cricketer in the world.[32] In 1933 the £20 per week paid to George Francis by Radcliffe was the highest wage paid by a league club in the Bolton area to a professional between the wars.

Vast crowds flocked to see Constantine play league cricket. Between 1929 and 1933 Nelson's fixtures were one seventh of those of the Lancashire League but accounted for 75% of the League's total match receipts.[33] Probably more than 75,000 paid to watch the home matches of Nelson in 1929, over 65,000 in 1930 over 50,000 in 1932, 1934 and 1935. In 1934 and 1935 Nelson had more paying spectators at its home matches than either of the first-class counties Leicestershire and Northamptonshire. Rochdale had its highest match receipts for the 1930s in 1938 when Constantine was its professional. The impact of Constantine on the gates of Nelson probably persuaded other Lancashire League clubs to sign West Indian test players.

It can be argued that Constantine rarely fulfilled his potential in test cricket. In his 18 test matches he scored over 50 runs on only four occasions and as a bowler took five wickets in an innings only twice. In first-class matches other than test matches for the West Indies he could be a devastating big hitter and a very fast bowler. Many judged him the greatest fielder of all time. Cardus described the movements of Constantine in the field as 'strange, almost primitive, in their pouncing

32. Howat, G. (1975), *Learie Constantine,* London: Allen & Unwin, 1975, p. 75; Constantine, *Cricket in the Sun,* pp. 65, 131; *[Bolton Evening News] Buff,* 9 January 1936.

33. *Nelson Leader,* 2 February 1934.

voracity and unconscious beauty, a dynamic beauty, not one of smooth curves and relaxations.'[34] Against Middlesex in 1928 he scored 86 runs in an hour, took seven wickets for 57 runs and then scored 103 runs in an hour to win the match. In league cricket his performances were astounding. In 1934 he took ten wickets for ten runs for Nelson against Accrington. In 1929 he scored 124 in just over an hour. In 1937, he scored 192, a vast number of runs for a league match, against the East Lancashire club. In 1938 he scored a century for Rochdale in only 33 minutes.

Constantine's drawing power in league cricket was based on his realisation that playing cricket in a highly spectacular style appealed to local tastes. Indeed Jack Hobbs felt that he played to the gallery too much and sometimes descended to clowning. Sir Home Gordon considered Constantine to be 'a shrewd chap, who felt that it paid to clown . . . when talking to me about his League experiences, he once broadly hinted as much. Why should he be blamed, when it brought him, annually, sums of money larger than anyone else has obtained from actual matches?'[35] The writer Don Haworth, born in 1924, watched Bacup play in the Lancashire League. When Constantine walked down the pavilion steps, he recalled that the 'whole crowd rose in a buzz of excitement' and added that when he made a good score 'he performed antics. He would play balls through his legs, go down the wicket and volley them, hook off-breaks, and run desperate singles. Everybody loved him.'[36] This style, Haworth suggests, appealed to spectators more interested in football who wanted cricket played 'fast and violently.' One Nelsonian has recalled that Constantine 'generated excitement like a man walking a tightrope without a safety net.'[37] The other black West Indian cricketers who played as professionals in the Lancashire League before the Second World War did not inspire the same level of public interest, possibly because they did not play with such flamboyant style.

Constantine's appeal was also due to his colour. A black man was still a novelty in much of Lancashire. Constantine was first black man that Don Haworth saw. When Constantine arrived in Nelson he thought of himself as 'a coloured curiosity'[38] and claimed that a black man was such an unusual sight that a boy asked whether he had just fallen down a coal cellar. C.L.R. James, who lodged with Constantine in Nelson in the early 1930s, says that they were the only black men in Nelson except for a road sweeper. Much of Constantine's attraction stemmed from the novelty of seeing a black man play cricket to such a high standard when blacks were still so very rare in Lancashire.

34. Cardus, *Good Days,* p. 33.
35. Gordon, *Background of Cricket,* p. 105.
36. Haworth, D. (1986), *Figures in a Landscape: A Lancashire Childhood,* London: Methuen, p. 29.
37. Giuseppi, U. (1974), *A Look at Learie Constantine,* London: Nelson, p. 43.
38. Wild, N. (1992), *The Greatest Show on Earth,* Nelson: Hendon, p. 7.

Constantine became a great hero in Nelson. During the nine seasons he was the Nelson professional, the club were the Lancashire League champions seven times and won the Worsley Cup, the League's knock-out competition, twice. Constantine wrote that he and his family made many friends in the town. He was invited to speak at local cricket and non-cricket functions. Jeffrey Hill has shown that Nelsonians took great pride that Constantine had helped to boost the town's reputation. It became regarded nationally as the leading club in league cricket. Probably no other person associated with Nelson in the 1930s had such celebrity. Constantine's status as a local hero in Nelson overrode his colour and his Catholic religion at a time when there was still hostility towards Catholics in Nelson. In 1937 a visitor to Nelson from New Zealand reported that 'His personality is tremendous, wonderful . . . to say that he has been a godsend to Nelson is to put it mildly. He has, to all people, both living in and out of Nelson, *been Nelson itself.*'[39] The respect and tolerance accorded to Constantine were a source of pride to the white population of Nelson. He was made a freeman of the borough in 1963. In 1969, when Constantine became a life peer, he chose the title Baron of Maraval in Trinidad and Tobago and of Nelson in the County Palatine of Lancaster. The white cricketer George Dawkes, who played as a professional for Leicestershire and Derbyshire, played cricket with Constantine during the Second World War. He remembers Constantine with respect and affection and speaks fondly of his pleasant and engaging personality but recalls that Constantine was very conscious of his colour and very aware when he was being slighted because of his colour. Constantine's book *Colour Bar,* published in 1954, is clearly the work of a man who had thought long and hard about the nature of racist prejudice. It seems unlikely that a man such as Constantine would have included Nelson in the title of his peerage had he experienced sustained racist animosity whilst living there, but he and his wife did encounter some hostility. One of Constantine's biographers has claimed that Constantine and his wife thought that it was 'a long, long time' before they felt part of the town, but that when he returned to Nelson in 1931 after the West Indian tour of Australia, he felt that he was returning home, to a place where he had genuine friends.[40] Shortly before his death Constantine recalled that for every insult he encountered in the Lancashire League, there were '10,000 human expressions of warmth and friendship towards me',[41] an exaggeration no doubt but an indication that he did not feel that he was often the victim of racist feeling.

The popularity of Constantine in Nelson seems unlikely to have increased racist animosity in that part of Lancashire and suggests that racial prejudice in this part of

39. *Nelson Leader,* 10 September 1937; Hill, J. (1997), *Nelson: Politics, Economy and Community,* Edinburgh: Keele University Press, p. 123.

40. Giuseppi, *Learie Constantine,* pp. 44–5.

41. *Lancashire Evening Telegraph,* 11 July 1989.

Lancashire between the wars was not so intense to prevent a black cricketer who played cricket in an exciting style becoming a local hero. In Haslingden George Headley encountered some prejudice, such as condescending remarks being made in his presence, but had a warm welcome from club members and supporters. His biographer claims that much of the prejudice was innocuous rather than sinister. When a child said 'Mummy, look at a black man!' the mother replied 'Oh no, dear. That's Mr Headley, our professional cricketer.'[42] Constantine's wife also experienced offensive remarks. Undine Giuseppi has mentioned that as Mrs Constantine approached a group of white women at a cricket function, she heard one woman comment 'I see they've let the jungle in on us', but he does not say where or when this occurred nor it is clear how many of those present shared this view.[43]

One can only speculate about what the reaction to Constantine would have been had he not played in such an exciting manner or not brought such success to the Nelson club. Other parts of England may not have been so tolerant. Nelson's long tradition of political radicalism may have made it more tolerant than other places. Don Haworth has remembered that a spectator at Bacup commented on Constantine that 'Australians we had come to expect, but did we really have any need for niggers to come here to teach us to play cricket?'[44] Such sentiments may have been widely held. In Blackburn, a larger town less than fifteen miles from Nelson, it was boasted in the 1950s that its East Lancashire Cricket Club, one of the great rivals of Nelson CC in the Lancashire League, had always been able to afford a white professional, which reflected an assumption that West Indian or Asian professionals would not usually be paid as much as whites with similar playing abilities but also a belief that in some respects having a white professional was a mark of superiority.[45]

Supporters of Lancashire League clubs were fiercely partisan. After the Second World War Constantine described the matches between the teams from the neighbouring towns of Colne and Nelson as 'not like cricket; it was more like a bloody war',[46] but there are no reports of racist barracking being directed at Constantine or other black players. A few weeks before his death in 1971 Constantine recalled to a Lancashire journalist two instances of racist prejudice he experienced in the Lancashire League. He remembered that in one match against Colne, he was so angry from the start that 'I bowled hard and fast at the batsman's ribs, kept the ball short on every batsman's body – and most of them got hits!' Constantine added that he had no 'derby day hatred for Colne . . . I did not feel that chronic, long-standing historical rivalry which existed between the two towns which excited between the

---

42. Lawrence, B. (1995), *Master Class: The Life of George Headley,* Leicester: Polar, 1995, p. 53.
43. Giuseppi, *Learie Constantine,* p. 69.
44. Haworth, *Figures in a Landscape,* p. 30.
45. I am grateful to Professor Mike Brogden for mentioning this to me.
46. *Lancashire Evening Telegraph,* 13 June 1989.

two towns to a point where it was almost enmity.' Constantine had become so angry because Colne players had deliberately set out to provoke him by making 'insults which were meant to wound', presumably of a racist nature. The Colne professional Archie Slater had played for Derbyshire against the West Indies in 1928 when Constantine believed that as a preconceived and concerted plan the whole Derbyshire team appealed like a 'well-trained Male Voice choir' for LBW each time a ball from Slater hit Constantine on the pad, even when he was a yard down the pitch or six inches outside the leg stump. In one innings of this match Slater had his career-best bowling return of eight wickets for 24 runs. In the Colne-Nelson match one of the Colne players said that he had never seen such a sustained attack on the body as that produced by Constantine. A special meeting of the clubs' two committees was held at the home of the Colne president and the two professionals were asked to behave differently.[47]

There was also unpleasantness in 1929 at a match between Nelson and East Lancashire whose professional was Jim Blanckenberg, a white South African who had played in 18 test matches for South Africa and from 1925 until 1928 had been the professional of Nelson. Constantine had met Blanckenberg only once before the match when Blanckenberg assured him that he had 'no animosity as regards my colour' though Constantine had heard 'second-hand stories to the contrary.' At the match, when Constantine came out to bat, Blanckenberg turned his back and walked away when Constantine offered to shake hands. Constantine recalled that he was 'Hurt, insulted, but above all furious. And that day I bowled "bodyline" before the term had been invented . . . I gave him a terrible beating and at the end of it he walked into our dressing room, naked except for a rain coat, and said to our skipper "Look what that bloody pro of yours has done to me." I am a black man, but that day he was black and blue. I will say this for him though – I have never seen a batsman stand up to the short ball and take blows to the body with so much courage. He never flinched as the ball thudded into him, never gave a sign of pain. He had tremendous guts.' Blanckenberg scored 77 runs before he was bowled by Constantine.[48] George Headley when playing for Haslingden in the Lancashire League also experienced prejudice from Blanckenberg. In 1934 when they were playing in a benefit match for Jack Iddon, the Lancashire CCC and England professional, Blanckenberg refused to shake the hand of Headley when they were introduced. Headley was further embarrassed when Blanckenberg said 'I am a great admirer of your cricket but where I come from we do not fraternise with you fellows.'[49]

47. *Lancashire Evening Telegraph*, 13 June 1989.
48. *Lancashire Evening Telegraph*, 11 July 1989.
49. Lawrence, *Master Class*, p. 54.

Cricket and White Supremacy between the Wars

The 1920s and 1930s were crucial turning points in the growth of black political activism in the Caribbean. After returning from the United States, the Jamaican Marcus Garvey established the United Negro Improvement Association, an organization concerned especially with attempting to improve working conditions and to end the economic exploitation of black workers. In 1929 Garvey founded the People's Political Party. The 1920s also witnessed growing restlessness and assertiveness among the black middle class, especially teachers and small farmers who established their own organizations. These forms of black political assertion reflected an ideology of decolonisation and challenged the traditional authority of whites in the Caribbean.

Michael Manley, prime minister of Jamaica from 1972 to 1980, has shown how black cricketing achievement had a key role in strengthening this black political assertiveness. He argues that in the late 1920s and 1930s the attainments in test cricket of the African-Caribbean George Headley, often called the 'black Bradman', and considered by C.L.R. James to be a better batsman on wet wickets than Bradman, came for

> the black masses . . . the focus for the longing of an entire people for proof: proof of their own self-worth, their own capacity. Furthermore, they wanted proof to be laid at the door of the white man who owned the world which in turn defined their circumstances. What better place to advance this proof than in cricket? This was a game uniquely and peculiarly the preserve of the white man, springing as it did from the very centre of the empire of which they were still part.

Through his achievements in a cultural space of such symbolic importance to whites and blacks, the achievements of Headley gave an added confidence to black political activism.[50] Hilary Beckles has argued that a tremendous sense of injustice among blacks in the Caribbean that neither Constantine nor Headley had become captain of the West Indies contributed to an anti-imperialist culture in the West Indies.[51]

West Indian cricket success did not cause English whites to abandon their assumptions of racial superiority over blacks. Cricket discourse in England remained patronizing and condescending towards black cricketers. Instead of seeing how cricket represented black support for decolonization, cricket observers in England tended

---

50. Manley, M. (1988), *A History of West Indies Cricket,* London: Guild, pp. 35–7. The links between cricket and decolonization in the Caribbean are a recurring theme in Beckles, H. McD. (ed.) (1994), *An Area of Conquest: Popular Democracy and West Indies Cricket Supremacy,* Kingston: I. Randle.

51. Beckles, H. McD. (1998), *The Development of West Indies Cricket: Volume 1 The Age of Nationalism,* London: Pluto, p. 69.

to assume that cricket helped to preserve imperial unity, but they tended to interpret imperial unity as maintaining the existing power structures of the Empire, which implied a continued acceptance of white metropolitan authority. The comments of leading white West Indian cricketers helped to strengthen the assumption that imperialist loyalties were supported through cricket. In 1923, for instance, at a dinner in Belfast given by the Northern Cricket Union, H.B.G. Austin, the white captain of the West Indian touring Britain which played county sides but not test matches and included black as well as white players, said that his team hoped that it would be felt that 'they of the West Indies were worthy to belong to the Mother Country' and that there was 'no more patriotic part of the Empire than the British West Indies, and . . . they wanted, they demanded to be left with the Flag under which they bred. They did not want and they would not part with their birthright and with their privileges; they were going to stay with the Flag under which they were born.'[52]

The campaigns in India for political independence attracted more attention and created more concern in Britain than the growth of black political assertion in the West Indies. Whilst at first sight it may seem that a national Indian cricket team, usually called All-India when it played against England, may have strengthened Indian national consciousness and demands for an end to English rule in India, cricket tended to have the opposite effect and helped to uphold the Raj and white authority. Much of Indian cricket between the wars was dominated by the maharajas. The Indian teams that toured England were captained by maharajas. Notable English cricketers between the wars, such as Jack Hobbs, Herbert Sutcliffe, Wilfred Rhodes, spent winters in India playing for or coaching the Maharaja of Patiala's team. Hirst, Leyland, Larwood and Waddington also played in India. Learie Constantine was employed to coach in Hyderabad by the Nawab Moin-ud-Dowlah.[53] In many ways the princes were the group in India who stood to lose most if India gained independence from Britain, especially as they were the rulers of independent states but who could on most occasions count on the support of Britain. Ranjitsinhji complained more than once that the British government in India ought to have co-operated more with the princes, but in 1930 he said that the princes of India

> have been very old members of Great Britain's team; and both on easy and on difficult wickets they have tried their best to play with a straight bat for the Empire . . . Throughout the period of adjustment of relations between Great Britain and India, upon which we are now entering, I am certain that the Indian Princes will do their best to play a part worthy of their best traditions . . . You can rely on us in the future . . . to play the game, and to give every support in our power to the harmony and to the success of the Imperial Team.'[54]

52. *Belfast Telegraph,* 26 July 1923.

53. Bose, *History of Indian Cricket,* p. 49; for a discussion of the princes' role in Indian cricket, see pp. 40–107.

54. *Cricketer Annual 1939–40,* (n.d.), London: Cricketer Syndicate, p. 49.

Mihir Bose has claimed that in the 1920s the British and the princes realized that cricket was a means of promoting their political interests, that 'in any fight with the Indian nationalists the princes would always support the British.'[55] Whilst no statement has been found of a British government encouraging India to be granted test match status in order to foster the loyalty of the princes and discourage support for Congress, test matches against India do seem to have emphasised the mutual dependency of the British and the maharajas. Cricket became entwined with the policy of using the princes to prop up white British rule in India

The organization of cricket in India also limited the game's capacity to boost support for independence. The Ranji Trophy, a competition for teams representing different regions in the sub-continent, was started only in 1934, but in cities where cricket was especially strong, much interest centred on quadrangular and triangular tournaments contested by teams based on religious affiliation. The Bombay Quadrangular Tournament, contested by Parsee, Hindu, Muslim and European teams was perhaps the most prestigious of these. In 1937 it became the Pentangular Tournament with the addition of a team called the Rest representing other groups such as Jews and Indian Christians. Ramachandra Guha has argued that by the 1930s such competitions were adding to the animosities associated with religious communalism and so helped to intensify the strategy of divide and rule which the British used to maintain their authority in India.[56] In 1940 Gandhi was reputed to have asked the 'sporting public of Bombay to revise their sporting code and to erase from it communal matches.'[57] Reports in England of Indian cricket and of the Indian teams touring England, however, suggest that English cricket world was very much ignorant of how cricket may have been adding to the difficulties of making Congress a movement with equal support from all religious groups in India.

Cricket suggests that assumptions of innate white supremacy were deeply entrenched in England between the wars. The cricketing achievements of black West Indian and Asian cricketers were respected but none, not even the great George Headley, received a level of adulation approaching that attained by Ranjitsinhji at the turn of the century. No black or Asian cricketer seems to have caused most whites to have had second thoughts about the supposed natural superiority of whites. In part this may have due to the relatively poor performance of the West Indian and Indian teams in test matches played in England. The ways in which cricket had encouraged support for decolonization in the Caribbean was largely ignored but so too was the ways in which cricket had helped to sustain the Raj in India. There were rumblings

---

55. Bose, *History of Indian Cricket,* p. 45.

56. Guha, R. (1998), 'Cricket and Politics in Colonial India', *Past & Present,* 161, November. Guha also points out how support for the Hindu team in Quadrangular cricket helped to weaken caste identities as a source of political disunity among Hindus between the wars.

57. *Bombay Chronicle,* 7 December 1940, quoted by Guha, 'Cricket and Politics', p. 178.

in England about the desirability of having the England team always captained by an amateur, but hardly any whites in England argued that the West Indies should have been captained by a black player. At the annual general meeting of Yorkshire CCC in 1925, Lord Hawke was said that he prayed to God that no professional would ever captain England. A headline in the *Daily Herald,* the only national newspaper to support the Labour Party, called these comments 'A Gratuitous Insult' and reported that the English professionals in Australia had condemned Hawke's remarks as 'disparaging' to professionals.[58] In 1924 Hawke's *Recollections and Reminiscences* had been published in which he described an incident concerning Kirk, one of the English players on the tour of the West Indies in 1896–7, who

> was a great handler of the native. At Barbados he gave a nigger eighteenpence for doing some job. The fellow, full of voluble expostulation, indignantly held out the money in his hand.
> 'All right,' said Kirk, 'wait a bit.'
> And on returning after nearly an hour, took back the shilling with the remark:
> 'Now you have sixpence, and with that you can go.'
> And it was all the fellow obtained from him.[59]

These remarks passed almost without comment and provoked nothing like the controversy of his speech about England always having an amateur captain. In 1935 Jack Hobbs wrote that the Middlesex and England professional batsman Patsy Hendren 'is of a most cheery disposition, a great humorist, popular alike with players and spectators on every ground he visits. He is cricket's Prime Minister of mirth, and we all gather round to listen to his stories, he tells them so well. Perhaps his speciality is his nigger stories.'[60] The making of such comments by Hobbs, so widely regarded as one of nature's gentlemen, a man of great courtesy who hated to hurt the feelings of others, shows how little whites in England realized how offensive their attitudes could be to coloured people and indicates that the achievements of coloured cricketers had not weakened assumptions of white superiority.

58. *Daily Herald,* 22, 23 January 1925.
59. Lord Hawke, (1924), *Recollections and Reminiscences,* London: Williams & Norgate, p. 162.
60. Hobbs, J.B. (1981 reprint of the 1935 edition), *My Life Story,* London: Hambledon, p. 236.

—3—

The D'Oliveira Affair and the Stop the Seventy Tour Campaign

In the 1960s race relations caused bitter political controversy in Britain. African-Caribbean and Asian migration provoked much resentment among whites. At the general election of 1964 Patrick Gordon Walker, about to be appointed foreign secretary in Harold Wilson's Labour Government, was defeated in what had been the safe Labour of Smethwick by a Conservative candidate whose election campaign had called for strict immigration controls. In 1968 the Conservative shadow cabinet minister Enoch Powell made his 'rivers of blood' speech which forecast communal violence unless African-Caribbean and Asian immigrants were repatriated. London dockers marched through the streets shouting their support for Powell. Although the Conservative leader Edward Heath disassociated himself from Powell's remarks, it has been alleged that Powell's views were decisive in helping the Conservatives to win marginal seats in the West Midlands at the 1970 general election. The unilateral declaration of independence by Ian Smith's government in Rhodesia as a means of perpetuating white rule was a recurring difficulty for the Wilson and subsequent governments. Much sympathy was expressed for the Smith regime in Britain but the decision of the Wilson government to use economic sanctions rather than military force to overturn the Smith government UDI was seen by others within and outside Britain as largely ineffective and covert co-operation with the Smith regime.

The Non-selection of D'Oliveira

First-class cricket in England during the late 1960s fostered racial harmony in Britain. Large numbers of African-Caribbeans had watched the test series that the West Indies won in England in 1963 and 1966, but there were few reports of racist disorders at matches. There were few if any protests at the selection in 1967 for the England team of Basil D'Oliveira, a Cape Coloured born and raised in South Africa who played county cricket for Worcestershire. For the 1968 season the regulation which had meant that overseas cricketers who played county cricket could no longer play test cricket was scrapped and a number of the leading West Indian, Indian and Pakistani test cricketers came to play county cricket. Players such as Clive Lloyd and Farouk Engineer at Lancashire, Garfield Sobers at Nottinghamshire, Asif Iqbal at Kent and Rohan Kanhai at Warwickshire were among non-white cricketers who became immensely popular with the supporters of the counties for which they played. Sobers was immediately made captain of Nottinghamshire at a time when non-whites in many occupations within Britain were not usually appointed to positions of authority over whites.

Much of this racial harmony was overshadowed by disputes about whether England should have played test match cricket against all-white South African teams selected in accordance with overtly racist apartheid policies. In the 1950s there had been hardly any protests in Britain about English cricketing links with South African teams selected on a racial basis, but in the early and mid 1960s, disquiet about playing against racially selected South African teams began to grow, stimulated by greater awareness of the nature of apartheid and influenced in part by the activities of SANROC, the South African Non-racial Olympic Committee formed in 1962, which argued that an international boycott of South African sport could help to overturn apartheid. The 1965 South African cricket tour of England passed off relatively free from incident, but by the late 1960s much controversy surrounded the England-South Africa series arranged for 1968–9 and 1970. The case of David Sheppard, the Anglican Bishop of Woolwich, who had captained Cambridge University, Sussex and England in the 1950s, indicates how unease about playing against racially selected South African teams grew in the 1950s and 1960s. In 1951 and 1955 he had played against the South African tourists in England, but declined to be considered for the 1956–7 tour of South Africa and refused to play against the South African team touring England in 1960.[1] By the late 1960s he was among the most prominent advocates for the cessation of cricketing links with South Africa until cricket in South Africa became multi-racial. Many others in English cricket wanted to retain links with South Africa.

Those who controlled the MCC wanted the tour of South Africa arranged for 1968–9 to take place. This would have been the last England touring team to have been selected by the MCC, the private members' cricket club established in 1787, which was about to share its authority over first-class cricket in England with the Cricket Council and the Test and County Cricket Board. The MCC had strong connections with the economic and social elite. In popular imagination, the MCC and its ground at Lord's were bastions of class privilege and political reaction. In the 1950s, Walter Monckton, the Conservative minister, had claimed that the right-wing opinions of the MCC committee made Macmillan's Cabinet seem like 'a band of pinkos'.[2] Until 1969 the MCC chose the captain and the members of the overseas

1. Sheppard, D. (1964), *Parson's Pitch,* London: Hodder & Stoughton, pp. 157–65.

2. Swanton, E.W., Plumptre, G. and Woodcock, J. (eds) (1986), *Barclays World of Cricket: The Game from A to Z,* London: Guild, p. 51.

touring parties on which England played test matches. On such tours the England tourists played under the name of the MCC in all matches except test matches. In 1968 the MCC rejected appeals from opponents of apartheid not to send a touring party to South Africa, but instead argued that 'keeping bridges open', retaining sporting ties with South Africa, would be a more effective means of persuading the South African government to abandon apartheid. It seemed likely that the England party would include Basil D'Oliveira. In South Africa D'Oliveira, as a non-white, had not been eligible to play first-class cricket but showed sufficient cricketing ability for the cricket journalist and broadcaster John Arlott to arrange for him to play as the professional for Middleton CC of the Central Lancashire League in 1960. In 1964 he became a professional county cricketer with Worcestershire, scoring centuries in his first two county championship matches. In 1966 D'Oliveira was selected for England and became the second coloured cricketer to have played for England since Second World War. The first was the Anglo-Indian Subba Row, who had played as an amateur for Cambridge University, Surrey and Northamptonshire and for England from 1958 until 1961. In the 1967 season D'Oliveira appeared in five of the six test matches played by England and in all of the test matches on the 1967–8 tour of the West Indies.

As it seemed probable that D'Oliveira would be selected for the tests against Australia in England in 1968, the MCC Committee's South African Tour Sub-committee resolved in December 1967 to seek assurances from the South African Cricket Association, the governing body for white cricket in South Africa and which controlled South African test cricket, that no preconditions or restrictions would be placed on the selection of the MCC tour party.[3] It was recognized in England and South Africa that a decision about whether D'Oliveira would be allowed to play would be taken by B.J. Vorster's Nationalist government. By March 1968 no reply had been received from SACA and the MCC asked Sir Alec Douglas-Home, the former Conservative foreign secretary and prime minister and current shadow foreign secretary who was visiting South Africa, to raise the matter with Mr Vorster, the prime minister of South Africa. In the 1920s Sir Alec had played cricket for the Eton first XI and for Oxford University and Middlesex, and had been president of the MCC in 1966. Sir Alec was very much an advocate of the view that bridge-building would be the most effective means of ending apartheid not only in sport but in other areas of South African life. In his memoirs he wrote 'experience confirmed my belief that precept and example must be better than ostracism, and that perception and understanding would bring apartheid to an end far more quickly than boycott. The more tourists and sportsmen, businessmen and politicians whom

---

3. MCC Committee Minutes, 20 December 1968.

we can send to South Africa the quicker will be the process of the dilution of "apartheid" – the more we send them to Coventry the more obstinate they will become and the more they will retire into their hard protective shell of intolerance.'[4] At his meeting with Vorster, Sir Alec formed the impression that the South African government had not reached a final decision on whether D'Oliveira would be admitted into South Africa as a playing member of the MCC touring party. He informed the MCC committee that in his opinion the odds were 5/4 on D'Oliveira being allowed to play in South Africa.[5]

Two weeks later, Vorster summoned Lord Cobham, who had been president of the MCC in 1954 and treasurer from 1963 to 1964, Governor-General of New Zealand from 1957 to 1962 and whose family had been very much involved with Worcestershire County Cricket Club, D'Oliveira's county, to a meeting where he was told that an MCC team including D'Oliveira would not be acceptable to the South African government. Cobham passed this message to S.C. Griffith, secretary of the MCC, G.O. Allen, the treasurer and Arthur Gilligan, president of the MCC, captain of England in the 1920s, and who, along with Allen, was also a member of the committee which would select the MCC side for the tour of South Africa. Most members of the MCC Committee and of the selection committee for the South African tour were not informed of Vorster's message to Cobham. It also seems that neither Denis Howell, the Minister for Sport in the Wilson government, nor D'Oliveira was informed of Vorster's message to Cobham.

Cobham made public that he had passed on Vorster's message to the MCC in April 1969.[6] Griffith was quoted as commenting that Cobham had given him a 'rather casual warning' and that 'Apart from Lord Cobham, all sorts of people were bringing us comments and reports of what they had heard in South Africa.'[7] A statement from the MCC issued on 10 April 1969 mentioned that Vorster's message to Cobham had not been passed on to the full MCC Committee or the selection committee because it 'appeared not to coincide with the impression which Sir Alec Douglas-Home gained from his discussions with Mr. Vorster', an indirect admission that Griffith, Allen and Gilligan placed more reliance upon the advice of Sir Alec than upon Cobham's information. The statement also mentioned that although two of this group were members of the selection committee, the rest of the committee were not informed of Cobham's message because the brief for the selectors was to select the best possible team. David Gray, the *Guardian* journalist, believed that the MCC Committee placed such reliance on Sir Alec's advice because they 'wanted to save

4. Lord Home (1976), *The Way the Wind Blows: An Autobiography*, London: Collins, p. 228.
5. Swanton, E.W. (1985), *Gubby Allen: Man of Cricket*, London: Hutchinson/Stanley Paul, p. 289.
6. *The Times*, 8, 11 April 1969; Hollis, C., 'Bowled Out', *Spectator*, 18 April 1969, p. 499.
7. *Guardian*, 8 April 1969.

the tour and to avoid an argument about D'Oliveira's eligibility until it was absolutely necessary.' As the selection of D'Oliveira was probable rather than certain, Sir Alec had argued that pressing the South African authorities for an answer upon whether D'Oliveira would be accepted 'might even produce a premature reply detrimental to the prospects of the tour taking place.'

A statement issued by the MCC in December 1968 claimed that pressing for a firm indication from South Africa upon D'Oliveira's acceptability would have appeared 'not only hypothetical but politically inspired. After careful consideration, we agreed that arrangements for the tour should be finalised on the assumption that the selected team would be accepted by the South African Government when the time came. It was our opinion that this would provide the best chance of the tour taking place.' Although the MCC Committee did not obtain a clear statement from South Africa on whether D'Oliveira would be acceptable, there were reasonable grounds for ignoring Cobham's message and thinking that D'Oliveira would be accepted. Vorster had agreed that a New Zealand Rugby Union side including Maoris, who were classified as non-white in South Africa, would be allowed to play against whites in South Africa and in April 1967 had stated that multi-racial teams from countries with whom South Africa had 'traditional sporting ties' would be permitted to play in South Africa. He added the rider, however, that this would not be extended to those who wished to make political capital out of sending multi-racial teams to South Africa.[8] Sir John Nicholls, the British ambassador in South Africa, reported to the Foreign Office that although Vorster 'did not say so specifically, it is a reasonable assumption from what he said that – and one that everyone has made – that Mr Basil D'Oliveira may come here as a member of an MCC team.'[9] Bruce Murray, however, has shown despite the speech of April 1967, by March 1968 or possibly earlier Vorster had decided that D'Oliveira would not be allowed to play in South Africa if he were selected by the MCC, though this was not emphasized in public.[10]

It may also have been hoped that D'Oliveira would have declared himself unavailable for the tour, although the account in his ghosted autobiography of what happened in 1968 and comments to the press do not suggest that pressure had been put on him by English cricket authorities to do this. He was offered the large sum of £4,000 from the South African Sports Federation to coach coloured cricketers in South Africa. Accepting this would have meant that D'Oliveira could not have been selected for the tour. This money was made available by Mr Tienie Oosthuizen of Rothmans. Rembrandt International, who controlled Rothmans, denied that this

8. *Guardian,* 4 December 1968.

9. Sir John Nicholls to Foreign Office, 14 April 1967, PRO FCO 25/709.

10. Murray, B.K., (1999), 'The D'Oliveira Affair 1968/9: Thirty Years After', Paper presented to the Twelfth Bi-ennial Conference of the Australian Society for Sports History, Queenstown, New Zealand, 1–5 February, p. 18. I am grateful to Professor Murray for providing me with a copy of his paper.

was a bribe to prevent D'Oliveira being selected for the tour or that Rothmans had anything to do with it.[11] For Christopher Hollis, the former Conservative MP, writer and publisher, expressed what was probably a widely held view when he wrote in *The Spectator* that the sum involved was so large that it appeared 'self-evidently a bribe'.[12] In his book *The D'Oliveira Affair*, D'Oliveira explained that Oosthuizen had stressed that the offer had to be accepted before the selection of the South African tour party,[13] which seems to strengthen suspicions that it was intended to ensure that he would not be a member of the tour party. Oosthuizen's approach to D'Oliveira did not become public knowledge until April 1969.[14]

D'Oliveira was selected for the first test match against Australia in the summer of 1968. England lost the match but he scored 87 in the second innings, the highest score by an England player in the match and also took two wickets. At first sight it would appear that he had played well, but he was one of six England players not chosen for the next test match. The report in *Wisden* on the match claimed that his second innings score was 'difficult to appraise' and that 'England needed him as an all-rounder and he had failed as first-change bowler.'[15] For Worcestershire, D'Oliveira's performances were below his best form. At the end of season, he was only fifth in the county's batting averages for county championship matches though top of the bowling averages, but Michael Melford pointed out in *Wisden* that many of his victims had been obtained on 'imperfect pitches'.[16] He was not originally selected for the fifth and final test but somewhat surprisingly was chosen when Prideaux, an opening batsman, withdrew through injury. In the first innings D'Oliveira scored 158 runs, a crucial contribution to England's winning the match and so squaring the series. The selection committee for the South African tour met in the evening of the day on which the final test match was won. They began their deliberations at 8 p.m. and dispersed only at 1:50 a.m. The next day the full committee of the MCC confirmed the selection of the tour party.[17] D'Oliveira was not included in the party. He called this 'a bitter disappointment'.[18]

Many found it incomprehensible that a cricketer who had just scored a hundred in a test match against Australia could not be selected for the tour, but cricket journalists were divided over whether D'Oliveira should have been selected. Some pointed out that D'Oliveira's innings in the final test was not so very impressive because he

11. *The Times*, 14 April 1969.
12. Hollis, 'Bowled Out'.
13. D'Oliveira, B. (1969), *The D'Oliveira Affair*, London: Collins, chapters 11 and 12.
14. *Daily Mail*, 4 April 1969; *Sunday Times*, 13 April 1969.
15. *Wisden Cricketers' Almanack 1969*, London: Sporting Handbooks, p. 296.
16. *Wisden Cricketers' Almanack 1969*, p. 74.
17. Swanton, E.W., 'South African Tragedy', *The Cricketer Winter Annual 1968–69*, 49, pp. 4–6.
18. *The Times*, 29 August 1969.

had been dropped after scoring 31 runs. In *The Times* John Woodcock thought that the selectors had made the correct decision, but in the *Guardian* John Arlott declared 'There is no case for leaving out D'Oliveira on cricketing grounds.' E.W. Swanton, very much the doyen of cricket journalists and whose sympathies usually lay with the cricket establishment, favoured D'Oliveira's selection because of 'his temperament for the testing occasion'. In the *Daily Sketch* Brian Scovell accepted the decision 'with equanimity'.[19]

D'Oliveira's exclusion from the test party stimulated immense public controversy and criticism. An editorial in *The Times* stated that it was being alleged 'with great vigour from many different quarters that this decision is a concession to racial prejudice', that D'Oliveira had not been selected in order to ensure that the tour went ahead.[20] The *Daily Mail* columnist Jim Manning was convinced that the omission of D'Oliveira stemmed from a desire by the MCC to avoid creating awkwardness in South Africa[21] and to Learie Constantine it was 'positively suspicious'.[22] The fact that none of the selectors was known in public as an opponent of bridge building added to suspicions of D'Oliveira being left out to ensure the tour went ahead. A week after the announcement of the tour party, E.W. Swanton wrote in the *Daily Telegraph* that he had not met anyone or received any letters supporting D'Oliveira's omission.[23] By mid September the MCC had received a thousand letters criticizing D'Oliveira's omission.[24] The day after the announcement of the tour party, the Anti-Apartheid Movement sent telegrams requesting the Prime Minister to intervene and to Arthur Gilligan, president of the MCC, asking for the tour to be cancelled. It also announced that all the selected players would be asked 'not to be part of a racialist team and to withdraw from the tour'. The Anti-Apartheid Movement claimed that 'not only is our team condoning apartheid by going to South Africa to play against a team for which only whites may be selected, but we are importing apartheid principles in the selection of our team.'[25] In the *Church of England Newspaper,* David Sheppard was highly critical of the MCC Committee and wrote that before the start of the cricket season it should have made sure that it had received 'an answer with no ifs and buts that whatever team we selected would be accepted.' Sheppard agreed to chair a group of MCC members who had come together in response to an article in the *Guardian* and an announcement in the personal column of *The Times* by

19. *The Times,* 29 August 1969; *The Cricketer Winter Annual 1968–69,* vol. 49, pp. 4–6.

20. *The Times,* 30 August 1968.

21. Marlar, R., 'D'Oliveira and the Press', *The Cricketer Winter Annual 1968–69,* 49, p. 6.

22. Howell, D. (1990), *Made in Birmingham: The Memoirs of Denis Howell,* London: Macdonald Queen Anne, 1990, p. 202.

23. *Daily Telegraph,* 4 September 1968.

24. *The Times,* 9 September 1968.

25. *The Times,* 29 August 1969.

Charles Barr, an MCC member, and who were unhappy with the MCC's handling of D'Oliveira's omission from the touring party. For Barr, the omission of D'Oliveira was not the whole issue but merely 'the spark which has set off what are perhaps broader issues – the sending of a team to South Africa.'[26]

Despite appearances, it seems that D'Oliveira was not selected for cricketing reasons. David Sheppard thought that the selectors had made 'a dreadful mistake', but added that they 'are friends of mine. They are people of honesty, and don't suffer from racial prejudice.'[27] Allen and Gilligan, who knew of Vorster's message to Cobham and as MCC officers were members of the selection committee, did not reveal this to the other selectors in order to ensure that it did not influence their deliberations. None of the selectors – Douglas Insole, Peter May, Alec Bedser, Colin Cowdrey, the tour captain, Leslie Ames, the tour manager, and the MCC officers Gilligan and Allen – were ever known to be public opponents of the policy of bridge-building. Insole, chairman of the selection committee, explained that D'Oliveira had been omitted because on the tour he would have been required as a batsman and that the other batsmen chosen were better batsmen than D'Oliveira.[28] In his autobiography published in 1985, Peter May, another selector, explained that D'Oliveira's batting form with Worcestershire had been disappointing and that 'he had not had a great tour of the West Indies the previous winter.' Like Insole, May also took the view that 'We were already overstocked with batting candidates.'[29] Following his relatively poor batting form, D'Oliveira's selection for the final test against Australia as a replacement for Prideaux, an opening batsman, appears surprising, but the original team included Colin Milburn who had sufficient experience of opening for him to take over this role. It seems unlikely that D'Oliveira was selected for the final test match against Australia in the hope that having been in relatively poor form he would not play very well and that there would then appear to be no strong reason to pick him for the tour. The desire not to lose a series against Australia was always so intense that what was thought to be the best side would always be picked. But even if all the discussion at the tour selection meeting had been concerned with cricketing ability alone, every selector must have known that by not selecting D'Oliveira they would improve the prospects of the tour going ahead.

The tour party for South Africa included Tom Cartwright, a Warwickshire bowler, who had been injured for nine of his county's last ten matches before the selection of the touring party was announced. On 14 September Cartwright played in a one-day match at Edgbaston and found that as his shoulder had not responded to treatment, he would not be fit for the tour. On 17 September D'Oliveira was chosen

26. *The Times*, 5 September 1968.
27. Howell, *Made in Birmingham*, p. 202.
28. *Wisden Cricketers' Almanack 1969*, p. 76.
29. May, P. and Melford, M. (1985), *A Game Enjoyed*, London: Stanley Paul, p. 191.

to replace Cartwright. A statement issued by J.A. Bailey, the assistant secretary of the MCC with special responsibility for the press and public relations, explained that as there was no direct replacement for a bowler with Cartwright's specialist abilities, the selectors had felt that the 'whole balance of the touring party had inevitably to be altered' which meant that an extra batsman was selected.[30] But to many the replacement of Cartwright by D'Oliveira seemed to confirm that the MCC had originally omitted D'Oliveira out of desire to accommodate the South African government and that only the strength of the public outcry over D'Oliveira's omission had caused his final inclusion in the tour party. Denis Howell, the Minister for Sport, pointed out that the omission of D'Oliveira and then his selection to replace Cartwright had been taken 'by the MCC on their own and without any pressure from the Government or interference from me.'[31]

The response from South Africa was swift. Following his original non-selection the *News of the World* had hired D'Oliveira to report on the tour and had he been allowed to do so, he would have been the first non-white allowed in the press boxes at the South African test grounds other than in 'a menial capacity', but Vorster had already commented that D'Oliveira might not have been permitted to report on the cricket. On 18 September, Vorster announced that an MCC team including D'Oliveira would not be admitted to South Africa. He declared 'We are not prepared to receive a team thrust upon us by people whose interests are not the game, but to gain certain political objectives which they do not even attempt to hide.' From his initial non-selection D'Oliveira had become 'no longer a sportsman but a political cricket ball. From then on it was political body-line bowling all the way. From then on the matter passed from the realm of sport to the realm of politics . . . the team became the team of South Africa's political opponents.' Vorster added that it was not the MCC team but the team of SANROC and of Bishop Reeves, the Anglican bishop of Johannesburg who had been deported from South Africa because of his opposition to apartheid.[32] Even though the MCC had specified that it would call off the tour if not all of its party was acceptable to South Africa, it did not do this until Jack Cheetham and Arthur Coy of SACA flown to London and held a four hour meeting with the MCC Committee on 24 September. After this meeting the MCC issued a statement saying that it had been informed 'that the side selected to represent MCC in South Africa is not acceptable for reasons beyond the control of SACA. The MCC committee therefore decided unanimously that the tour will not take place.'[33] This delay in cancelling the tour suggests that at least some influential figures within the

30. *The Times,* 17 September 1968.

31. *The Times,* 17 September 1968.

32. *The Times,* 18 September 1968.

33. MCC Committee Minutes, 24 September 1968; 'Dates in the Story', *The Cricketer Winter Annual, 1968–69,* 49, p. 6.

MCC were hoping that some formula could still be found for the tour to go ahead. D'Oliveira mentioned that he had thought of standing down, but added 'you get so many letters from people saying that it is not your decision.'[34]

The group formed by Charles Barr and chaired by David Sheppard had sufficient support for an extraordinary meeting of the MCC to be held at Church House in December 1968. Three resolutions were presented to the meeting. The first regretted the committee's 'mishandling of affairs leading up to the selection of the team' for the intended tour, the second urged that no further tours of South Africa be undertaken until there was evidence of 'actual progress' towards non-racial cricket in South Africa and the third wanted the appointment of a special committee to examine the nature and progress of SACA's proposals for non-racial cricket.[35] The meeting was described in the *Guardian* as 'acrimonious' and John Arlott summed it up as a parade of prejudice. Sheppard argued that the committee's decisions over D'Oliveira made it appear to the world that 'English cricket was bending to a racialist wind'. Ronald Aird, president of the MCC took the chair and claimed that unlike the Committee who wanted the tour to take place, Sheppard and his friends were opponents of apartheid rather than those wishing for the advancement of cricket. Dennis Silk, a public school teacher and a member of the MCC Committee, declared that 'We do not stand as the social conscience of Great Britain any more than our Government stands as the social conscience of the world' and mentioned that South Africa was Britain's third largest export market. Opponents of the resolutions laid great stress upon the advice received from Douglas-Home, who was not present at the meeting, whilst Vorster's message to Cobham was not mentioned. John Arlott commented that Douglas-Home 'was referred to from time to time in terms of reverence, once as far as one could make out, as somewhere on a level with the Almighty; but no one presumed to explain why he gave the MCC Committee the advice which led to the ultimate breakdown and protests.' MCC members were able to register their votes on the resolutions by post. All three resolutions were defeated by clear majorities, though on a show of hand in the hall the voting was much closer. About half of the MCC members voted in the postal ballot. The first resolution was defeated by 4,357 votes to 1,570, the second by 4,664 to 1,214 and the third by 4,508 to 1,352.[36] These votes suggest that a high proportion of MCC members, the premier cricket club in England, wished to retain cricketing links with South Africa, even though it was known that cricket in South Africa was played and organized on the basis of racial segregation.

34. *The Times,* 24 September 1968.
35. *The Cricketer Spring Annual 1969,* 50 (1), p. 23.
36. *Guardian,* 6 December 1968.

The Effects of the D'Oliveira Affair

In retrospect the MCC Committee can be seen to have mishandled events in 1968. No doubt the committee was sincere in its beliefs that making the tour and building bridges with South Africa would be the most effective method of combating apartheid. The fact that this was also the view of Sir Alec Douglas-Home, a former Conservative prime minister, foreign secretary and shadow foreign secretary probably helped to reaffirm the view of the Committee's members that they were right to try to ensure that the tour took place. Jack Bailey, the assistant MCC secretary, has written that the 'cricket world was strongly inclined towards getting on with the game with South Africa – or anybody else – leaving politics to the politicians. It was, and always will be, an attitude of substance, if your brief is the administration of your sport and the well-being of your sport and your penchant is loyalty to good, time-honoured and trusted friends, and if you believe that contact is more productive than isolation.' In Bailey's view the MCC was 'in the business of protecting tours and fostering cricket, not cancelling tours.'[37] The cricket establishment in England would also have been aware that the survival of county cricket was largely dependent on the distribution of profits from test matches and test tours.

The MCC Committee can be accused of political naiveté in 1968. By concerning itself so much with cricketing issues, it ignored the wider political implications involved with playing cricket against South Africa. The Committee seems to been unaware, or preferred to disregard, how sending a touring team to play against racially segregated teams would appear to many as conniving with the racism of apartheid. The handling of the D'Oliveira issue strengthened suspicions that the cricket establishment was too eager to co-operate with, and so help to prop up, the apartheid regime. Whilst politicians usually evade answering hypothetical questions, more insistent attempts could have been made before the start of the 1968 English cricket season to establish whether a side including D'Oliveira would have been allowed to play in South Africa. Whatever Vorster's answer may have been, a blow could have been struck against apartheid in South African sport. Had Vorster agreed to accept a side including D'Oliveira, the presence of a Cape Coloured born and raised in South Africa playing cricket against white teams in South Africa would have been an open challenge to apartheid in sport. Had Vorster been forced to declare that he would not accept a team including D'Oliveira, the refusal of the MCC to send a team would have emphasized to white sport followers in South Africa that retaining apartheid in sport would lead to the exclusion of South Africa from international sport.

The touring side for South Africa appears to have been selected on cricketing grounds, but it can be argued that the political considerations of selecting D'Oliveira

---

37. Bailey, J. (1989), *Conflicts in Cricket,* London: Kingswood, p. 48.

ought to have been taken into account. Selecting D'Oliveira for the tour, especially after he had just scored a century and played a key part in the defeat of Australia, would have avoided creating the impression that the cricket establishment was seeking not to antagonize Vorster and would also have prevented the great groundswell of public condemnation that enabled Vorster to declare that the subsequent selection of D'Oliveira as a replacement for Cartwright was due to protests from anti-apartheid activists. By being able to claim that D'Oliveira' selection had been the result of pressure from political activists, Vorster did not have to face criticism in South Africa from the *verkrampte* or more extreme wing of his party, which was opposed to any relaxation of apartheid.

It was not the intention of the cricket establishment in England to strengthen the sporting boycott of South Africa in 1968, but this was the result of the D'Oliveira affair. In 1961 the all-white Football Association of South Africa had been suspended from FIFA, a suspension that was confirmed in 1964. Also in 1964 South Africa was excluded from international fencing, but as neither soccer nor fencing had a mass following among white South Africans, these moves had only limited impact in South Africa. The suspension of the South African National Olympic Committee from the Olympic movement and prohibition from the Olympic Games of 1964 were more serious for many white South Africans. When the South African Olympic Committee proposed to send a multi-racial South African team to the Mexico Olympics of 1968, the IOC re-admitted South Africa to the Olympic movement, but a threatened boycott by black African states and pressure from Mexico caused the invitation for South Africa to compete in the 1968 to be withdrawn. In 1967 a New Zealand rugby tour of South Africa was cancelled because the South African government would not accept a team including Maoris who were classified in South Africa as non-white.[38] Given the enthusiasm for rugby among white South Africans and especially among Afrikaners, this must have caused much resentment in South Africa. The England cricket tour of 1968 was the second proposed tour by a team of overseas sportsmen playing one of the major South African sports, and the first proposed cricket tour, and by a country with whom South Africa had a strong tradition of playing sport, that was cancelled because the South African government would not admit a coloured player. The cancellation of the England tour ratcheted up the isolation of South Africa from international sport. In England it seems that opposition to the proposed South African tour in 1970 was strengthened by resentment over the South African government's refusal to admit D'Oliveira in 1968.[39]

---

38. Hain, P. (1971), *Don't Play with Apartheid: The Background to the Stop The Seventy Tour Campaign,* London: Allen & Unwin, pp. 54–67.

39. Memorandum of W. Wilson, Southern African Department, 9 May 1969, PRO FCO 45/311.

Supporters of the 1970 Tour

The South African cricket tour of England scheduled for 1970 brought the issue of sporting relations with South Africa to the centre of British politics. By 1970, a new body, the MCC Cricket Council, which was known as simply the Cricket Council although it did not adopt this title until 1974, had replaced the MCC as the supreme authority for cricket in England. The Cricket Council consisted of twenty-seven members. Eleven were nominated by the MCC, ten by the National Cricket Association and six by the Test and County Cricket Board. Nine, including the current England captain Colin Cowdrey, had played cricket for England as amateurs and two others had captained county sides as amateurs. Raman Subba Row was one of the MCC nominees.

The Cricket Council was determined that the tour should take place. In December 1969, Derek Brutus of SANROC had written to all county clubs asking them not to support the proposed tour. Brutus claimed that he had no objection to an all-white South African side coming to Britain provided that it was selected from the best players and regardless of their racial background. He argued that receiving a side from which four-fifths of the population were arbitrarily excluded would be conniving with racial discrimination on the sports field. David Sheppard also expressed his opposition to the tour, claiming that opponents of the tour were not calling for a general improvement in the apartheid laws, but simply wanted the South African Cricket Association to 'show their good faith'. He could not see why 'they cannot stick their necks out a little and choose a multiracial side'. Some members of the Cricket Council expressed little sympathy with the requests from Brutus and Sheppard. Wilfred Wooller, who had captained Glamorgan as an amateur and who was a powerful figure in the administration of the Glamorgan club and a nominee of the TCCB on the Cricket Council, replied to Brutus that 'We have no sympathy with your cause in any shape or form, and regard it as an utter nuisance. You do far more damage than good, and I have yet to come across any first-class cricketer, active in the game at the present, who has any use for your activities.' When asked for a more specific comment about Brutus he was reported to have said 'I do not like these people any more than I like these other who come over for the Commonwealth Prime Ministers' conference; they should put their own house in order first.' He mentioned that he greatly respected David Sheppard, but thought that he 'was one of those for whom everything was either black or white with nothing in between.'[40]

40. *The Times*, 14 January 1969.

The D'Oliveira affair and the cancellation of the MCC tour to South Africa had not weakened the determination of the English cricket establishment to play test cricket with South Africa. At its inaugural meeting held on 22 January 1969 the Cricket Council voted unanimously to invite SACA to send a touring party to England in 1970. Only late in May 1970, and then only at the request of the government, did the Cricket Council withdraw its invitation to SACA. After the first meeting of the Cricket Council, S.C. Griffith, the secretary of the MCC, said that its policy was to 'play and foster the game as widely as possible' and that any player selected by South Africa would be welcomed. He declined to say whether the Cricket Council intended to talk with the government but mentioned that it had discussed the invest- igations being carried out at the provincial level in South Africa concerning future collaboration between the white and non-white cricket authorities.[41] In April 1970 the Cricket Council issued a pamphlet *Why the '70 Tour* explaining why it wanted the tour to take place. This stressed that the Cricket Council was totally opposed to apartheid and that 'To condone any such policy would be completely at variance with a tradition, long fostered by cricket administration in this country, that cricket is open, on equal terms, to all who wish to play.' It argued that severing cricketing connections with South Africa would not encourage multi-racial sport in South Africa and that a sporting boycott would 'serve to make those who are already inward-looking even more so.' Abandoning the tour because of 'pressure from a minority would subscribe to a victory for mob-rule in our public life. This could lead to serious repercussions for the future of the game not only in this country, but the world over.'[42] Even a week before the tour was cancelled, the Cricket Council was maintaining that 'bridge-building' or keeping sporting cricketing contacts with South Africa was the most effective method of promoting multi-racial cricket in South Africa and was 'in the long term . . . in the best interests of cricket, and of cricketers of all races in South Africa.'[43] When individual members of the Cricket Council spoke out, they usually supported bridge-building. Colin Cowdrey, for instance, stated that he had 'never believed in an isolation policy and never will' and described the decision of the Cricket Council on 20 May to go ahead with the tour as 'a bold decision and Christian good sense.'[44] Subba Row, who would probably have been classed as a non-white in South Africa, stated that he disliked apartheid but felt that the invitation to the SACA should stand because the South African tourists represented liberal opinion in South Africa and had shown that they were prepared to play against any cricketers regardless of race.[45] Jack Bailey summarized the MCC's attitude as the

41. *The Times,* 23 January 1969.
42. *Daily Telegraph,* 20 April 1970.
43. *The Times,* 20 May 1970.
44. *The Times,* 20 May 1970; *Daily Telegraph,* 20 May 1970.
45. *The Times,* 23 April 1970.

old-fashioned notion of not letting down in South Africa those who had contributed so much to the game internationally. In his view those who were nourishing cricket in South Africa found their government's laws anathema and they 'had fought side by side with England during the war. Now they needed our help and support. We should lend it to them.'[46]

Calls to cancel the tour received little support within first-class cricket. The Cricket Council believed that a clear majority of those who supported county cricket wanted it to go ahead. The opinion of Wilfred Wooller, a member of the Cricket Council who was also secretary of Glamorgan CCC, that 98% of the cricket world, by which he probably meant the membership of the county clubs, thought that the tour was in 'the best interests of the game' may have been an exaggeration but not a very wild exaggeration.[47] In February 1970 Griffith wrote to the secretaries of all the county clubs that 80% of all MCC members favoured maintaining cricketing ties with South Africa.[48] In February 1970 the AGM of Lancashire CCC rejected overwhelmingly a call for the club to withdraw from its scheduled fixture against the South African team. By the beginning of May only twelve of Lancashire's members had resigned from the club because of their opposition to the tour.[49] In April about 150 of Surrey's members wanted the invitation to the South African tourists to be withdrawn and there was a massive vote in favour of the tour at its AGM.[50] Of Kent's 6,200 members, 4,214 had replied to a questionnaire about their views on the tour: 3,497 supported the tour going ahead. Only 717 were opposed.[51]

Of the 287 members of the Cricketers' Association, the trade union for county cricketers, 152 had voted in a poll organized by the Association in January 1970: 124 had voted in favour of the tour and 28 against it. Of the 28 opposed to the tour, nine felt that the tour would be impracticable and three objected to it on moral grounds. These 28 were employed by 13 of the 17 first-class counties, which could mean that at four counties all players supported the tour going ahead. Those who took part in the poll tended to be those who would have been most likely to have been selected for matches against the South Africans: 130 out of 190 capped players voted but only 20 of the 95 uncapped members. Forty-two overseas players, many of whom were not white, took part in the poll, but how they voted is not recorded.

46. Bailey, *Conflicts in Cricket,* p. 56.

47. Humphry, D. (1975), *The Cricket Conspiracy,* London: National Council for Civil Liberties, p. 58.

48. S.C. Griffith to all county secretaries, 11 February 1970, Cricket Council Cancelled South African Cricket Tour to the UK 1970 – General File.

49. *The Times,* 6 February 1970; *Daily Telegraph,* 5 May 1970.

50. *The Times,* 23 April 1970.

51. Cricket Council Cancelled South African Cricket Tour to the UK – General File.

Jack Bannister, secretary of the Association from 1970 until 1989, was reported to have said that 'If a player wants to make a personal decision about not playing, we will advise him first of all to consider the terms of his contract with his club', which does not seem a call to boycott the tour.[52] Coloured cricketers employed by Lancashire, Warwickshire, Glamorgan and Surrey announced that they did not wish to be selected for matches against the South Africans, but it was also reported that threats to themselves and their families had affected their decision.[53] Garfield Sobers, the West Indian test cricketer who was playing for Nottinghamshire was criticized by the West Indian Standing Conference for saying that he was prepared to play against the all-white South African team. Peter Lever, the white Lancashire fast bowler, asked to be excused from playing against the South Africans because of his opposition to the tour.[54] Michael Brearley, who played for Middlesex, associated himself with the opposition to the tour. Raymond Illingworth, who would probably have captained the England side had test matches been played against South Africa in 1970, said that he 'rated my freedom to choose to play against South Africa, and the freedom of others who wish to watch in peace, every bit as important as any freedom to demonstrate.' He believed that the South African tourists had shown that 'they will gladly play against men of any race or colour anywhere in the world . . . These . . . are the men who should be welcomed as players in our mixed society and sent back to encourage our ways in their own country.'[55] In May 1970 Brian Close, the Yorkshire captain, addressing a rally of the Keep the Seventy Tour Campaign, claimed that all Yorkshire's players wanted to play against the South Africans and that he had spoken to 'a lot of coloured players who sincerely want to play first-class cricket against South Africa. But a lot are prevented by their own countries who say to them "If you play you will not be allowed back into your own countries."'[56] Basil D'Oliveira was prepared to play against the South African team because he believed that it 'essential to keep some contact open' if any influence was to be exerted upon apartheid.[57]

Opposition to the Tour

Opponents of the tour shared a detestation of apartheid but differed about how to oppose the tour. Peter Hain, a nineteen year-old Young Liberal student who had been raised in South Africa and who became the Minister of State at the Foreign

52. *The Times*, 21 January 1921.
53. *The Times*, 5, 7 15 May 1970.
54. *The Times*, 3 March 1970.
55. *Daily Express*, 21 April 1970.
56. *The Times*, 16 May 1970; *Daily Telegraph*, 16 May 1970.
57. *Guardian*, 23 May 1970.

and Commonwealth Office for Tony Blair's New Labour Government in 1999, and Louis Eaks, another Young Liberal, set up the Stop the Seventy Tour campaign. The STST campaign had little formal organization and received much support from student activists. The Anti-Apartheid Movement and SANROC, led by Derek Brutus, co-operated with the Stop the Seventy Tour campaign as did Church, a group of radical Christians committed to the overthrow of apartheid. The leaders of the STST campaign held demonstrations at matches played by the Wilf Isaacs XI, a team of white South African cricketers who had toured England in 1969 and played against sides including county cricketers in matches held at grounds where first-class cricket was played. At Oxford the demonstrators caused play to be abandoned for the day. Those who were to lead STST had also staged protests at the tennis Davis Cup match between Britain and South Africa at Bristol and had been active in the protests against the tour of Britain by the all-white South African rugby union team during the 1969–70 season, but although they had caused much disruption, they had not prevented any match being played.[58]

Hain regarded the disruptions to the rugby tour as a practice run for the campaign to have the cricket tour stopped. In February he was reported as saying that as it would be far easier to disrupt cricket matches, that 'We got involved in the rugby tour as a sideshow. We have learned our lessons, and know the tactics that will be used against us.'[59] The leaders of the STST campaign saw their attempts to stop the tour as part of a wider struggle against apartheid and believed that an international sporting boycott of South Africa could be crucial to the campaign to undermine apartheid. Equally they saw the attempts to stop the tour as a means of combating racism in Britain. Hain and his sympathizers did not advocate violence but were prepared to use direct action to stop the tour. They made it clear that they would interrupt play at matches and if necessary damage grounds so that matches could not be played. Some supporters of STST created the impression that they would be prepared to break the law in order to prevent the tour taking place. In April the *Observer* reported that tactics for interrupting matches could include blowing whistles and trumpets to distract players, releasing small animals such as mice or rabbits onto pitches, shouting obscenities, releasing stink bombs and even having remote control toy aeroplanes operated from outside grounds.[60] One student was reported to be breeding half a million locusts for release at cricket grounds. He claimed that 70,000 locusts could consume a hundredweight of grass in twelve minutes.[61]

58. Hain, *Don't Play with Apartheid*, chapter 10.
59. *The Times*, 3 February 1970.
60. *Observer*, 26 April 1970.
61. *The Times*, 11 May 1970.

Coloured groups in Britain opposed the tour. Jeff Crawford of the West Indian Standing Conference, which had 8,500 members in the UK, declared his support for STST. In March 1970, twenty West Indian organizations in London set up the West Indian Campaign against Apartheid Cricket which it was hoped would mobilize West Indian opposition to the tour. Gary Burton, who took the chair at the meeting where the Campaign was launched, called upon every black player to boycott the tour as 'participation would be an insult to every black person.'[62] Tasadduq Ahmed, chair of the League of Overseas Pakistanis, promised moral support for non-violent protests against the tour. J. Joshi, the national secretary of the Indian Workers' Association, argued that it would perhaps be more appropriate to combat racism in Britain rather than 'taking refuge in what is happening a long way off'.[63] No organization of coloured people was prominent in support of the tour.

There was much opposition from the churches. In April 1970 the British Council of Churches voted unanimously in support of further representations for the tour to be cancelled, but accepted only by 38 votes to 31 resolutions in favour of peaceful demonstrations against the tour.[64] David Sheppard, no doubt as a result of his status as a former England cricketer, emerged as the cleric whose opposition to the tour attracted most publicity, but his views upon the tour were broadly similar to those of other clerics who called for its cancellation. In a letter to *The Times,* which he wrote with the philosopher Angus MacIntyre of Magdalene College, Oxford, Sheppard argued that claims of support for multi-racial cricket from white South African cricketers would mean little until they made it clear that would not accept the application of apartheid to cricket. 'Only by an incomprehensible logic', the letter continued, 'can men whose lives are organised upon a racial basis be regarded as supporters of multi-racial sport in other countries.'[65] In an article printed in *The Times* Sheppard claimed that Christians had to speak out against the cricket tour because the leaders of apartheid in South Africa called themselves professing Christians. Expressions of opposition to the tour would help to convince black Africans that the Christian Church was not 'simply a trick to buttress white supremacy'. Whilst white cricketers continued to play in an all-white team, they were in Sheppard's view identifying themselves with all the injustices of apartheid. Sheppard was also worried that the proposed tour could harm racial relations in Britain. He admitted that joining demonstrations ran the risk of 'inflaming race relations' but urged that not joining them carried 'the greater risk of allowing the black population of this country to assume that white people tolerate racialism.'[66]

62. *The Times,* 23 March 1970.
63. *The Times,* 29 January 1970.
64. *Daily Telegraph,* 22 April 1970.
65. *The Times,* 10 April 1970.
66. *The Times,* 25 April 1970.

Sheppard set up the Fair Cricket Campaign, which was intended to hold peaceful demonstrations against the tour. It planned to demonstrate outside Lord's on the first day of the test match against South Africa and attracted support from across the political spectrum.

Trevor Huddleston, the Anglican bishop of Stepney, who had spoken out against apartheid during his ministry in South Africa, also felt that the tour could 'escalate racial tension' in Britain.[67] The bishop of Gloucester felt that the MCC was blind to go ahead with a series of matches which could be so distasteful to so many people and which could damage race relations.[68] Most clerical opponents of the tour advocated peaceful demonstrations against the tour. The Archbishop of Canterbury thought that the tour could strain race relations in Britain but also feared that violent demonstrations could stimulate support not for the protesters but for 'those against whom they are protesting'.[69] Canon Collins, the Anglican whose opposition to nuclear weapons was to attract much attention, was one cleric who came close to advocating more direct forms of action. He criticized the prime minister for not supporting calls for the digging up of cricket pitches, and launched an appeal for £200,000 to counter that of Newman and to assist the campaign against the tour.[70] Clerics who supported the tour attracted less attention than those who criticized it.

Attacks on eleven county cricket grounds during the night of 20/21 January 1970 were the first direct action against the tour. Posters were stuck to the main gates at Lord's. At Cardiff a four-foot hole was dug in the square and filled with tacks and the scoreboard was sprayed with paint. Paint was also sprayed on Wilfred Wooller's car. At Bristol weed killer was poured onto the playing area and at Taunton paint was sprayed on the covers and grandstand. Slogans were painted on buildings and walls at Leicester, Old Trafford, The Oval and Southampton. Peter Hain denied responsibility for these protests but Louis Eaks admitted to knowing that the protests were taking place and that Young Liberals had been responsible for the action at Old Trafford. Eaks warned that 'serious, irregular assaults' would have to be expected at cricket grounds.[71] In May sodium chlorate was sprinkled on Gloucestershire's pitch in Bristol.[72]

Opposition to the tour stimulated the formation of organizations to support it. Lieutenant-Colonel Sir Charles Newman, VC, a member of the Essex and Kent county cricket clubs, Subba Row and Jack Bailey launched an appeal for a fund of £200,000 to ensure that the tour would go ahead. The fund was intended to pay for

67. *The Times*, 29 April 1970.
68. *The Times*, 28 April 1970.
69. *Guardian*, 21 April 1970.
70. *The Times*, 20 April, 15 May 1970.
71. *The Times*, 21 January 1970.
72. *The Times*, 7 May 1970.

police protection at cricket grounds and for insurance cover, with 25% of the proceeds to go to encouraging 'cricket of all races and in all countries in which the game is played'. It was denied that the fund had formal links with the Cricket Council, but the fact that donations could be addressed to 'The 1970 Cricket Fund' at Lord's, suggests that that the Cricket Council approved of the Fund. The Fund Committee included M.J.C. Allom, a member of the Cricket Council and the president of the MCC in 1969, Colin Cowdrey, Brian Sellers, a former captain of Yorkshire and also a member of the Cricket Council, Jack Bannister of the Cricketers' Association, Alec Bedser, the former Surrey and England player and current chairman of the England selectors, Simon Kimmins, who had played for Kent as an amateur in 1950 and 1951, the race horse trainer Peter Cazalet, Derrick Robins, the chairman of Coventry City FC and who organized cricket tours to South Africa later in the 1970s, and K.A.C. Thorogood, a London businessman.[73] Patrons of the Fund included the Dukes of Norfolk and Beaufort, Lords Portal and Wakefield, the Bishop of Bath and Wells and the Bishop of Leicester, Judge Sir Carl Aarvold, the QCs P.D. Popplewell and John Stocker, the war hero Douglas Bader, Joe Mercer, the football manager and former captain of the England football team, the golfer Dai Rees, the rugby union internationals Gareth Edwards and Bob Hiller, who had played a little first-class cricket, Brian Close, Rachel Heyhoe, the England woman cricketer, and Tony Lewis, the captain of Glamorgan CCC and who was to captain the England cricket team in 1972–3.[74] By the beginning of May donations totalled only £15,000, though over 3,000 letters of support had been received.[75]

The right-wing Conservative group the Monday Club organized the Support the Seventy Tour campaign, with John Jackson, the prospective Conservative candidate for Erith and Crayford as its chairman.[76] It held rallies in different parts of the country to provide evidence of support for the tour. Peter Toombs formed the Anti-Demonstration Association. In the middle of April he claimed that this had 3,000 members who had each paid a subscription of one guinea. Toombs insisted that he had received no money from South Africa and that he had refused an offer of £10,000 from a West Midlands businessman. At the end of April Toombs named the prime minister and six others including John Arlott, Peter Hain, Derek Brutus and David Sheppard in a complaint the under the Race Relations Act that they were inciting unlawful race discrimination. The ADA threatened to photograph and prepare dossiers on those leading demonstrations against the tour. When the Home Secretary

73. *The Times*, 24 April: *Daily Telegraph*, 23, 24 April 1970.
74. *Guardian*, 24 April 1970.
75. *Daily Telegraph*, 2 May 1970.
76. *The Times*, 20 May 1970.

James Callaghan met the Cricket Council, the ADA declared that 'the South African tour must go on'. It promised to defend the South African tourists and also coloured cricketers in England who had been threatened with violence. It called upon 'ex-Service organisations, commandos etc, to assist us in a new battle of Britain freedom' [sic].[77] Early in May 1970 a parliamentary candidate for the National Front announced that the MCC and Scotland Yard could count upon support from the National Front if left-wing groups caused trouble during the tour.[78]

The Attempts to Save the Tour

The threats of disruption to matches and the example of difficulties caused by demonstrators during Isaacs' tour and during the rugby tour meant that as early as December 1969, the Test and County Cricket Board had enquired about the costs of extra policing and insurance cover if matches had to be cancelled. On 12 February 1970 a sub-committee of the TCCB recommended restricting the tour to twelve matches, with the first match starting as late as 6 June. There would be five test matches but only five counties would play against the tourists and instead matches between representative sides from Northern and Southern counties against the South Africans would be organized. Artificial pitches would be laid at each ground and the games played on wickets covered by matting. Revenue from all twelve matches and not merely the test matches would be pooled among the first-class counties. Spectators would not be allowed to sit on the grass. All seats were to be numbered and it would be stated on tickets that those trying to interrupt play would be removed from the ground.[79] When these proposals were made public, Peter Hain described them as 'round one to us' and claimed that the STST committee expected that 200,000 would take part in its demonstrations.[80] Late in April, Simon Hebditch, a 24-year-old Young Liberal, who had previously been arrested for carrying dye that he had hoped to spray onto a rugby field, was appointed the full-time organizer of the STST Committee.[81] At the Headingley ground in Leeds, Yorkshire CCC erected barricades with barbed wire borrowed from the Army.[82] The TCCB insured the tour for £140,000, but the terms of the policy specified that if the Cricket Council cancelled

77. *The Times*, 16, 30 April, 22 May 1970.

78. *The Times*, 4 May 1970.

79. Minutes of the Cricket Council Emergency Executive Committee, 16, 29 December, 12 February 1970, Cricket Council Cancelled South African Cricket Tour to the UK 1970 – General File.

80. *The Times*, 13 February 1970.

81. *The Times*, 27 April 1970.

82. *Guardian*, 9 April, 5 May 1970.

the tour, compensation would be paid only on account of 'riots, civil commotions, vandalism malicious damage and/or acts of demonstration' occurring during the tour. No compensation would be paid if the tour were cancelled by the Council before its scheduled commencement. The premium for this cover was £27,500.[83]

The Cricket Council launched a public relations campaign to defuse opposition to the tour. On October 1969, Subba Row, chair of the TCCB Public Relations and Promotions Sub-committee, had argued the need to stress that the Cricket Council and the TCCB disliked apartheid in sport but as they could not change the law in South Africa, playing against South Africa would be the best means of changing apartheid. To show that SACA's heart was in the right place, attempts could be made to persuade coloured cricketers in South Africa to accept the Trust Fund of £25,000 that SACA had offered them. In December the Cricket Council Emergency Executive Committee discussed how to get television publicity for the Trust Fund.[84] Though no proof has been found, the idea of the Trust Fund may have originated with the English cricket establishment. In the 1970s senior figures in English cricket suggested to SACA how it could create a more favourable public image in Britain.

During April various organizations urged cancellation of the tour. Frank Cousins, chair of the Community Relations Commission and formerly the leader of the Transport and General Workers' Union and a retired member of the Wilson cabinet, appealed on number of occasions for the Cricket Council to call off the tour.[85] At the National Union of Students annual conference in Bradford, resolutions of support for the campaign against the tour and calling for a total sporting boycott of South Africa were passed and in May Jack Straw, president of the NUS and later to be the Home Secretary in the Blair government, claimed that his 400,000 members would give 'maximum peaceful support to anti-apartheid demonstrations'.[86] Vic Feather, secretary of the TUC, speaking with the full support of the TUC Council, hoped that all trade unionists would show their 'dissent, distaste and repugnance' for apartheid by staying away from matches against the South Africans rather than by joining demonstrations at grounds in which 'other elements' could be involved.[87] The TGWU and USDAW were among trade unions calling for the tour to be cancelled.[88]

---

83. P. May to S.C. Griffith, 8 April 1970, Cricket Council Cancelled South African Cricket Tour to the UK 1970 – General File. Press reports claimed that the tour had been insured for £250,000 and that the premium for this had been £50,000. See, for instance, *Guardian,* 19 April 1970.

84. S. Row to S.C. Griffith, 22 October 1969, Cricket Council Emergency Executive Committee Minutes, 16 December 1969, Cricket Council Cancelled South African Cricket Tour to the UK 1970 – General File.

85. *The Times,* 7 May 1970.

86. *The Times,* 3 April 1970; *Guardian,* 21 May 1970.

87. *The Times,* 23 April 1970.

88. *The Times,* 10, 28 April 1970.

Trade unions of those working in the mass media were faced with the issue of whether reporting on the tour could be construed as conniving with the racialism. John Arlott, the radio commentator and newspaper journalist, announced that he would neither broadcast nor report on matches against the South Africans.[89] The Association of Cinematograph, Television and Allied Technicians promised support for members who refused to film or provide television coverage of the tour.[90] The book and magazine branch of the National Union of Journalists suggested that journalists should not report on the tour, a view that was soon supported by Paul Foot who was writing for *Private Eye*. At the NUJ annual conference in Harrogate one delegate argued that reporting the tour in the normal way would 'by implication, condone apartheid in sport'. The central London branch of the NUJ voted in favour of a veto, but this example was not followed in all areas. Branches in Birmingham and Harrogate voted against a boycott. At the Wolverhampton branch the voting was 38 to 1 against a boycott. The NUJ chapel of the *Guardian* voted for a boycott, though this majority included only one of the sports journalists. Clifford Makins, sports editor of the *Observer,* claimed that 'we can report the matches responsibly on the sports pages, while remaining alert to the wider implications.'[91]

There was a more or less clear party divide over whether the tour should take place. The Labour Government wanted the tour to be cancelled. In a television interview Harold Wilson said that the Cricket Council had made 'a big mistake' in inviting a South African team.[92] Detestation of racialism and apartheid in particular were at the root of Labour's opposition to the tour, but other considerations influenced government attitudes. In October 1969 Denis Howell, the Minister for Sport, said on the ITV's *Sports Arena* programme that his personal opinion was that the South Africa team should not come to Britain, because he had 'no time for any sport based on racial considerations'. After the cancellation of the tour, he claimed that the policy of bridge building had done nothing in over fifty years to change racial discrimination in South Africa.[93] On 14 May in an emergency debate in the House of Commons on the proposed tour, Howell urged the Cricket Council to cancel the tour on the grounds that going ahead with the tour could lead to racial disharmony, raise law-and-order difficulties, threaten the Commonwealth games and have long-term deleterious effects for British sport.[94] Some feared that demonstrations in support of or in opposition to the tour could heighten racial tension in Britain, and there

89. *Guardian,* 17 April 1970.
90. *The Times,* 20 April 1970.
91. *Observer,* 12 April 1970; *The Times,* 10, 14 April 1970.
92. *The Times,* 18 April 1970.
93. *The Times,* 5 June 1970.
94. Howell, *Made in Birmingham,* p. 207.

may have been a suspicion that, in what was expected to be the year of a general election, racial clashes could be an electoral asset for the Conservatives. The government was also aware that the tour could damage Britain's relations with African and Asian states. Linked to this was a threat by African and Asian nations to boycott the Commonwealth Games due to be held in Edinburgh in June, a move that would have ruined the Games as a celebration of multi-racial sport. At the beginning of May Harold Wilson said on television that it would be 'a tragedy if the Commonwealth Games are cut down and denuded to just a shadow of what they ought to be. I am sure it is right to go on with the Games anyway. But peace is indivisible and so is sport. I think that there is a duty on those concerned to think of this cricket decision on other sports.'[95] By 20 May, eighteen countries had stated that they would join a boycott.[96]

Until the last moment the government did not want to take the responsibility of cancelling the tour, but hoped that the Cricket Council might be persuaded to do this. Nora Beloff, the political columnist of the *Observer,* wrote at the beginning of May that for over a year the prime minister and Denis Howell had been 'privately trying to cajole the MCC into calling off the tour', but that after prolonged ministerial discussion, the prime minister had decided that he could not himself cancel the tour. The only legal procedure for doing this would have to have declared the South African cricketers 'undesirable aliens', but this could have disrupted economic relations with South Africa. South Africa was Britain's third largest export market and a recurring problem of the Labour government had been how to bridge the trade gap by boosting exports.[97] In public the Home Secretary, James Callaghan, denied that he was putting pressure on the Cricket Council.[98] Even on 21 May after a three-hour meeting with representatives of the Cricket Council, he mentioned that he had urged cancelling the tour on grounds of 'public policy' but still maintained that 'It must be their decision' to call off the tour. 'I have no power to ban a game of cricket in England,' he continued, 'I do not want such power. I would substantially stretch my powers on immigration if I were to deny admission to these young men on the grounds that they were undesirable aliens. I would not want such powers.'[99]

Edward Heath, the Conservative leader, stated early in May 1970 that he was glad that the South African tourists were coming to Britain.[100] In April he had argued that there were two approaches to South Africa – ostracism or making use of whatever means existed to influence South Africa. In modern times, Heath could think

95. *The Times,* 1 May 1970.
96. *The Times,* 21 May 1970.
97. *Observer,* 3 May 1970.
98. *The Times,* 12 February 1970.
99. *The Times,* 22 May 1970.
100. *Daily Telegraph,* 4 May 1970.

of no instance where ostracism had caused a regime to reverse its policies.[101] When the tour was cancelled Charles Morrison, the Conservative shadow minister for sport, expressed the mainstream Conservative attitude to the tour. He said that 'I come down on the side of being a bridge builder. This is more likely to have influence on South Africa's general views than by isolating them.'[102] During a visit to South Africa in March, Anthony Barber, chairman of the Conservative party, had said that the shadow cabinet believed apartheid to be totally wrong, but that it was a internal matter for South Africa and one that should not affect the mutual interests of Britain and South Africa in the South Atlantic. In his opinion it was up to the British government to ensure that the tour took place in peace and without illegal molestation.[103] Not all Conservatives wished the tour to take place. Edward Boyle, the former Minister of Education who was also a member of the MCC, the MP Nicholas Scott and Lena Townsend, the former chair of ILEA, were prominent Conservatives who joined David Sheppard in setting up the Fair Cricket Campaign.[104] Prominent Liberals opposed the tour. The Liberal leader Jeremy Thorpe thought that the Cricket Council had acted as 'stupidly as any body of men or women can' and that inviting the South African tourists would damage race relations by giving the impression 'that we don't mind about apartheid.'[105] Jo Grimond, the former Liberal leader, was opposed to the tour but did not like how the government had surrendered to threats of demonstrations when 'neither they nor the Cricket Council would give way to reason.'[106]

Perhaps in the hope of seeking an electoral advantage, Conservatives tried to convert the tour debate into a law-and-order issue. On the television programme *Sportsnight with Coleman*, the Prime Minister had said that 'Everyone should be able to demonstrate against apartheid – I hope people will feel free to do so.' Heath agreed that people should be free to demonstrate but emphasised that demonstrations could easily turn violent if large numbers attended them and shortly afterwards called for the law on demonstrations to be amended to prevent minorities using them for damage and disruption.[107] Iain Macleod described Wilson's television comments 'an act of utter irresponsibility' and added that 'hooligans and anarchists' thrived on demonstrations.[108]

The Cricket Council called off the tour on 22 May, only a little over a fortnight before the first match was due to be played on 6 June. On 21 May Callaghan had decided to meet representatives of the Cricket Council, claiming that the concerns

101. *The Times*, 1 May 1970.
102. *The Times*, 5 June 1970.
103. *The Times*, 11 March 1970.
104. *Guardian*, 13 May 1970; *Observer*, 17 May 1970.
105. *Daily Telegraph*, 22 May 1970.
106. *The Times*, 26 May 1970.
107. *The Times*, 18 April, 1, 5 May 1970
108. *Observer*, 26 April 1970.

expressed about the tour expressed by teachers, trade unionists, the churches and the police would have meant that 'I would have been failing in my responsibilities if I did not meet them.'[109] On 21 May he had a three hour meeting with Allom and Griffith where he pointed out the possible impacts of the tour upon relations with other Commonwealth countries, race relations within Britain, divisions within the community, the police and the Edinburgh Games, but reiterated that he had no authority to ban the tour himself. Wooller felt that the Cricket Council had 'virtually been given an ultimatum to call off the tour'[110] and, as *The Times* pointed out, the governing body of a sport had no option but to accept what the government requested.[111]

Up to the meeting with Callaghan the Cricket Council gave the impression in public of being determined that the tour would go ahead. The *Observer* believed that day-to-day handling of the tour issue was conducted by Allom, Allen, Griffith and Aiden Crawley, the former MP and chairman of London Weekend Television. It implied that they favoured a hard line whilst other members of the Council took a 'more detached' view.[112] On 11 May the Council replied to Peter Shore's request for the tour to be cancelled with the message that it intended 'the tour to proceed as arranged in accordance with the wishes of the large majority of people in this country.' A meeting with representatives from the High Commissions of Jamaica, Trinidad, Barbados, India, Pakistan and Ceylon did not cause the Council's attitude to change.[113] The next day, after meeting the chairman of the Edinburgh Games committee, Griffith re-iterated that the tour would go ahead.[114] Against a mounting number of calls for the tour to be cancelled, the Cricket Council met again on 18 May. Twenty-six of the 28 members were present. The Council agreed once more that the tour would go ahead. When this was announced to a press conference, the *Guardian* reported that most journalists listened 'with mounting incredulity as it became clear that the tour was still on'.[115] A group of no more than eight, the 'bronzed group', burst into applause. Denis Compton, the former England professional cricketer who had a column in the *Sunday Express* and who was wearing a Springbok badge in his lapel, shouted 'bloody marvellous!' and shook two South African journalists by the hand. On the same day the Cricket Council had refused to meet a delegation consisting of Lord Walston, the chair of the Institute of Race Relations, Lord Gore-Booth, Lord Hunt and the Bishop of London. Walston had

109. *The Times*, 21 May 1970.
110. Humphry, *Cricket Conspiracy*, p. 59.
111. *The Times*, 22 May 1970.
112. *Observer,* 17 May 1970.
113. *The Times*, 12 May 1970.
114. *The Times*, 13 May 1970.
115. *Guardian*, 20 May 1970.

earlier claimed that it would be madness to hold the tour during a general election and for the first day of the Lord's test match to be on election day itself.[116] On 19 May the Council refused to meet a delegation of MPs which led Arthur Latham, the Labour MP for Paddington, to write that to it that it had put itself in 'the indefensible position of appearing to have closed ears, closed eyes and a closed mind.'[117]

Despite giving the impression in public of being determined that the tour would take place, the Cricket Council may have been looking for an excuse to call off the tour. John Arlott claimed that the terms of the insurance policy, which specified that the compensation of £250,000 would not be paid if the Cricket Council called off the tour, could have explained why the Cricket Council had been so reluctant to cancel the tour.[118] There can be little doubt that the Cricket Council would have been aware of the terms of the insurance policy and at his meeting with Allom and Griffith, Callaghan mentioned that he would raise the matter of compensation with the Chancellor of the Exchequer but made it clear that he could make no promises. In the event the government paid £70,000 compensation to the Cricket Council,[119] a far smaller sum than the £140,000, which the insurance company would have paid had the government called off the tour. A series of matches between England and a Rest of the World team were arranged for the summer to help compensate the county clubs for losing their share of any profits from the tests against South Africa. The Cricket Council may have hoped that appearing to be determined for the tour to take place may have been a tactic for stampeding the government into prohibiting the tour, but no newspaper analyses of why the tour was cancelled argued that intransigence on the part of the Cricket Council had been motivated by a hope that this could have provoked the government to cancel the tour.

Was the Cricket Council Condoning Racism?

Members of the Cricket Council and prominent cricketers usually argued that they wanted to see multi-racial cricket in South Africa, which seems to be far from being a statement of support for racism or for apartheid. The *Observer's* assessment was that one or two members of the Cricket Council were open supporters of apartheid, some were 'authoritarian' but most were 'political babes in the racial jungle' and 'well-intentioned' though 'apt to be paternal in attitude to non-whites'.[120] The line of the cricket establishment was that bridge building, or retraining cricketing links

---

116. *Observer,* 24 May 1970.
117. *The Times,* 21 May 1970.
118. *Guardian,* 19 May 1970.
119. Humphry, *Cricket Conspiracy,* p. 60.
120. *Observer,* 24 May 1970.

with South Africa would be the most effective method of promoting multi-racial cricket in South Africa. In the late 1960s and in 1970 belief in bridge building as the means of persuading SACA and the South African government to accept multi-racial cricket owed much to assumptions that playing cricket in accordance with the English canons of sportsmanship could promote moral reformation. A statement issued after the Cricket Council's meeting on 18 May 1970 rebutted accusations that the tour posed a threat to community relations in Britain by claiming that 'cricket has made an outstanding and widely acknowledged contribution to the maintenance of good relations between all people among whom the game has been played'.[121] This statement also mentioned that SACA had been informed that there could be no subsequent test tours between England and South Africa until 'South African cricket is played and teams selected on a multiracial basis', which, of course, prompted the question of why the Council wanted the 1970 series to take place but then stipulated that there could be no subsequent tours by teams not selected on a multi-racial basis. When the proposed South African tour was eventually cancelled, the *Observer* reported that the Cricket Council was 'supported, not only by out-moded Colonial Office ideals about the supreme virtue of gradualism in racial affairs, but also by extraordinary notions of the beneficent influence of cricket on those who play and support the game. They see it as not only bringing people of different races closer to each other, but also closer to God and to humane standards generally.' The *Observer* continued 'Nothing has been more important in the long-drawn-out Springboks crisis than the innocence of many Council members in believing, sincerely, that cricket is somehow capable of reducing hatred and notions of white superiority in South Africa.'[122]

The Cricket Council's confidence in bridge building was probably strengthened by the support in the Conservative party for bridge building. In outlook and back-ground most members of the Cricket Council were sympathetic to the Conservative party. The Conservative policy towards South Africa in general was that retaining contacts rather than isolation would be more likely to undermine apartheid. The Cricket Council also seems to have believed that the public supported its stance. Griffith's statements often stressed the high level of public support for the tour. It is not possible to assess the exact level of public support for the tour, but an opinion poll published during the first week of May 1970 showed that over the past three months the numbers wanting the tour to take place had been double those who wanted it called off.[123] The *Observer* thought 'a faith widely held by the cricketing public' was that playing cricket with South Africa could help to overturn apartheid.[124]

121. *The Times*, 20 May 1970.
122. *Observer*, 24 May 1970.
123. *The Times*, 4 May 1970.
124. *Observer*, 24 May 1970.

Callaghan thought that the tour was 'one of the few issues of recent times where public opinion has been divided right down the middle.'[125] Whilst the Labour government wanted the tour cancelled, its reluctance to take direct responsibility for doing this could mean that senior Labour politicians were mindful of the extent of public support for the tour in a general election year. It has already been mentioned how the financial dependence of county cricket clubs on test match revenues and the fact that the insurers would not have to pay compensation if the Cricket Council cancelled the tour could have been other reasons why the Cricket Council was so reluctant to call off the tour.

For the Cricket Council the 1970 tour quickly became entangled with the issue of law and order and whether demonstrations, or the threat of demonstrations, should have been allowed to prevent groups and individuals from pursuing an activity that was not against the law. The threat of disorder at cricket matches has to be seen against rising concerns about the rise of violent political protest around the world such as the anti-Vietnam demonstrations in the United States, the French uprising of 1968, confrontation in Northern Ireland and campus demonstrations and sit-ins throughout much of the Western world. The *Guardian* believed that the members of the Cricket Council had come to 'see themselves as bastions of law and order against a violent fringe of activities [sic]'.[126] In 1989 Jack Bailey wrote 'We were fighting for the world of cricket as we knew it; for the right to play cricket under the law of the land. There was nothing but discouragement from Harold Wilson's Labour government, but a vast wave of encouragement from the cricket-loving public, and all the time there was the feeling that here was something worth fighting for, even if defined as vaguely as freedom under the law.'[127] When the Cricket Council announced on 19 May that the tour would still go ahead, an editorial in the *Daily Telegraph* claimed that 'Those who really care about liberty and law and order are greatly in debt to the Cricket Council . . . The issue is not really about cricket at all, but rather about civil liberty in our country, threatened as it is on the cricket field as it is in other fields by a fascist-minded anti-democratic minority.'[128] When the Council cancelled the tour, Allom said he deplored 'the activities of those who, by intimidation of individual cricketers and threats of violent disruption have inflamed the whole issue.'[129]

Conservative politicians and the Conservative press blamed the government for allowing demonstrators to ensure that the tour was cancelled. Quintin Hogg, calling 'the whole operation . . . a classic illustration of the inability of this government

125. *The Times*, 22 May 1970.
126. *Guardian*, 20 May 1970.
127. Bailey, *Conflicts in Cricket*, pp. 57–8.
128. *Daily Telegraph*, 20 May 1970.
129. *The Times*, 23 May 1970.

to preserve freedom in this country, or to maintain law and order', argued that Wilson and Callaghan had bowed to threats of violence and blackmail.[130] On the eve of the tour's cancellation, a *Times* editorial declared that a major issue of public policy had been decided by 'the threat of mob action' and that in the long run allowing 'intimidation to become a successful means of political persuasion' would have 'grave consequences . . . far beyond cricket or even race relations.'[131] When the tour was called off, a *Daily Telegraph* editorial described it as 'a glorious red-letter day for intimidation, civil violence and disruption by a noisy and determined minority of peaceful pursuits wanted by a majority. The victors, ranging from the loud-mouthed organisers of demonstrations to the more furtive enemies of our society, have just cause for celebration.'[132]

Many saw support for the tour as upholding or at least condoning racism. The opposition of most Afro-Caribbean and Asian organizations to maintaining cricket links with South Africa shows that mainstream non-white opinion in Britain saw bridge building as co-operation with the overt racism of apartheid. Leaders of the Fair Cricket Campaign and most Labour and Liberal MPs seem to have thought that accepting a South Africa cricket team that had been selected upon the basis of race rather than cricketing ability alone would indicate to coloured people in Britain that the cricket world and British whites in general were unconcerned about the extent of racial injustice in South Africa. The leaders and presumably the supporters of the Stop the Seventy Tour movement believed that the Cricket Council's support for the tour condoned the racism of apartheid and agreed with SANROC that calling off the tour would strengthen the sporting boycott of South Africa and so help to bring about the collapse of apartheid. Opponents of the 1970 tour were also worried that it could have undermined attempts to promote racial harmony in Britain, especially when Enoch Powell's views had placed race and immigration on the agenda of national politics. Linked to this was the fear that any violent clashes that accompanied the tour might have led to widespread racial violence. An editorial in the *Guardian* suggested that had the tour taken place, it would have been accompanied with 'Paki-bashing, police-baiting, racial violence and vigilante groups.'[133] The desire of the Cricket Council for the tour to take place and its explanation that the tour had been called off because of pressure from the government and the threat of disorder suggest that the effects of the tour upon racial relations within Britain did not figure very highly in the calculations of the Cricket Council.

When the Cricket Council announced that the 1970 tour would take place but that there could be no further test match cricket with South Africa until South African

130. *The Times,* 23 May 1970.
131. *The Times,* 22 May 1970.
132. *Daily Telegraph,* 23 May 1970.
133. *Guardian,* 22 May 1970.

teams were selected upon a multi-racial basis, it may have wanted this statement to be seen as evidence that it was repudiating racism. The *Guardian* believed that the statement was an admission that 'the real issue is apartheid in sport', which meant that it was the 1970 tour rather than one in the future which ought to have been called off.[134] A cynical interpretation of this announcement was that it could have been a ruse to persuade the SACA to cancel the tour which would have meant that the insurance company would have been obliged to pay compensation to the Cricket Council. Although the statement of the Cricket Council emphasized that opinion polls showed that a majority of the public wanted the tour to take place, it is possible that the level of opposition to the tour may have influenced this decision.

The determination of the Cricket Council for the 1970 to take place can be interpreted as a strong desire to accommodate the racist policies of the South African government. The Cricket Council did have several opportunities to cancel the tour without incurring any loss of face. The refusal of the South African government to accept the MCC party including D'Oliveira in 1968, the scale of the disturbances on the South African rugby tour and the opposition to the tour from the prime minister and the home secretary could have been used as opportunities to cancel the tour. But persisting with the desire for the tour to take place, and the decisions to hold matches only at grounds that could be better defended and to reduce the programme of matches suggest that the cricket establishment was not aware of, or not concerned about, how the tour gave the impression that the cricket establishment was incapable of appreciating why non-whites and also whites objected to the tour. The fact that the Cricket Council and many of its supporters allowed other issues such as the maintenance of law and order and a determination not to give way to the threats posed by demonstrations to take precedence over the racial dimension can be taken to show that antagonism to racism was not its prime concern. To many non-whites and also those who supported the Fair Cricket campaign, indifference to the injustices that accompanied apartheid was a form of complicity with apartheid. First-class cricket between 1968 and 1970 may not have been racist but the conduct of its governing body created an impression that many in English sport, whilst expressing a dislike of racism, did not detest it to such an extent that they would support the banning of South Africa from international sport.

The Consequences of Cancelling the Tour

The cancellation of the 1970 tour had profound effects on international sport and on cricket in South Africa. In May 1970 the Pakistan Cricket Board of Control wrote to six Pakistan test cricketers who were also playing county cricket to suggest

134. *Guardian,* 20 May 1970.

that they did not play in matches against the South African tourists and also called off the tour to England of the Pakistan under-25 side. Pakistan and India also threatened to call off their cricket tours of England scheduled for 1971. The West Indies Board of Control also expressed its opposition to the South African tour.[135] By cancelling the tour the Cricket Council helped to ensure that test cricket would continue as a multi-racial sport and not spilt into separate white and non-white groups.

When Cricket Council announced on 19 May that it was not intending to withdraw the invitation to SACA, it re-emphasized that no further representative cricket would be played against the official South African side either in South Africa or in Britain unless multi-racial cricket had been introduced in South Africa. England played no test matches against South Africa until Nelson Mandela was released from jail and the African National Congress announced that the sporting boycott could be lifted. The refusal of English cricket to resume test cricket with South Africa during the apartheid years, even though in 1970 it had given the impression of having been dragooned into calling off the tour, helped to strengthen the sporting boycott of South Africa. Cricket was the first major sport of white South Africa to abandon international matches with South Africa. Cricket severed its international sporting links with South Africa far sooner than rugby union, the other major sport of white South Africa. In 1984 England played rugby internationals in South Africa.

The English cricketing boycott of South Africa, occurring when South Africa had an especially strong side, encouraged some progress towards multi-racial sport in South Africa. In May 1970 John Woodcock wrote that for 'far too long little has been done by the white South African Cricket Association to recognise the moral and technical claims of non-white cricketers.'[136] In December 1969, as a result of the D'Oliveira affair, SACA had offered to SACBOC (the South African Board of Cricket Control), which administered cricket among Coloureds, Malays and Indians and which had African delegates although most Africans played under the auspices of SAACB (the South African African Cricket Board), a grant of R50,000 to assist the promotion of non-white cricket. As SACA had previously taken little interest in non-white cricket, this grant may have resulted from expediency and fears about the effects of racial discrimination upon South African test match cricket. The grant was rejected by SACBOC, which saw it as an attempt to 'perpetuate colour different-iation'. But African cricket did receive some help from SACA. Coaching facilities were provided by SACA. An African team was allowed to play in the SACA Gillette Cup competition and an African team toured Rhodesia. In 1971 the white players

135. *Cricketer International,* July 1970, p. 5; *Observer,* 3, 17 May 1970.
136. *Cricketer International,* May 1970, p. 6.

in the final test trial for a projected tour of Australia, which never took place, walked off the field as a protest against apartheid in cricket. In 1972 Boon Wallace, who had just become president of SACA, announced that he had a mandate from the nine white provincial unions that the national side should be selected upon merit alone. By 1975 a mixed club had been formed when it was not clear whether this violated South African law. Mixed friendly matches were being played and plans were made for a mixed league in the Transvaal.[137] In 1976 representatives of SACBOC, SACA and SAACB agreed to establish a single governing body for all South African cricket and that in future all cricket in South Africa would be played on integrated basis regardless of race or colour. The resulting South African Cricket Union was formally began its existence in September 1977, with Rashid Varachia, of Asian descent, as its chairman but a group within SACBOC, led by Hassan Howa, did not accept this new body and shortly afterwards formed a rival body, the South African Cricket Board. Basil D'Oliveira who was a member of a Sports Council fact-finding mission to South Africa in 1980 thought that 'tremendous strides' had been made in South African cricket but the view of Howa was that there could be 'no normal sport in an abnormal society', which implied that truly integrated sport could come about only with the dismantling of apartheid in all aspects of South African life.[138]

No one can be sure whether these steps towards multi-racial cricket would have occurred had cricket and other sports not boycotted South Africa, but the fact that such progress occurred only after imposition of the boycott suggests that the sporting isolation of South Africa had been a major factor in breaking down the more rigid forms of apartheid in cricket. It is also difficult to avoid thinking that these moves towards to multi-racial cricket were inspired in part by expediency, by the realization among some white cricketers and administrators that unless they expressed opposition to apartheid in cricket, the opportunities for white South Africans to play international cricket would be slight. The steps taken by white South African cricketers challenged apartheid law but this did not mean that discrimination in other areas of life ceased. The admission by Dr Piet Koornhof, the South African Minister of Sport from 1972 until 1978, that it had been a mistake not to admit D'Oliveira in 1968 and that he was glad to see 'cricket paving the way in getting us back', prompts the suspicion that some whites in South Africa supported

137. Swanton, *Barclays World of Cricket*, pp. 119–20; *Wisden Cricketers' Almanack 1983*, London: John Wisden, p. 104.

138. Merrett, C. and Nauright, J. (1998) 'South Africa', in Stoddart, B. and Sandiford, K.A.P. (eds) (1998), *The Imperial Game: Cricket, Culture and Society*, Manchester: Manchester University Press, p. 73; (1980) *Sport in South Africa: Report of the Sports Council's Fact-finding Delegation*, London: Sports Council, p. 75.

moves towards multi-racial cricket as a means of achieving a return to test cricket whilst retaining apartheid in other areas of life.[139] It can also be argued that the changes which had occurred in cricket had been restricted to a part of life which was not of such very great importance. Control of the state and the economy remained a monopoly of white South Africans. To some it seemed that the progress to multi-racial cricket was little more than window dressing, the granting of concessions in one part of life to scale down the level of international criticism of apartheid and so help it to survive in those aspects of life where the impact of racialized power had deeper repercussions. But cricket in South Africa during the 1970s shows that isolation was more effective than bridge building in promoting change within South African cricket. The advocates of bridge building had claimed that they wanted to retain cricketing links with South Africa in order to bring about multi-racial cricket in South Africa. Ironically the opposition to the retention of cricketing contacts with South Africa, stimulated by the D'Oliveira affair and the proposed tour of 1970, led to a boycott of South Africa, which helped to promote the growth of multi-racial cricket on more or less the lines desired by the bridge builders.

139. *The Times,* 21 July 1984.

−4−

Playing with Apartheid: The Rebel Tours to South Africa

England did not play test match cricket against South Africa from 1965 until 1994 but this did not mean that there were no links between English and South African cricket. Leading white South African cricketers such as Eddie Barlow, Barry Richards and Mike Procter, whose test careers were cut short by the expulsion of South Africa from international cricket, played county cricket with great success. White South Africans of English descent, such as Tony Greig, Allan Lamb and Chris and Robin Smith, played for England. Greig captained England from 1975 to 1977. English county cricketers played and coached in South Africa during the English winter. Derrick Robins, chairman of Coventry City Football Club and a prominent supporter of Warwickshire CCC, organized tours of English county players to South Africa in 1973, 1974 and 1975. The first included only white players and was described as the equivalent to an England third eleven. It was managed by Jack Bannister, secretary of the Cricketers' Association.[1] The South African government allowed the African-Caribbean John Shepherd, a Kent player, to play for the second and third Robins' tours. Younis Ahmed, a Pakistani, played for the second tour and Mushtaq Mohammed, also a Pakistani, for the third. The second Robins' tour was the first occasion when the South African government had allowed coloured cricketers to join a predominantly white cricket tour of South Africa. The Robins' team was permitted to play against an African XI in Soweto. In 1975 a privately organized party of English public schoolboys, including the future England captains David Gower and Christopher Cowdrey, toured South Africa and also played a match in Soweto. In 1976 the International Wanderers team, managed by the former Australian captain and cricket journalist Richie Benaud, which included John Shepherd and the England players Derek Underwood, Phil Edmonds and Mike Denness, toured South Africa.

By the late 1970s and 1980s calls for the ending of such links with South African cricket from opponents of apartheid inside and outside South Africa provoked recurring turmoil and acrimony in English cricket. The governments of Guyana, India, Bangladesh and Zimbabwe cancelled test matches against England or tours to their

---

1. *Cricketer,* April 1973, p. 17.

countries by England because of English players having links with South Africa. The rebel tours of 1982 and 1990, that is tours of English players to play against representative South African teams in defiance of the TCCB's policy, brought cricket to the forefront of national political debate in England and led the TCCB to ban the rebels from test cricket and so undermined the strength of the England test team.

Support for a Cricketing Boycott of South Africa

In the late 1960s and at the start of the 1970s opponents of apartheid had argued that there could be no international cricket with South Africa until South African cricket became multi-racial. By the late 1970s and the 1980s organizations in South Africa such as SANROC, the South African Council on Sport (SACOS) and many of their supporters in the rest of Africa, the Caribbean and Asia were calling for the severing of all sporting links with South Africa and for no resumption of these until all forms of apartheid had been dismantled. 'No normal sport in an abnormal society' became increasingly the rallying cry as it was argued that multi-racial sport could be achieved only through full political racial equality. Opponents of a total boycott did not expect that this in itself would bring about the collapse of apartheid but they realized that it was a major irritant to white South Africans, which had led the Nationalist government to modify some features of apartheid. In 1975 Norman Middleton, the first president of SACOS, claimed that opponents of apartheid had to use whatever 'platforms' were available to 'confront and embarrass the whole system'.[2] The passion for sport of so many white South Africans led the white South African MP Helen Suzman to observe that the international sporting boycott of South Africa was 'the only thing that really hurts South Africans where they feel it.'[3] Whereas an international sporting boycott could emphasize to white South Africans the detestation of apartheid felt outside South Africa, disregarding a boycott would signal to the supporters of apartheid that much of the white world did not find apartheid so objectionable as to justify breaking sporting links with South Africa. Many in English cricket in the late 1970s and 1980s still believed that bridge building, retaining sporting contacts with South Africa, was the most effective method of persuading white South Africans to abandon apartheid.

Coloured cricketers born or raised in England supported the cricketing boycott of South Africa, though none took a very prominent public role in it. The Lancashire player John Abrahams, a Cape Coloured born in South Africa who had arrived in

2. Archer, R. and Bouillon, A. (1982), *The South African Game: Sport and Racism,* London: Zed, p. 307.

3. Jarvie, G. (1985), *Class, Race and Sport in South Africa's Political Economy,* London: Routledge & Kegan Paul, p. 6.

Britain as a boy when his father came to play league cricket as a professional in the 1960s, refused an invitation to play for one of the Robins' tours because he realized that acceptance could have been interpreted as evidence of support for apartheid but his refusal did not become widely known.[4] Gladstone Small, the black Warwickshire and England fast bowler born in Barbados, told *Cricket Life International,* the short-lived cricket magazine edited by the Pakistan test player Imran Khan, that he had declined an invitation to tour South Africa and that he would never go there whilst apartheid remained intact. He said that he could not contemplate visiting a country where 'someone like me would only be able to enjoy the privileges of amenities in the capacity of an "honorary white" and then have to look across the road into the eyes of a fellow black man who fell on the wrong side of the fence.'[5] When the two rebel tours of white English cricketers to South Africa were announced, comments in the press by coloured cricketers qualified to play for England were rare. In 1980 Simon Hughes, the white Middlesex player, thought that black cricketers in county cricket were not 'remotely tempted' to ostracize white South Africans in county teams and wrote of the warmth shown by West Indians to white South Africans. In 1982 Hughes thought that the five African-Caribbean Middlesex players appeared to have 'no hard feelings . . . not on the surface, anyway' towards John Emburey for joining the Boycott rebel tour and even though they may have felt 'a bit betrayed', considered the three year ban from test cricket for the rebels as harsh.[6] The attitude of the African-Caribbean England player Chris Lewis to the rebel tourists was perhaps typical of many coloured county cricketers raised in England. In an interview in 1997 Lewis said that he would not have gone to South Africa in the 1980s 'for any amount of money . . . But you cannot expect everyone to feel the same way as you do. Other people have their problems, maybe financial . . . I wouldn't have encouraged anyone else to have gone, but people make their own decisions and live by that.'[7]

Prominent black West Indian cricketers who played county cricket in England were outspoken in their opposition to playing or coaching in South Africa. Clive Lloyd, the West Indian captain, told the United Nations that he adhered to 'the principle of non-discrimination in sport'. For him, racism was 'contrary to humanity . . . It is my personal conviction that to the extent to which I play before separate audiences and separate spectators, to that extent I make a direct contribution to the

---

4. Interview with J. Abrahams, 16 February 2000.

5. *Cricket Life International,* October 1989, p. 13.

6. Hughes, S. (1997), *A Lot of Hard Yakka: Triumph and Torment: A County Cricket's Life,* London: Headline, pp. 40, 80.

7. Chris Lewis interview with Huw Edwards, 20 July 1997, in H.M. Edwards, '"Friends for Life": English Cricket's Relationship with Apartheid South Africa during Her Period of Sporting Isolation', Southampton University B.A. dissertation, p. 42.

strengthening of apartheid. My own personal conviction compels me instead to fight for the elimination of that system.'[8] Viv Richards, Lloyd's successor as captain of the West Indies, said 'Our people have been bought and sold throughout history . . . I will never play cricket in South Africa. One must have principles.' In his view those who played in South Africa during the apartheid years 'were used. They were used to make the South African system look better. It was blood money.'[9] The West Indian fast bowler Michael Holding who played county cricket for Lancashire and Derbyshire was so opposed to apartheid that he refused £166,000 to play in South Africa.[10] Joel Garner, another West Indian test match fast bowler, wrote in 1988 that like professionals in every field, he was prepared to sell his skills for the highest price, but not in South Africa. He would not 'accept that status of "temporary white" while the majority Black population lived under what I consider to be unjust circumstances.'[11] In 1981 Imran Khan refused terms to play in South Africa which 'would have been offered to only Paul Newman' because this would have meant 'endorsing apartheid – a system I have always abhorred.' He did not believe that the rebel tours to South Africa would 'do anything significant for the integration of black people in white-dominated South Africa.'[12]

Some black and Asian cricketers who played county cricket in England went to South Africa. It has already been mentioned that John Shepherd, Younis Ahmed and Mushtaq Mohammed played on the Robins' tours. Eight of the 20 who played on the West Indian rebel tours of South Africa in 1982–3 and 1983–4 had played county cricket and another was later to play county cricket. Only white players went on the England rebel tours to South Africa. Roland Butcher and Phil DeFreitas were among those who were to join the Gatting tour, but withdrew before the tour took place. The London-based African-Caribbean newspaper the *Voice* claimed that had it not been for concerted pressure from black people, 'they would have sold their souls for the rand'. Its correspondent thought that their reasons for withdrawing from the tour, mainly fears about threats to their families, showed 'little understanding or no concern for the millions of black people suffering under the apartheid state' which had 'sentenced millions of black people to a life of degradation and poverty.'[13] In the opinion of Michael Holding, black West Indian cricketers who joined the rebel West Indian tours and were granted 'honorary' white status in South Africa, 'in effect . . . were denouncing their race and colour to become, even if only in

8. McDonald, T. (1985), *Clive Lloyd: The Authorised Biography*, London: Granada, p. 140.
9. McDonald, T. (1984), *Viv Richards: The Authorised Biography*, London: Pelham, pp. 124, 126.
10. *Voice*, 23 July 1983.
11. Garner, J. (1988), *'Big Bird' Flying High*, London: Barker, p. 53.
12. *Cricketer Life International*, September 1989, pp. 8–9.
13. *Voice*, 15 August 1989.

name, something they were not. If it was an "honour" to be white, then they must have felt it was a dishonour to be black.'[14]

English Players and Cricket in South Africa

From the 1970s to the 1990s no white county cricketer appears to have expressed public support for apartheid. Some white England cricketers not only expressed opposition to apartheid but declined invitations to play in South Africa. Ian Botham, the biggest star of English cricket in the 1980s, refused to join the rebel tours arranged to South Africa, saying that had he joined he would no longer have been able to look his friend Viv Richards in the eye.[15] David Gower, another England super star, refused to join the rebel tours to South Africa but was placed on the United Nations blacklist for touring South Africa with the England Schools Crocodile team in 1974–5.

Whilst hardly any white county cricketers expressed support for apartheid, very few campaigned in public for the sporting boycott of South Africa to be made more rigorous. The former England captain, Mike Brearley, wrote at length in 1982 of his opposition to those who joined the 1982 rebel tour. Whilst acknowledging the efforts of SACU to foster multi-racial cricket, he felt that 'we should lean over to lend our psychological support to the black majority rather than to the whites.' Recognizing the symbolic importance of cricket, he supported the sporting isolation of South Africa on the grounds that 'If sport is the only usable weapon, however feeble, with which to dent apartheid and irritate its proponents, let us not leave it hanging on the wall.'[16] In 1985, Brearley and the Somerset cricketer Peter Roebuck, along with the sports journalists John Arlott and Peter Woods, formed the Campaign for Fair Play, which wanted no sporting contact with South Africa until apartheid was dismantled. A statement of the Campaign argued that sporting contacts helped to 'cement an evil system' and argued that any relaxation of apartheid in sport was irrelevant. What was required was 'not a nicer form of Apartheid . . . but its abolition.'[17] The fact that relatively little was heard of this campaign suggests that it did not receive strong support from English cricket. In 1989 when England agreed to accept an ICC ruling that all who took part in future in any form of cricket in South Africa would be banned from test cricket, many from English cricket complained but Roebuck wrote that it 'is political freedom, not sporting freedom, that is in debate. County cricketers must bite the bullet and accept their responsibility in the war against racism.'

14. Holding, M. and Cozier, T. (1993), *Whispering Death: The Life and Times of Michael Holding,* London: Deutsch, p. 118.

15. *Sunday Times,* 9 October 1994.

16. *Sunday Times,* 7 March 1982.

17. *Cricketer International,* June 1985, p. 17.

Mike Edwards, a former chairman of the Cricketers' Association who had played for Surrey from 1961 to 1974, felt that the ICC ruling ought to have been stronger and argued that 'Cricket springs from the community and any community's affairs ought to be part of the political process.'[18]

Many white English cricketers played and coached in South Africa during the 1970s and 1980s. Of the seventeen England players who toured the West Indies in 1980–1, Jackman, Bairstow, Boycott, Gower, Gooch and Downton had played in South Africa, though Downton and Gower had done so with the schoolboys' Crocodile tour.[19] In April 1981 David Turner (Hampshire), Bob Woolmer (Kent), Keith Pont (Essex), Geoff Boycott (Yorkshire), Geoff Cook (Northamptonshire) and Tony Pigott (Sussex) were included in a list compiled by SANROC of 125 British sportsplayers and officials who had taken part in sport in South Africa or had tried to arrange sporting events with South Africa since September 1980.[20] At the end of 1982, the SANROC list included 40 English cricketers.[21] By 1986 between 70 and 75 English cricketers, around a quarter of county cricketers, spent the winter playing or coaching in South Africa. The Cricketers' Association, the trade union for county cricketers, opposed representative tours to South Africa but contended that cricketers should be allowed to play or coach in South Africa in an individual capacity. In the 1970s the Association had voted to accept more than £2,000 from the Transvaal Cricket Union's profits from playing against the first Robins' touring team.[22] In 1986 the Association supported four players selected for the England A team who had played in South Africa and who refused to give an undertaking to the Bangladeshi government that they would not play in South Africa again, a refusal that caused the Bangladeshi government to cancel the England A team tour to Bangladesh.

When West Indian delegates to the ICC pressed in 1987 for all who played, coached or administered cricket in South Africa to be banned from test cricket, Geoff Cook, chairman of the Cricketers' Association, whose playing in South Africa had almost caused the England tour of India to be cancelled in 1981, claimed that county cricketers might strike if such a resolution were passed and implemented. County cricketers, he argued, had always accepted the Gleneagles Agreement, but took the view that individuals had the right to choose where they played and said that the 'West Indies are turning the screws on us and attitudes among cricketers are hardening.' Simon Hughes, the Middlesex representative on the Cricketers' Association, said that players felt that they were being pushed into a corner and

18. *Cricketer International,* March 1989, p. 5.
19. *The Times,* 27 February 1981.
20. *The Times,* 23 April 1981.
21. *The Times,* 3 November 1982.
22. Edwards, '"Friends for Life"', p. 10.

'seem to be unanimous in their opposition to the West Indies proposal.'[23] By 1990 only twelve English cricketers were coaching or playing in South Africa on an individual basis,[24] perhaps as a result of the 1989 ICC ruling that all who played or coached in South Africa would be banned from test cricket, but possibly also because of the more disturbed political situation in South Africa. In 1989 a poll published in *The Cricketer* showed that 94 per cent of past and present cricketers, though it was not stated how many were polled, thought that cricketers from the UK should have been allowed to play or coach in South Africa.[25]

Women's cricket in England was also affected by some of its leading players having links with South Africa. In 1983 the English Women's Cricket Association tour to the West Indies was cancelled by the Caribbean Women's Cricket Federation because three of the England party had played on a private cricket tour of South Africa. When asked whether the West Indies should have been excluded from the forthcoming men's World Cup because of this, Rachel Flint, probably the best known English woman cricketer, said that this would be a tragedy but that 'perhaps the time has come for a stand to be taken against the removal of our freedom and rights'. She felt that it would be hypocritical for the West Indies men to play against players such as Lamb, Gower, and Wessels who had played in South Africa.[26] In 1987 the WCA banned twelve women from playing for England because they had played in South Africa.[27]

In 1982, fifteen white male English cricketers took part in the first rebel tour. Its programme included matches against representative South African teams for which the South African players were awarded test caps. Five of the fifteen – Boycott, Gooch, Emburey, Lever and Underwood – had just been on the England tour of India and Sri Lanka and only three had never played for England. Because he had played for Northern Transvaal in 1971–2, Boycott, who had a key role in organizing the 1982 rebel tour, had been granted an entry visa by the Indian government only after assuring Mrs Gandhi of his opposition to apartheid. A second rebel tour of English cricketers, captained by Mike Gatting, was held in 1990 and was intended to be followed by another tour in 1991 but this did not take place because of the demonstrations in South Africa surrounding the 1990 tour. In 1982 the Cricketers' Association by 190 votes to 35 resolved to support the TCCB decision to ban the rebels from playing for England for three years, but its resolution also stressed the right of individual cricketers to 'follow their profession wherever they chose'.[28] It is

23. *The Times*, 12 June 1987.
24. *The Times*, 19 January 1990.
25. *Cricketer International*, November 1989, p. 21.
26. *The Times*, 19, 24 February 1983.
27. *The Times*, 11 April 1987.
28. *The Times*, 14 April 1982.

also probable that the Association was aware that had no ban been imposed, India and Pakistan may have cancelled their tours of England arranged for 1982 and that the subsequent loss of test match revenue, a vital source of income for several counties, could have led some counties to employ fewer players. In 1986, Jack Bannister, secretary of the Association, pointed out that whilst the Association had supported the bans in 1982, it had also sought an assurance that they would not be extended 'whatever shifts there might be in world opinion' and that not selecting for tours those who had played or coached in South Africa would be 'an illegal restraint of trade.'[29] In 1997 one cricket journalist who had played cricket for England in the 1980s, believed that 'at a conservative estimate 75 per cent of English county cricketers would have leapt at the chance' to join the rebel tours and that some 'actively offered their services.'[30] No report has been found of white cricketers in the 1980s calling for those who had played or coached in South Africa to be banned from county cricket.

White English cricketers who played or coached in South Africa often argued that they were pursuing their careers and like those in other professions had the right to earn their livelihood where they wished. As Graham Gooch, arguably the best England batsman of the 1980s, had captained the rebel England tour of 1982 and played for Western Province in South Africa in 1982–3, his views on playing in South Africa attracted more publicity than those of most others. Just after the 1982 rebel tour he was reported to have asked 'What have I done wrong? I am a professional cricketer with a living to earn.'[31] Gooch called the three year ban 'a hell of a long sentence, especially when you are convinced of the innocence of your "crime." No law broken, no contract abused, no chance to state your case in "open" court.' For him playing in South Africa was not condoning apartheid.[32] In 1984 when still banned from playing for England, Gooch said 'I don't agree with apartheid . . . I hate it. I've spoken out against it when I've been in South Africa.' He added that though the rebels had not expected to be banned, he did not regret going to South Africa and had not missed test cricket as much as he had expected.[33]

Geoffrey Boycott also took the line that 'we were professionals earning our living with the talent we possessed.' He felt that most of the Gatting tour rebels 'were worried about their financial security and felt that they could not rely on the game to provide them with a good living.'[34] In 1986 the England bowler Greg Thomas

29. *Cricketer International,* March 1986, p. 10.
30. Edwards, '"Friends for Life"', p. 12.
31. *The Times,* 20 March 1982.
32. Gooch, G. and Keating, F. (1995), *Gooch: My Autobiography,* London: Collins Willow, p. 106.
33. *The Times,* 7 June 1984.
34. Boycott, G. (1991), *Boycott on Cricket,* London: Corgi, pp. 141, 144.

who was about to play in South Africa, asked 'what sort of a choice do I have? I've got bills to pay, and what else could I do this winter?' The Sussex player Alan Green who was also going to South Africa said 'I am just doing a job like anybody else. We know lots of English miners and engineers out there, and nothing is said about them going to South Africa, only us.'[35] Boycott also argued that 'the whole of South Africa and cricket is persistently distorted by hypocrisy' and that being able to visit South Africa was 'a democratic right that no-one should be able to take away.' He noted that British athletes who complained about the rebel tour of 1982 had not hesitated to take part in the 1980 Moscow Olympics, even though the USSR had invaded Afghanistan.[36]

Estimates of payments made to the 1982 rebels varied between £30,000 and £50,000 per player.[37] In 1995 Gooch admitted that he had been paid £60,000 and wrote that 'the deal and the money were very good . . . for a month's work it was six times as much as I'd get in five years or more as a county pro.'[38] The 1990 rebels were thought to have received between £80,000 and £120,000 each.[39] Even if such figures are exaggerations, they still represented considerable sums, especially to those nearing the end of their first-class cricket careers.

Details of the amounts paid for playing for provincial or club sides or for coaching are hard to find but Simon Hughes, who had played for Northern Transvaal, thought in 1987 that young county cricketers, who were not paid by their counties during the winter, could be paid at least £3,000 for coaching in schools and playing club cricket in addition to receiving free air fares, accommodation, and a car plus living expenses.[40] Moreover, the playing skills of younger players, and consequently their earning potential in England, could be sharpened by playing in South Africa. In 1982 Mike Brearley, who supported the sporting boycott of South Africa, advised Simon Hughes to play in South Africa rather than New Zealand, because 'the Currie Cup will be harder cricket.'[41] The insecurities of professional sport no doubt increased the attractions of the money offered for playing in South Africa. Whilst it is easy to see those who played in South Africa as mercenaries who turned a blind eye to the iniquities of apartheid, TCCB regulations did not prohibit individual cricketers from paying or coaching in South Africa in an individual capacity until 1989.

35. *The Times,* 3 October 1986.
36. Boycott, *Boycott,* pp. 134, 136.
37. *Guardian,* 5 March 1982.
38. Gooch and Keating, *Gooch,* pp. 95, 98.
39. *The Times,* 29 December 1990.
40. *The Times,* 12 June 1987.
41. Hughes, *Hard Yakka,* p. 95.

English cricketers who played or coached in South Africa, and those from the English cricket world who sympathized with them, maintained that having cricketing links with South Africa, by promoting multi-racial cricket, was weakening apartheid, although it is possible that expressing such views may have been self-justifying and attempts to deflect criticism of their actions. Graham Gooch thought that apartheid was 'totally unfair, revolting and distasteful', but that through his rebel team, 'every group in South Africa – black, white, coloured, Indian – [is] learning from and enjoying our cricket and our bridge-building in international sporting relations.'[42] In 1984 the cricket journalist Christopher Martin-Jenkins argued that the West Indian rebel tours had 'aided rather than set back' 'the cause of non-whites' because multi-racial sport was opening the minds of less liberal whites in South Africa.[43] Whilst admitting the importance of the money for the Gatting rebels, David Graveney, the manager of the tour, stressed that 'For us', SACU's promotion of township and integrated cricket was 'as important as the money.'[44] In 1990, on first day of the Gatting rebel tour, an editorial in *The Times* argued that the sporting boycott of South Africa had helped to promote multi-racial sport in South Africa, but that for further progress, carrots as well as sticks were needed. It thought that 'the occasional unofficial tour' should have been encouraged and not seen 'as a political *casus belli.*'[45] After his rebel tour, Gatting was particularly upset that fears of being banned had led English professionals to stop coaching in the townships and so were no longer promoting non-racial sport.[46]

White English cricketers who played in South Africa often argued that sport and politics should be kept separate. When the 1990 rebel tour was announced Mike Gatting said 'I know very little about apartheid. I do believe there shouldn't be any politics in sport.'[47] The white England player Robin Smith, born and raised in South Africa, who had not played on the rebel tours but had played provincial cricket in South Africa for Natal, said in 1997 that he did not endorse apartheid but 'I don't think that sport and politics should be as one.'[48] The view that sport and politics should not be mixed was linked to a belief that hypocritical politicians made political capital out of South Africa. Graham Gooch said that 'Cricket is a lovely medium for the politicians. They make all their public outcries against cricket, and let all trade with South Africa go on under the table.'[49] After the rebel tour of 1990 Mike Gatting

42. Gooch and Keating, *Gooch*, p. 106.
43. *Cricketer International*, March 1984, p. 3.
44. *Sunday Times*, 6 August 1989.
45. *The Times*, 19 January 1990.
46. *The Times*, 14 March 1990.
47. Marqusee, M. (1994), *Anyone but England: Cricket and the National Malaise*, London: Verso, p. 205.
48. Robin Smith interview with Huw Edwards, 17 July 1997, Edwards, "' Friends for Life'", p. 41.
49. *The Times*, 7 June 1984.

was reported to have said of South Africa that 'The blacks should have the vote, but black majority rule would be difficult. A lot of them are not well educated, and there should be some from of compromise. I am glad I have seen the country for myself. Neil Kinnock criticises us for going, but he has not been there, so he would not know what it is like.'[50] The opposition to apartheid from overseas governments, especially those in the Third World, was condemned as hypocritical and a form of blackmail against English cricket. Boycott wrote 'The Indians, who are all too ready to adopt threatening poses, should look at the apartheid in their own back yard, where discrimination on grounds of race is common. Life for many Indians is much worse than it is for most blacks in South Africa' and described India's demand that only those who declared in public that they would never play in South Africa as 'a monstrous demand from a government trying to take the lead among the Third World countries.'[51]

Many from the world of cricket other than current players also argued that cricket and politics should have been kept separate and that the boycott of South Africa was shrouded in political hypocrisy. In 1982 the sports journalist Tony Pawson wrote in the *Cricketer* that recognizing the progress towards multi-racial cricket in South Africa 'would deprive politicians of the ability to use sport as a *political* weapon' and of 'the obsessive concentration on South Africa, while ignoring the much greater abuses by a score of states from Russia to Uganda to Guyana.'[52] When the Bangladeshi and Zimbabwean governments refused to accept the England B touring party in 1986, Christopher Martin-Jenkins, editor of *The Cricketer,* claimed that only 'hard-line anti-apartheid agitators who enjoy seeing international cricket administrators once again squirming in the deep and murky waters of politics' would gain by these 'killjoy eleventh hour decisions'.[53] In the 1980s, E.M. Wellings, who had played for Oxford University from 1929 until 1931 and been cricket correspondent for the *London Evening News,* had a regular column in *Wisden Cricket Monthly.* In 1985 he wrote that he disliked apartheid but that handing political power to blacks would 'spread the famine areas of Africa southward, for South Africa is the granary of those parts, and corrupt one-party Black governments cannot manage such affairs efficiently.' In 1988 he wrote that more England cricketers developed links with South Africa and 'so get themselves entered on that childish list [the UN blacklist], the stronger will be the English hand in opposing the SANROCs and Rajiv Gandhis of the modern world . . . Modern Democracy and its methods of interference are blinding everyone to the fact that playing cricket is all-important.'[54]

50. *The Times,* 14 March 1990.
51. Boycott, *Boycott,* p. 148.
52. *Cricketer International,* June 1882, p. 12.
53. *Cricketer International,* February 1986, p. 2.
54. *Wisden Cricket Monthly,* March 1985, p. 7, December 1988, p. 19.

The Thatcher government proclaimed its commitment to the Gleneagles Agreement of 1977 which called on Commonwealth governments to discourage sporting links with South Africa, but argued that, as Britain was a democracy, individuals and organizations were free to trade with South Africa if they wished and that the government could do no more than persuade British sportsplayers not to have sporting ties with South Africa. The corollary of Thatcher's refusal to join an economic boycott of South Africa was that British cricketers should have been able to earn their livelihood in South Africa. In 1982 a front page headline in *The Times* described Thatcher's condemnation of the rebel tour as 'lukewarm.' In the Commons she reaffirmed her government's support for the Gleneagles Agreement but emphasized that 'the decision is up to each of the persons concerned because they are in a free country.'[55] In many ways, cricketers who went to earn their livelihood in South Africa were acting in harmony with the *Zeitgeist* of Thatcherism, the conviction that not maximizing the earnings potential of a talent was moral weakness whereas willingness to go anywhere in pursuit of wealth was a virtue.

Most Labour and Liberal MPs and trade union leaders were highly critical of those who played in South Africa, but a minority of Conservative MPs were outspoken in encouraging sporting links with South Africa and their views may well have led English cricketers to play and coach in South Africa. John Carlisle, the MP for Luton West and chairman of the Conservative Sports Committee, was the most prominent of this group. In 1981 when Mrs Gandhi was prevaricating over whether the England team could be admitted to India, Carlisle wrote that the Gleneagles Agreement was 'a worthless treaty' and called on the ICC to readmit South Africa to test cricket.[56] Carlisle was among forty Conservative MPs who expressed support for the 1982 rebel tour. In 1981 he had been one of those who set up the Freedom in Sport campaign. In 1982 Lord Chalfont, the former Labour minister, agreed to become president of Freedom in Sport because international sport was being 'hijacked by political extremists' who were 'entitled to state their views but are not entitled to blackmail people by threatening their livelihoods for exercising their rights as individuals.'[57] In 1982, Carlisle described the TCCB's banning from test cricket those who played on the rebel tour of South Africa as 'a sorry day for international cricket' and argued that in order to extricate cricket from 'the blackmail and hypocrisy of government interference', South Africa should be readmitted to test cricket.[58] Fifty Conservative MPs were reported to have deplored the decision of the ICC in 1989 to ban from test cricket all who subsequently played, coached or

55. *The Times*, 3 March 1982.
56. *The Times*, 21 October 1981.
57. *The Times*, 12 March 1982.
58. *The Times*, 28 August 1982.

administered cricket in South Africa.[59] In 1990, when chairman of the British-South African Parliamentary Group, Carlisle called the premature ending of the Gatting tour 'a tragedy for cricket and for sport that political influence has cut short what was a very useful tour.'[60]

South African whites such as Ali Bacher, the managing director of SACU and who had been the captain of South Africa when South Africa last played test cricket, hoped that the formation of the multi-racial SACU in 1977, which was contrary to the racial segregation of apartheid, would bring about South Africa's readmission to test cricket. Bacher stressed, however, that he had never voted for the Nationalist Party and recognized that it was impossible to have normal sport in an abnormal society. In 1986 he professed that 'big political changes' had occurred in South Africa and that cricket had played 'a big part' in bringing them about. In his view a non-racial society was bound to come in South Africa and that the playing of cricket together by different racial groups would help to achieve this sooner and more peacefully. Jack Bannister called Bacher 'a straightforward, honest man' who had done 'so much to improve the lot of black, white and Coloured cricketers in South Africa.'[61] In 1990, Bacher, speaking about the Gatting tour, mentioned that during the past three years SACU had introduced 60,000 township children to cricket and that 2,000 had been given coaching. Bacher accepted that apartheid was still on the South African statute book, and that SACU did not wish to portray South African society as normal, but he felt that SACU was building for 'the future, for a post-apartheid society'. In his view, the Gatting tour was not an attempt to whitewash Pretoria, but part of SACU's campaign to promote change.[62] Even some of those who had long advocated a sporting boycott of South Africa accepted that SACU had done much to promote multi-racial cricket. An editorial in the *Guardian,* which had long campaigned against apartheid, argued that the Gatting rebel tour was 'a very considerable coup for . . . a South African political establishment – which, while trumpeting modifications has continued to sustain the grotesque essentials of apartheid', but added that Bacher and others had 'an irreproachable record in trying to beat down racial divisions in South African sport.'[63] Some white South African cricketers argued that the rebel tours helped to promote multi-racial sport. In 1994 Mike Procter, the white South African all-rounder, arguably one of the greatest of all-rounders of all time but whose test career had been cut short by the sporting

59. *Cricketer International,* March 1989, p. 5.
60. *The Times,* 14 February 1990.
61. *The Times,* 10 October 1986.
62. *The Times,* 20 January 1990.
63. *Guardian,* 2 August 1989.

boycott, said of the rebels 'I never saw them as rebels: to me they were brave men, supportive of multi-racial cricket in South Africa and they were right to make a stand against the hypocrisy that hangs around the whole question of sporting links with each other. Those tours were the best thing that could have happened to all South African cricket at that time.'[64]

By no means all critics of apartheid were impressed by SACU's claims that it was challenging apartheid by promoting multi-racial cricket. Some in South Africa suspected that SACU's promotion of multi-racial cricket was not meant to be part of a campaign to overthrow all forms of apartheid, but an attempt to abolish it only in cricket in order for South Africa to return to test cricket. Other South Africans saw the establishment of SACU as little more than tokenism and set up the South African Cricket Board, a rival cricket authority that refused to have any dealings with SACU and argued that the cricketing boycott of South Africa had to continue until apartheid was dismantled. SACB banned its members from grounds where cricket was played under the auspices of SACU and refused financial assistance from SACU even though this would probably have raised the standard of SACB cricket.[65] SANROC argued that there could be no normal sport in an abnormal society. Christopher Merrett, a white South African, wrote in 1982 about the 'hypocritical compartmentalisation of life and morality' of those who played under the auspices of SACU and insisted that normal cricket was possible when 'outside the cricket ground we have, obediently, to fit into our allotted place in apartheid society.'[66] Mluleki George, the national co-ordinator of the National Sports Congress, argued that SACU's promotion of cricket in the townships was 'fighting to preserve white privileges enshrined under different guises . . . in fact they are buying our black kids with millions of blood money . . . These people have gone to the townships not because they are sincere in helping our kids. They have gone there simply because they want to buy our kids for propaganda mileage overseas.'[67] In 1989 the London-based *Asian Times* saw SACU's attempts to persuade black cricketers from overseas to play in South Africa as an attempt to 'sanitize' apartheid, to 'prop-up the self-confidence of the government as well as that white-controlled South African Cricket Union.'[68] David Sheppard, after visiting South Africa, had no doubt about Ali Bacher's 'genuine enthusiasm' to promote cricket among black youngsters, but thought that it was 'a pretence to suppose that equal opportunities now exist in cricket.' In his view the Gatting tourists were wrong to

64. Gooch and Keating, *Gooch*, p. 110.

65. Swanton, E.W., Plumptre, G. and J. Woodcock, (eds) (1986), *Barclays World of Cricket: The Game from A to Z*, London: Guild, p. 117.

66. *Cricketer International*, April 1982, p. 58.

67. *Voice*, 7 February 1989.

68. *Asian Times*, 11 August 1989.

imagine that cricket could be kept in 'a separate box from major human injustice. It is impossible to play normal cricket in an abnormal society.'[69]

The TCCB and South Africa

By not playing test cricket with South Africa from 1966 until 1994 and by accepting the ICC ruling in 1989 that all who subsequently played, coached or administered cricket in South Africa would be banned from test cricket for three years if aged under nineteen, for four years if over nineteen and for five years for playing on representative tours, the English cricket establishment supported the cricketing boycott of South Africa. In March 1982 the twenty-one members of the full board of the TCCB voted unanimously to ban from test cricket for three years the fifteen players who had played on the 1982 rebel tour, a decision which weakened the England team, though the TCCB had originally proposed a two-year ban but West Indian pressure had caused this to be raised to three.[70] In 1984, the TCCB banned Monty Lynch, who was born in Guyana but had become qualified to play for England, from being selected by England for four years because he had played for a West Indian rebel tour to South Africa.[71]

By calling off the South African tour in 1970 and by its announcement that there could be no further test cricket with South Africa until South African cricket was played and administered on a multi-racial basis, the Cricket Council had a key role in strengthening the international sporting boycott of South Africa. The Cricket Council and the TCCB, however, often gave the impression of being eager to resume test cricket with South Africa and of having needed to be pushed and prodded into stiffening the exclusion of South Africa from test cricket. Indeed in the 1970s and 1980s the Cricket Council and the TCCB strove behind the scenes to help South Africa regain test status. The moves to establish multi-racial cricket in South Africa have been outlined in Chapter Three. The declared policy of the Cricket Council was to maintain test cricket without polarization, which meant observing the boycott of South Africa in order to ensure that test cricket continued to be multi-racial, but at the same time it wished to 'help SACU and others in South Africa who were striving to achieve integrated cricket there.'[72] The England cricket authorities did not want to risk splitting the ICC and test cricket by taking a unilateral decision to resume representative cricket with South Africa, but seemed to be convinced that

69. *Cricket Life International,* April 1990, p. 40.
70. Marqusee, *Anyone but England,* p. 197.
71. *The Times,* 23 March 1984.
72. Cricket Council Minutes, 19 January 1982.

the progress made towards multi-racial cricket justified South Africa's return to test cricket, or at least to some form of representative cricket. They showed little sympathy for the view of SACB that there could be no normal sport in an abnormal society and that all forms of apartheid had to be scrapped before South Africa could return to test cricket. In the 1970s officials of SACA saw the England representatives as their supporters at the ICC and the Cricket Council advised SACA on the types of changes to South African cricket that would be most likely to expedite a return to test cricket. In 1973 after the England representatives had persuaded the ICC to delay taking a decision on whether there could be a South African tour of England in 1975, Boon Wallace, secretary of SACA, wrote to S.G. Griffith, secretary of the MCC, that 'I know just how much you contributed to this decision and can only say how lucky we are to have you at Lord's.'[73]

In the 1970s the Cricket Council and the TCCB encouraged links with cricket in South Africa. In the winter of 1971–2 Jack Cheetham, president of SACA, invited the Cricket Council to send a touring side to South Africa in February and March 1972 which would have played against white, coloured and African teams and could have included Basil D'Oliveira. The coloured cricketers were reported to have been offended that Cheetham had not consulted them before issuing the invitation. The Cricket Council suggested that the tour be delayed for a year in order to give the differing cricket authorities in South Africa more time to come together and insisted that D'Oliveira be included in the team. The tour did not take place, perhaps because D'Oliveira had visited South Africa and had been dismayed by criticism of his presence there by coloured groups.[74] The minute books of the Cricket Council do not indicate that it tried to discourage the Robins' tours to South Africa, although in 1979 when Robbins was trying to organize a tour to England by South African cricketers who would have played against county teams, Donald Carr, secretary of the Cricket Council, wrote to him that 'we do not want to be a party to any provocative proposals' before the forthcoming ICC meeting which was to discuss South Africa.[75] In the early and mid 1970s the Cricket Council stressed to SACA how a multi-racial administration and governing structure for all cricket in South Africa could ease the return of South Africa to the ICC. In 1972 the secretary of the Cricket Council wrote to try and persuade the SACB to join the recently established Cricket Council in South Africa.[76] On a visit to South Africa in 1974 Lord Caccia,

73. B. Wallace to S.C. Griffith, 23 May 1975, Cricket Council Lord Caccia's Visit to South Africa File 1974.

74. Cricket Council Minutes, 30 December 1971, 6 January 1972.

75. D. Carr to D. Robins, 19 December 1979, Cricket Council South Africa (1) January 1978 – December 1980 File.

76. S.C. Griffith to S. Reddy, 4 September 1972, Cricket Council Lord Caccia's Visit to South Africa File 1974.

Provost of Eton College, a former British ambassador to Washington and president of the MCC, had meetings with officials of differing cricket bodies in South Africa and with Piet Koornhof, the South African Minister for Sport, which seem to have been secret or at least attracted very little attention in Britain. He stressed to Koornhof the need for multi-racial administration in addition to multi-racial teams. Caccia wrote to Koornhof that 'you know the lines of communication between South Africa and us are always open.'[77]

The Cricket Council welcomed the formation of SACU, the multi-racial governing body in 1977. When SACU representatives complained at a meeting with the Cricket Council's Emergency Executive Committee in 1978 about the ICC not rewarding its progress towards multi-racial cricket, it was agreed that F.R. Brown, chairman of the Cricket Council, would write personally to the chairmen of all the ICC full member boards about how impressed the Cricket Council had been with developments in South Africa and to suggest that Rashid Varachia, the president of SACU, be allowed to address the ICC.[78] In 1979, the Cricket Council delegates had a key role in persuading the ICC to send a fact-finding commission to South Africa, headed by Charles Palmer, the chairman of the ICC who had captained Leicestershire as an amateur in the 1950s. As India, Pakistan and the West Indies refused to support the commission, it included representatives from only England, Australia, New Zealand, the USA and Bermuda.[79] The report argued that 'cricket had been at the forefront in attempting to achieve conditions wherein games can be played on a basis of equality between races' in South Africa and recommended that as many ICC countries as possible send a strong team to play representative matches in South Africa in 1979–80.[80] For the next meeting of the ICC the Cricket Council prepared an appendix to the agenda calling for member countries to be allowed to send to South Africa a representative team of first- class calibre to play not against national South African teams but provincial sides and multi-racial teams and only where apartheid laws did not apply to spectators. The appendix argued that without such encouragement 'those who had laboured to promote multi-racial cricket may lose heart, with the result that the situation deteriorates rather than improves.'[81] The proposal was not accepted by the ICC.

77. Lord Caccia to P. Koornhof, 10 April 1974, Cricket Council Lord Caccia's Visit to South Africa File 1974.

78. Cricket Council South Africa (1) January 1978 – December 1980 File.

79. Swanton, *Barclays World of Cricket*, p. 117.

80. Report of the Palmer Commission, pp. 21, 26. The full text of the Report is in Cricket Council South Africa (1) January 1978 – December 1980 File.

81. Cricket Council South Africa (1) January 1978 – December 1980 File.

Some England players and journalists, as well as administrators, argued that the establishment of SACU and the steps towards multi-racial cricket in South Africa justified the resumption of test cricket with South Africa. Bob Willis, the England fast bowler who became the England captain in 1982, was reported to have said that the South African cricket authorities 'appear to have done what they were asked to do in the last 10 years. Nothing seems enough for some people.'[82] Bob Woolmer, another England player, who had visited South Africa six times and was coaching a mixed-race club in Cape Town, said in 1982 in South Africa that 'cricket has done enough here to warrant full international status again.'[83] In *The Times* John Woodcock, who was also editor of *Wisden* from 1981 to 1986, stressed his dislike of apartheid but suggested that delegates to the ICC would have welcomed South Africa back into test cricket had not governments had exerted pressure on them to keep out South Africa.[84] He wrote in 1981 'I would rather we played South Africa again, where more genuine efforts have been made in cricket than in most other games to mix races, than lay ourselves open to a repetition of what has just happened in Guyana' where a test match arranged between England and the West Indies had been cancelled when the Guyanese government deported the England player Robin Jackman because he had played cricket in South Africa.[85] Sir Clyde Walcott, the African-Caribbean former test player and West Indies cricket administrator, suspected in the 1970s and 1980s that 'some of the predominantly white countries' would have resumed test cricket with South Africa 'if the politicians had allowed them.'[86]

The TCCB's refusal until 1989 to ban from test cricket all who played or coached in South Africa caused friction with the West Indies, India and Pakistan. In the 1970s and for much of the 1980s the TCCB policy was that cricketers from England had contractual obligations to their counties only for the summer months and for the rest of the year were free agents who could sell their services where they wished. After the ICC refused to admit South Africa to test cricket in 1981, rumours began circulating that business interests in South Africa might finance a tour of South Africa without the approval of the TCCB. Perhaps in the hope of discouraging such a tour, the Cricket Council wrote in August to all first-class cricketers that they could still play or coach as individuals in South Africa but that joining a representative side of test calibre could jeopardise their chances of being selected for England. Fears of being in restraint of trade and of subsequent legal action may explain why the

82. *The Times,* 12 August 1981.
83. *The Times,* 9 March 1982.
84. *The Times,* 24 July 1981.
85. *The Times,* 7 March 1981.
86. Walcott, C. and Scovell, B. (1999), *Sixty Years on the Back Foot: The Cricketing Life of Sir Clyde Walcott,* London: Gollancz, 1999, p. 152.

TCCB did not to take a stronger line, but *The Times* also mentioned that the TCCB may have been hoping that after a meeting of the Commonwealth heads of government in Melbourne, it might have been possible to have arranged a tour of South Africa. No decisions at the Melbourne conference made it possible for a TCCB side to be sent to South Africa. The comments of some of the 1982 rebel tourists that they had not expected to be banned from test cricket for three years suggest that firmer threats from the TCCB might have made it more difficult to organise the tour. Fears for the financial wellbeing of county cricket seem to have been a key factor in the TCCB decision to ban the 1982 rebels. India and Pakistan made it clear that they would cancel their tours to England in the summer of 1982 unless strong action were taken against the rebels. Had India and Pakistan not toured England in 1982, about two million pounds of assorted test match revenues would not have been available for distribution among the English counties and some counties could have gone to the wall.[87] In 1989 it was more or less an open secret that a second English tour was being planned. Before accepting the captaincy of the rebel side, Mike Gatting asked the England manager Mickey Stewart for assurances about his test future[88] which suggests that the England cricket establishment knew what was being planned, but the TCCB appeared to do very little to discourage the tour.

In 1986 the TCCB advised four England players not to accede to the request of the Bangladeshi government and sign declarations that they would never play or coach in South Africa again, even though this led to the cancellation of the England B tour to Bangladesh and Zimbabwe. The TCCB was reported not to have wanted such declarations to create a precedent. A *Times* editorial suspected that the Bangladeshi government's action was retaliation for the Thatcher government's refusal to implement 'full-blooded economic sanctions against Pretoria'.[89] In 1988 the projected England tour of India was called off when the Indian government objected to eight of the sixteen England players who had played or coached in South Africa. The selection of Gooch as captain and Emburey as vice-captain, who had both played on the 1982 rebel tour of South Africa, was seen by some as deliberate provocation by the England selectors, but as the Indian government had allowed these two players into India a few months earlier to play in the World Cup, others accused the Indian government of hypocrisy. It later became known that Gooch had planned to spend the winter playing in South Africa but had been persuaded out of this when he was asked to captain the England team to India.[90] Although

87. *The Times*. 14 April 1982.
88. Marqusee, *Anyone but England*, p. 204.
89. *The Times*, 3, 4 January 1986.
90. *Wisden Cricketers' Almanack 1989*, London: John Wisden, p. 47; *Asian Times*, 16, 23 September 1988.

the chairman of the England selectors Peter May claimed that 'We don't pick teams for political reasons', A.C. Smith of the TCCB was reported to have rejected a compromise which would have allowed visas to be granted to the eight players had they promised not to play or coach in South Africa again.[91]

Until 1989 the policy of the Cricket Council and TCCB was that no test playing country could object to players selected by another country. In 1970 when the South African government refused to accept an England touring party including D'Oliveira, this policy could have been interpreted as opposition to, or at least non-co-operation with, apartheid but by the 1980s it was seen as condoning apartheid, as a refusal to tighten the cricketing boycott of South Africa. In February 1981 the Cricket Council ordered the England party not to play a test match in Guyana when the Guyanese government deported Robin Jackman because he had played first-class cricket in South Africa. In July 1981 the ICC decided unanimously that team selection was a matter solely for the cricketing governing body of a team, but governments that saw sporting boycotts of South Africa as a means of combating apartheid continued to object to the selection of players with South African connections.[92] In October 1981 it seemed likely that the England tour to India might be cancelled when the Indian government threatened to refuse visas to Geoffrey Boycott and Geoff Cook because of their South African connections. The tour did go ahead after the TCCB reiterated its announcement of August that players might not be eligible for selection by England if they played in international or representative matches in South Africa. Boycott and Cook were reported to have expressed their opposition to apartheid but a few days earlier Cook had refused to stand down from the tour as this would have appeared to be an admission of guilt and he felt no guilt about having played in South Africa.[93] An editorial in *The Times* claimed that it would have been 'an intolerable infringement of individual rights' if the TCCB had done more than warn players about taking part in representative matches in South Africa.[94] In 1986 the TCCB, including representatives from all seventeen first-class counties, voted unanimously not to support a resolution of the West Indian Board to ban from test cricket all who played or coached in South Africa.[95]

In January 1989 the England representatives at the ICC agreed to accept that all players who played, coached or administered cricket in South Africa be banned from test cricket. The report in *Wisden* suggests that the English cricket establishment reached this position with reluctance. Some county chairmen opposed the decision, but the dependence of county cricket on a regular programme of test matches gave

91. *Asian Times,* 23 September 1988.
92. *Wisden Cricketers' Almanack 1982,* London: MacDonald Queen Anne, p. 1248.
93. *The Times,* 4 August, 19, 20, 31 October 1981.
94. *The Times,* 31 October 1981.
95. *The Times,* 17 June 1987.

England little alternative but to accept the West Indian proposal. The editor of *Wisden*, Graeme Wright, felt that an important principle had been conceded. In his opinion 'citizens of the United Kingdom have had a freedom curtailed at the insistence of other countries. It can be argued that a freedom which allows trade with an unjust society is not so valuable a freedom. None the less it is a freedom within British law.'[96]

Prominent figures in the administration of English cricket had contacts with South Africa. Some went to South Africa as guests of SACU. In 1988, Ted Dexter, who a year later became chairman of the England Cricket Committee, and his wife were guests of SACU when he was a member of its television commentary team. The chairman of the ICC in 1989, when it adopted the policy of banning from test cricket all who played, coached or administered cricket in South Africa, was Field Marshal Lord Bramall, the president of the MCC who was a director of the Diamond Trading Company, part of the gem-selling group owned by the South African De Beers mining company.[97] In 1989 twelve former first-class cricketers, ten of whom had played for England, attended the centenary celebrations in South Africa of the first test match between England and South Africa. From the headquarters of the Freedom in Sport International organization, the body associated with the Conservative MP John Carlisle and Lord Chalfont, they wrote to *The Times* of their distaste for apartheid but applauded the efforts of SACU to 'promote the interests of cricket to all races in South Africa' and 'to break down the constitutional barriers between races by sporting contact.'[98] This group included Peter May, who had been the chairman of the England selectors from 1982 to 1988, and M.J.K. Smith, who was president of the National Cricket Association from 1990 to 1996.

South Africa's Readmission to Test Cricket

In the changing political climate of South Africa after Nelson Mandela's release from prison in 1991, SACU and SACB merged to form the United Cricket Board of South Africa, a non-racial governing body for cricket in South Africa. In June 1991 Ali Bacher, managing director of UCBSA, and Steve Tshwete, the ANC sports liaison officer who had been imprisoned on Robben Island for fifteen years, came to Lord's to press for South Africa's re-admission to the ICC and to test cricket. Tshwete wanted the ICC to know that UCBSA was to 'cast aside any discrimination and to promote cricket on multi-racial lines' and had the full support of the ANC and of the South African government.[99] A few days later the Conservative Foreign

96. *Wisden 1989*, pp. 48–9.
97. *Guardian*, 2 August 1989.
98. *The Times*, 6 January 1990.
99. *The Times*, 22 May 1991.

Secretary Douglas Hurd confirmed that the British government was supporting South Africa's readmission to the ICC. The government also donated cricket bats worth 25,000 rands to young cricketers in the black townships.[100] South Africa was readmitted to the ICC at a meeting in June 1991 when Colin Cowdrey, the English chairman of the ICC, ruled that the meeting could accept a proposal from Australia and India calling for this, even though no such resolution was on the agenda. Clyde Walcott, leader of the West Indian delegation, was reported to have said that South Africa's readmission had been rushed through and taken on political grounds. 'It is clear to us' he said, 'that the decision was taken from a political point of view as against any other reason. We had nothing in front of us, no constitution. We knew nothing of the structure of cricket in South Africa. It was not on the original agenda and only included at the last moment by the chairman. Our position was that we were not give an opportunity to discuss the matter with our board.'[101]

The formation of UCBSA and the return of South Africa to test cricket was cheered by many as a new dawn in South African politics and sport. As part of the celebrations of the establishment of UCBSA, Sir Gary Sobers and Sunil Gavaskar visited South African townships where cricket was being played. After visiting South Africa, the former West Indian captain Clive Lloyd advocated that South Africa be allowed to play in the 1992 World Cup. He had no doubt that things had changed, apartheid was no longer on the statute book and South African leaders were trying 'to get things together'.[102] In November 1991 South Africa played three one-day internationals in India and in April 1992 played a test match against the West Indies in Barbados. Initially the ICC decided that South Africa would not play in the World Cup to be held in Australia and New Zealand during February and March 1992, but in October 1991 it was agreed that South Africa could take part.

Some detected racist undertones in South Africa's rapid return to test cricket. They argued that until apartheid was abolished, South Africa should not have been readmitted to test cricket. In July 1991, Norman Cowans, the black England cricketer born in Jamaica, noting that Mandela still could not vote, said that he would not play in South Africa until apartheid was lifted.[103] The former West Indian captain Viv Richards was puzzled why the ANC was still supporting economic sanctions but had dropped the sporting boycott. He wanted more information about the situation in South Africa before he would consider touring there. Michael Holding feared that the white South African government's moves to democracy might have been reversed and felt that the return of South African to test cricket should have been delayed.[104]

100. *The Times,* 26 April, 13 June 1991.
101. *Caribbean Times,* 23 July 1991.
102. *Voice,* 29 October 1991.
103. *Voice,* 16 July 1991.
104. Holding and Cozier, *Whispering Death,* p. 123.

When the ICC decided to allow South Africa to take part in the 1992 World Cup Adam Licudi, a *Caribbean Times* sports journalist questioned whether the ANC had been in a muddle in backing UCBSA and asked whether the re-introduction of sporting links would 'gloss over the vices which are still being perpetrated in that society.'[105] When the ANC and Mandela approved the playing of three limited-overs internationals between India and South Africa in November 1991, Nigel Carter argued in *Caribbean Times* that not even the ANC and Mandela were infallible and that by reversing their doctrine of 'no normal sport in an abnormal society', had dropped 'a huge political clanger. Blacks are still being slaughtered by the hundreds every day in South Africa, the courts have proven the complicity, orchestration in fact, of the massacres by President De Klerk's security forces. The De Klerk regime has snubbed its nose at any suggestion of fundamental redistribution of wealth from parasitically bloated whites to impoverished blacks.'[106] *Asian Times* regretted that India, the first country to have closed its embassy in Pretoria and the first to have imposed sanctions against South Africa, had been the first country to resume international cricket against South Africa.[107]

South Africa's return to the ICC was seen in some quarters as part of a scheme to ensure that the balance of power in international cricket politics remained with England. In the *Muslim News,* far removed from a sensationalist journal, Anver Azaad argued that England and Australia had had tried to change the rules of test cricket in order to weaken the West Indies fast bowling whereas India and Pakistan had developed batsmen who could cope with such bowling. Given the assumption that power on the field led to power off the field, poor performances by England and Australia against the West Indies had been making it more difficult for England and Australia to maintain control of test cricket. With more and more money coming into international cricket and as Indian and Pakistan had the financial and organizational structures to challenge England and Australia, the English cricket establishment had been determined to maintain control over the hosting of events such as the cricket World Cup. In Anver Azaad's opinion, the admission of South Africa had been organised 'to prevent the "Black" members from taking control of the ICC and wielding greater influence in it than the "White", old powers – England and Australia.' The English cricket establishment had 'embarked on a well-thought out strategy of running down the "Black" members of the ICC and laundering England's poor [playing] performance.' With the connivance of the British press, the quality of the game in South Africa had been praised whilst teams, management, facilities

---

105. *Caribbean Times,* 29 October 1991.
106. *Caribbean Times,* 19 November 1991.
107. *Asian Times,* 19 November 1991.

and pitches in the Third World had been denigrated. Press stereotypes of the "Black" countries had been 'Pakistanis – cheaters; Indians – sly and cunning; the West Indies – brutal and savage.'[108] The fact that India had proposed that South Africa be readmitted to the ICC weakens the force of arguments such as those of Anver Azaad, but the constitution of the ICC gave great power to England and could easily be seen as a hangover from the heyday of Empire. As founder members of the ICC, England and Australia could veto proposals. The president of the MCC was automatically the chairman of the ICC. The headquarters of the ICC were at Lord's and the MCC provided, and paid for, the offices of the ICC and its secretariat. In 1993 the constitution of the ICC was reformed when England and Australia abandoned their power of veto and it was agreed that the members of the ICC would chose its chairman though the ICC administration continued to housed at Lord's. England's refusal to grant Zimbabwe test match status in 1989 may have been interpreted as evidence of fears that the ICC could become dominated by the 'black' countries.

At the ICC meeting that readmitted South Africa to test cricket, England representatives pressed for the bans on the rebel tourists from test cricket to be lifted but it was agreed only to review them in twelve months. Doug Insole of the TCCB said 'We felt that the sooner England could pick from a full-strength side the better it would be for us and for cricket as a whole.'[109] In July 1992 the ICC voted unanimously that the bans would be lifted from the following October, which in effect halved the original five-year ban. Sir Colin Cowdrey, chairman of the ICC, saw lifting the ban as 'part of the whole conciliatory move forward. The quicker it was done the better.' Among English first-class cricketers opinion was divided about the ban being lifted prematurely, especially as a return to test cricket by the rebels could mean that some of those who had not played in South Africa would lose their test places. Tim Curtis, chairman of the Cricketers' Association, thought that most players were against lifting the ban.[110] In July the vote in the Cricketers' Association on whether the ban should be lifted was split 120–120.[111] Even David Graveney, who had managed the Gatting tour but was also treasurer of the Cricketers' Association, said that his 'gut reaction' was that the time to lift the ban was April 1993, which would have been the same length as the ban served by the 1982 rebels. He further noted that it had been right for the decision about lifting the ban to have been taken by the ICC because playing in South Africa had been 'so sensitive politically' in the West Indies, India and Pakistan. Probably a desire to strengthen the playing

108. *Muslim News*, 23 October 1992.
109. *The Times*, 12 July 1991.
110. *The Times*, 9 July 1992.
111. *Asian Times*, 21 July 1992.

potential of England influenced the TCCB calls for the bans to be lifted but pressing for them to be lifted so soon after South Africa's readmission to test cricket gave the impression that revulsion over apartheid or support for a sporting boycott of South Africa had not been so very great.

Such impressions are strengthened by the subsequent careers of those who played in South Africa. In 1997 a former England player who had not joined either rebel tour commented that 'these expeditions to South Africa no longer appear to be a noose around their necks, but a passport for advancement which reflects a peculiar set of priorities.'[112] No player was sacked by a county for playing in South Africa, but as playing in South Africa was not against the law, dismissal for this could have been challenged in the courts. Five of the sixteen rebels from the 1982 tour and six of the fifteen from the 1990 tour played for England after completing their bans. It is perhaps fair to say that those who did not play for England after their bans had either passed their playing peak or had never been quite good enough for England. Emburey, the only player to go on both tours, even played for England after the second ban was lifted. Gooch and Emburey of the 1982 rebels were later to captain England. David Graveney, manager of the 1990 rebel tour, did not have to resign as treasurer of the Professional Cricketers' Association and in 1994 became its general secretary and in 1998 its chief executive. In 1992 and 1993 he captained Durham CCC. In 1995 he became a selector for the England team and in 1997 the chairman of the selectors. Graveney was also elected onto the MCC Committee for 1996–7. Gatting did not lose the Middlesex captaincy because of the 1990 rebel tour. He became an England selector in 1997 and was the team manager for the England A tour of Australia in 1996 and coach for the England tour of Kenya and Sri Lanka in 1996–7. Gooch captained Essex from 1986 until 1991 and England from 1988 until 1993. He was the tour manager of the England A team to Kenya and Sri Lanka in 1997–8 and of the England tour to Australia in 1998–9. In 1991 he was awarded the OBE. Emburey was manager of the England A tour to Pakistan in 1995. In 1999 Mike Gatting was president of the Professional Cricketers' Association. Gatting and Gooch were England selectors in the late 1990s. Alan Knott, one of the 1982 rebels, was engaged as a wicket-keeping coach by England. In 1999 Geoff Cook, whose playing in South Africa had almost led to the 1981–2 England tour to India being cancelled but who had refused to join the 1982 rebel tour, was the chief executive of Durham CCC and Dennis Amiss, one of the 1982 rebels, was the chief executive of Warwickshire CCC. Gatting was the director of coaching for Middlesex, Athey for Worcestershire and Emburey for Northamptonshire. Willey and Hendrick, also members of the 1982 rebel tour, became test-match umpires. In 1999 there

112. Edwards, '"Friends for Life"', p. 39.

were no African-Caribbean or Asian county chief executives and only one first team county coach. Those who went on the rebel tours had been banned from test cricket and it can be said that letting bygones be bygones is very much in keeping with the spirit of reconciliation that has accompanied the collapse of apartheid in South Africa. The competitive nature of test and county cricket may have meant that cricketing ability has taken precedence over political sensibilities in the appointment of test selectors and coaches. In 1997 Robin Smith said apropos of rebel tourists being England selectors, 'you have to forgive and forget, and look to the future. We are striving to make England a better side, and if they are the best men for the job, which I believe they are, and all that's gone should be forgotten.' Chris Lewis provided a different perspective when he said 'the people who went to South Africa put their financial gain over that of their country. That is not in doubt. OK I find it ironic that those people in charge will now question certain people's desire and willingness to play for their country, when at a time they had chosen the money over representing their country. So it is rather ironic.'[113] On the other hand, the prominent roles within cricket for those who accepted handsome payments for playing or coaching in apartheid South Africa add to the impression that that having sporting links with South Africa provoked little long-term resentment in English cricket and that English cricket had little sense of remorse or shame over its attitude towards South Africa during the apartheid years.

Cricket Followers and South Africa

What followers of cricket in England thought about a sporting boycott of South Africa is unclear but scraps of evidence suggest that many believed that cricketers should be free to play in South Africa. In 1983 John Carlisle, the Conservative MP, called for the MCC as a private club to tour South Africa. He wanted all sporting bodies 'to stand on their own feet and get rid of interference by governments' and thought that if the MCC as a private club toured South Africa, this would help to gauge whether recent opinion polls that suggested overwhelming support for the resumption of sporting ties with South Africa were right. Even though the MCC had ceased to be the supreme authority within English cricket in the late 1960s, its prestige and the symbolic significance of its ground at Lord's meant that an MCC tour to South Africa, though playing only against school and club sides, would have been interpreted as official approval from English cricket for the South African political regime.[114] Just over a thousand of the club's members attended a meeting in

113. Robin Smith interview with Huw Edwards, 17 July 1997, Chris Lewis interview with Huw Edwards, in Edwards, '"Friends for Life"', pp. 41–3.

114. *The Times*, 3, 24 February 1983; *Wisden Cricketers' Almanack 1984*, London: MacDonald Queen Anne, p. 322.

July to consider whether a touring party should be sent to South Africa in 1983–4: 535 voted against such a tour and 409 in favour. In a postal vote of the club's members 6,069 voted against the tour and 3,935 for it. Over 40 per cent of the MCC's 18,000 members did not appear to have felt so strongly over the tour as to register a vote, 40 per cent voted against the tour but 20 per cent wanted it to go ahead. In 1990, the chairman of Yorkshire's press and public relations subcommittee felt sure after discussion with Yorkshire's members that there was widespread support for the view that the Yorkshire bowler Paul Jarvis had a right to play for the 1990 rebel tour.[115] In order to ensure that the 1984 test series took place, the TCCB had asked English counties not to play any of the 1982 rebels in matches against the West Indian tourists. Only Yorkshire refused to do this which resulted in the match between Yorkshire and the West Indians, to be played at Hull in memory of the anti-slavery campaigner William Wilberforce, being cancelled.[116] There was no great outcry in Yorkshire at the county club's refusal to comply with this request of the TCCB.

Clues about the cricketing public's attitude to South Africa can be gauged from the *Cricketer* and *Wisden Cricket Monthly,* the leading cricket monthly magazines in England. Presumably their readers would have been more interested in cricket than the general public. In November 1982, 2,300 readers of the *Cricketer* took part in a poll that sampled their opinions about several aspects of cricket. Thirty-three per cent thought that English players should have been dissuaded from playing or coaching in South Africa but 88 per cent felt that it was right for players to be free to play where they wished. Sixty-two per cent wanted South Africa back in test cricket and over half of those who felt that South Africa should have not been readmitted to test cricket felt that the South African cricketers who had played multi-racial cricket in defiance of their government deserved some form of recognition.[117] Both the *Cricketer* and *Wisden Cricket Monthly* condemned apartheid. The usual editorial line of each magazine was that bridge-building would be more likely to bring about political change in South Africa than a boycott and that the efforts of SACU to establish multi-racial cricket in South Africa merited a sympathetic consideration of its requests for the restoration of official cricketing links. Both magazines printed articles and letters representing the full spectrum of opinion on cricket's relationship with South Africa, although those showing sympathy for SACU and the need for cricketing links with South Africa outnumbered those calling for a stronger boycott of South African cricket. David Sheppard's views on cricket and apartheid were often reported in the *Cricketer.* John Arlott, one of the first to campaign against apartheid, not only had a regular column in *Wisden Cricket Monthly*

115. *The Times,* 24 February 1990.
116. Steen, R. (1993), *Desmond Haynes: Lion of Barbados,* London: Witherby, pp. 128–9.
117. *Cricketer International,* November 1982, pp. 18–9.

Figure 1 Ranjitsinhji at the crease.

Figure 2 Framjee Patel, a leading patron of Parsee cricket, who was made a member of the MCC and of Surrey CCC in 1906. He called cricket 'the child of progress' of 'the friendly embrace of the East and the West' and wanted cricket to be 'one of the many links to unite the citizens of the greatest Empire the world has ever seen'.

Figure 3 C. A. Ollivierre was probably the first African-Caribbean to play county cricket. He played for Derbyshire from 1901 until 1907.

By kind permission of Mr Gerry Wolstenholme

Figure 4 How one cartoonist portrayed the defeat of the West Indian touring team by W.G. Grace's XI in 1906.

Figure 5 Learie Constantine at the nets. When playing as the professional for Nelson CC from 1929 until 1937, his exuberant batting and bowling attracted record attendances in the Lancashire League.

Figure 6 Learie Constantine, already knighted and the High Commissioner for Trinidad and Tobago, being granted the freedom of the borough of Nelson in 1963.

Figure 7 The barbed wire installed around the Headingley ground to protect the playing area against possible demonstrations from opponents of the proposed South African tour of England in 1970.

Figure 8 This cartoon shows how the high feelings surrounding the proposed South African cricket tour of 1970 were seen as a threat to law and order and racial relations.

Figure 9 The England opening batsman Brian Close facing a bouncer from the West Indian fast bowler Michael Holding at the Old Trafford test match in 1976. In the 1970s and 1980s West Indian fast bowlers were much criticised in England for using short-pitched balls.

Figure 10 West Indian supporters celebrating at The Oval in 1984 after the West Indies had just won all five of the test matches against England. Use of the term Blackwash suggests that they saw this victory as an expression of black achievement.

Figure 11 The confrontation between the England captain Mike Gatting and the Pakistani umpire Shakoor Rana during the test match at Faisalabad in 1987.

Figure 12 The Pakistani players confront the English umpires Roy Palmer and David Shepherd during the England-Pakistan test match at Old Trafford. Some observers likened the conduct of Pakistani players towards umpire Palmer to the incident between Gatting and Shakoor Rana in 1987.

Figure 13 Pakistani supporters at the World Cup match between India and Pakistan at Old Trafford in 1999. The enthusiasm of Asian supporters was considered a highlight of the World Cup.

Figure 14 Asian youths playing cricket in Bradford in the late 1990s. Such enthusiasm for cricket among white youths was rare in the late twentieth century.

Figure 15 Asians watching a match between Asian teams at a park in Blackburn in Lancashire in 2000. Similar numbers of spectators would be most unusual for a match between two white parks teams.

but was a member of its editorial board. As both magazines were commercial concerns, it may have been feared that more aggressive and more one-sided support either for or against the boycott could have lost readers. In the 1970s and 1980s the attitude of these magazines to South Africa never became the subject of comment in the national press on a scale similar to that provoked by Robert Henderson's article in 1995 in *Wisden Cricket Monthly*, which asked whether England players born overseas were fully committed when playing for England. The *Cricketer* and *Wisden Cricket Monthly* suggest cricket followers in England did not have exceptionally strong views about how far cricket should have been involved in the campaigns against apartheid.

The Balance Sheet of English Cricket and Apartheid in the 1980s and 1990s

The cricket establishment in England could claim that it stood by the sporting boycott of South Africa and by doing so signalled to white South Africa that apartheid was abhorred by even those countries with a tradition of friendship towards South Africa. Cricket was the first major British sport to stop playing international matches against South Africa during the apartheid years and did more at an earlier date than rugby union to support the boycott of South Africa. The banning of South Africa from test cricket persuaded white South African cricketers to promote multi-racial cricket in South Africa. Yet for much of the 1970s and 1980s English cricket gave the impression that its heart was not in the boycott of South Africa, that it would have welcomed some formula which would have allowed South Africa back into test cricket. The two rebel tours and the numbers of white English cricketers who played in South Africa showed to white South Africans that the sporting boycott of South Africa could be breached. The rhetoric surrounding the bans on the rebel tourists centred around expediency and pragmatism, around fears about how the disruption of test cricket could have threatened the survival of county cricket. At times eminent figures in English appeared to think that maintaining the tradition of test match cricket was more important than combating racism. In 1982 Christopher Martin-Jenkins argued that it was 'hardly just' to ban the Gooch rebels form test cricket for three years whilst the '"Packer Pirates", who seriously jeopardised Test cricket' should have escaped a ban. In 1991 Vic Marks reflected that in the early 1980s those who played in South Africa were 'subjected to far less opprobrium than the Packer players, which reflected a peculiar set of priorities.'[118] In 1982 Donald Woods, a white South African journalist who had fled to Britain in 1977, wrote that two thirds of the human race,

---

118. *Cricketer International,* September 1982, p. 8, May 1991, p. 26.

with a deeply personal sense of affront over apartheid, cannot easily stomach the sight of Englishmen playing cricket in South Africa as if South Africa had the kind of amiable society where the batting and bowling of a ball seemed a logical extension of other national amiabilities . . . what seems to many white Britons to be the most harmless of activities, the simple playing of cricket, is an outrage to the black man everywhere – a dancing on the grave of apartheid's victims.[119]

Throughout the 1980s many from English cricket found it hard to appreciate this.

White cricketers may have persuaded themselves that playing and coaching in South Africa was undermining apartheid, an even more powerful case can be made for the view that they were helping to prop up its underlying racism. Whilst many who played and coached in South Africa may have hoped, or even believed, that the efforts of SACU to promote multi-racial cricket could have led to greater ethnic understanding which in turn could have persuaded whites to vote to overturn apartheid, their presence in South Africa can be seen as condoning apartheid and helping to create a cosmetic view of South African society outside South Africa. Those who played and coached in South Africa may have found apartheid distasteful, but their presence in South Africa showed that their objections to apartheid were not so great as to prevent them going to South Africa. English cricketers in South Africa helped to weaken the international sporting boycott of South Africa. The South African government's tax concessions to companies that organized rebel tours shows that that it wished to undermine the boycott and that it must have assumed the boycott was challenging apartheid. Had it not been for the English rebel tour of 1982, setting up the Sri Lankan and West Indian rebel tours may have been harder if not impossible. The rebel tours and also overseas cricketers playing in the Currie Cup showed that with money, the boycott could be circumvented, that it was possible for white South Africa to retain apartheid in so much of South African life and have contact with high-quality cricketers from overseas.

English cricket was in an unusually strong position to have shown to white South Africa that whites in England detested the racism underlying apartheid. In the late twentieth century football had a much stronger hold on the public imagination in England than cricket, but cricket has continued to be seen inside and outside England as a distillation of Englishness and an expression of English moral worth. Cricket still had close links with the social and business elite in Britain. As cricket represented so much more than a merely a sport, thoroughgoing condemnations of apartheid from English cricket could have been a declaration of unequivocal and unqualified opposition from English whites to apartheid. By adopting only a half-hearted and

---

119. *The Times*, 3 March 1982.

often apparently reluctant opposition to apartheid, English cricket gave the impression to all ethnic groups in South Africa that opposition to apartheid in England was not so very intense. By delaying a prohibition on cricketers playing in South Africa in an individual capacity and by arguing that the progress towards multi-racial cricket justified the readmission of South Africa to test cricket, English cricket helped to insulate white South Africa from the revulsion which so much of the world felt for apartheid. The actions and attitudes of English cricket can be seen as helping to persuade white South Africa that sporting contact could be resumed without abandoning the essence of apartheid. More forthright support from English cricket would have made the sporting isolation of South Africa more effective and a stronger weapon in the campaign to overthrow apartheid. Whilst English cricket helped to undermine apartheid in cricket, its failure to emphasize to white South Africa that apartheid was a system with which there could no compromise may well have prolonged the survival of apartheid in more important areas of life.

–5–

'Fast and Brutish': Reactions to the West Indian Pace Attack

The West Indies dominated test cricket from the mid 1970s until the early 1990s. They won eighteen of the twenty-two test match series they played between 1976 and 1990–1. Only two test series were lost and that against India in 1978–9 was when the West Indian side was below full strength because most of the leading players had defected to Kerry Packer's World Series cricket. Of the 112 tests played by the West Indies, fifty-five were won and only thirteen lost, a staggering wins to losses ratio. In the seven England-West Indies test series played between 1976 and 1989–90, the West Indies won twenty-two matches and England one. The West Indies won all five tests in each of the series against England in 1984 and 1985–6. The West Indies also won five of the six test series against Australia with the remaining one being drawn. The West Indies won the first two cricket World Cups and it was a major surprise when India defeated them in the final of the third. The West Indian teams in the late 1970s and 1980s were hardened, highly professional sides. The basis for their success in test cricket was a bowling attack of four fast bowlers supported by strong batting and superb fielding.

Disparaging the West Indies' Success

This West Indian success in international cricket attracted more condemnation than praise in England. Michele Savidge and Alastair McLellan in their sympathetic study of West Indian fast bowling claim that the West Indian team was 'the most vilified and maligned in sporting history.'[1] In 1984 in the *Sunday Times* Robin Marlar, captain of Sussex from 1955 to 1959, wrote of the West Indians 'brutalizing the game' and threatening to destroy it and called the West Indian fast bowler Malcolm Marshall 'a cold blooded assassin.' John Woodcock, as editor of *Wisden,* claimed that the West Indies, though not the only offenders, were the worst offenders in the 'viciousness' of the fast bowlers who were changing 'the very nature of the game' and resorting

---

1. Savidge, M. and McLennan, A. (1995), *Real Quick: A Celebration of the West Indies Pace Quartets,* London: Blandford, p. 13.

'ever more frequently to the thuggery of the bouncer'.[2] In 1987, David Miller, chief sports correspondent for *The Times,* wrote of West Indian fast bowlers 'aiming at the heads of anyone and everyone.'[3] Christopher Martin-Jenkins, in an editorial in the *Cricketer* in 1986, argued that whilst not wanting to penalize the West Indies for their success, 'all who cherish the game which once had beauty, variety and subtlety as well as thunder and blood should deplore the increasing violence of professional cricket.'[4] In 1991, David Frith, editor of *Wisden Cricket Monthly,* described the forthcoming West Indian tour as 'Another invasion . . . by a West Indian team which is the most fearsome, the most successful and the most unpopular in the world. Their game is founded on vengeance and violence and fringed by arrogance.'[5]

This animosity towards the West Indies contrasted sharply with responses to West Indian cricket in earlier decades. Until the late 1970s West Indian test-match sides were praised for their immense talent and for playing in a less cautious and more flamboyant manner than other test countries. In Britain West Indian cricket was often described as 'calypso' cricket, an expression resonating with assumptions about the Caribbean as a tropical paradise where West Indian cricketers played an uninhibited, carefree style of cricket reflecting their natural exuberance. In 1976 the cricket journalist Henry Blofeld had claimed in *Wisden* that the West Indians had 'always tended to play their cricket in the same way as they live their lives. Because they are by nature, gay, excitable and flamboyant, their approach to cricket has captured the imagination in a way that no other country has done.'[6] Although the West Indies had great success in test cricket in the 1960s, West Indian sides were thought to have often played below their potential and what were assumed to be West Indian character defects were frequently used in England to explain the comparatively disappointing results of West Indian test sides. In 1970 Blofeld had attributed the strength of West Indian cricket to cricket in the Caribbean being 'less stylised' with players building their game on 'eye rather than technique'. Even West Indian test cricketers, he wrote, 'played the game by ear rather than by design', which gave their cricket 'the sense of adventure and fun which they show playing cricket at a far lower level on the corners in Barbados . . . or anywhere else in the West Indies.' But Blofeld also saw such qualities as the weakness of West Indian test cricket. In his view when 'everything is going right the wave of enthusiasm is all-enveloping and gets higher and higher, but when things go wrong it subsides at an even faster rate.' The West Indies were not able 'to regroup mentally and take stock of the situations and problems in front of them when things start going wrong'. He saw 'temperament' as the weakness of West Indian cricket. In losing a series against Australia, they had been

2. *Wisden Cricketers' Almanack 1984,* London: MacDonald Queen Anne, p. 50.
3. *The Times,* 10 December 1987.
4. *Cricketer International,* April 1986, p. 2.
5. *Wisden Cricket Monthly,* June 1991, p. 3.
6. *Wisden Cricketers' Almanack 1976,* London: Sporting Handbooks, p. 71.

temperamentally unable 'to buckle down and slowly to fight their way back to an even keel'.[7]

West Indian cricketers and their supporters resented the criticisms levelled against their teams of the late 1970s and 1980s. Wes Hall, the retired fast bowler who was managing the West Indian tour to New Zealand in 1984–5, asked 'Why are they always getting at us?'[8] Clive Lloyd, captain of the West Indies from 1974–5 until 1984, described his team as furious over the critics from across the world who were 'trying to degrade our excellence and our achievements. That is the real reason behind statements that we bowl too many bouncers . . . But it's all being said by people who wish to deny us our rightful title as the best team around. It really makes me hopping mad.'[9] Viv Richards, Lloyd's successor as captain of the West Indies, wrote that West Indian fast bowling had been 'continually maligned as a negative force by many in the cricket establishment and much of the Press'.[10] The West Indian fast bowler Michael Holding wrote that West Indian players objected to the impression that 'our success is based not on skill but on intimidation and brute force'.[11] In 1988 Joel Garner, another great West Indian fast bowler, complained that in England there had been 'little praise for West Indian cricket over the past ten years. Constant criticism. Short-pitched bowling and slowing down the game, and a bunch of other rubbish. If the English or Australian had experienced the same level of success, you would read and hear words like dynasty and comparison with history's best. Not in our case. There was a jealousy and selfishness among English players and commentators.'[12] Failure to give full recognition to the West Indian playing abilities seemed to West Indians to smack of racism, to belittle the quality of West Indian achievement. Clive Lloyd thought that his West Indian team had never been given the credit its playing achievements merited and said that this could be called 'all sorts of things, call it prejudice, call it racism, I don't know.'[13]

West Indian players and their supporters felt that criticism of fast bowling underestimated the other great playing strengths of the West Indian team. Michael Holding felt that the quality of the fielding supporting the fast bowling was rarely recognized.[14]

7. Blofeld, H. (1970), *Cricket in Three Moods: Eighteen Months of Test Cricket and the Ways of Life behind It,* London: Hodder and Stoughton, pp. 168–9.

8. Savidge and McLennan, *Real Quick,* p. 110.

9. McDonald, T. (1985), *Clive Lloyd: The Authorised Biography,* London: Granada, p. 155.

10. Savidge and McLennan, *Real Quick,* p. 11.

11. Holding, M. and Cozier, T. (1993), *Whispering Death: The Life and Times of Michael Holding,* London: Deutsch, p. 149.

12. Garner, J. (1988), *'Big Bird' Flying High,* London: Barker, p. 196.

13. Steen, R. (1993), *Desmond Haynes: Lion of Barbados,* London: Witherby, p. 26.

14. Holding and Cozier, *Whispering Death,* p. 149.

In the late 1970s and early 1980s Viv Richards was usually considered to be the best batsman playing test cricket. Ian Botham thought Richards a better batsman than Bradman. Clive Lloyd must have been among the greatest left-handed batsmen of all time and was a magnificent fielder. Few batsmen are thought to have hit the ball harder than Lloyd. Gordon Greenidge was probably the best opening batsman in the world. West Indian batsmen such as Desmond Haynes, Gus Logie, Roy Fredericks, Larry Gomes, Richie Richardson, Lawrence Rowe and Alvin Kallicharran would probably have walked into the teams of other test-playing countries. As captain of the West Indies Clive Lloyd won more test matches than any captain in the history of test cricket, but in England he was not always recognized as a great captain. It was implied that Lloyd was fortunate to have such fine bowlers and batsmen at his disposal and Mike Brearley, revered in English cricket as a captain of genius, was reported to have said that Lloyd's limitations as a captain had been exposed by Lancashire's mediocre record under his leadership in county cricket. Such criticisms overlooked the fact that Lloyd had managed to wield the West Indies into a highly efficient side and that under his captaincy the West Indies lost the reputation for being a test side whose collective performances so often failed to match the individual talents of players. Trevor McDonald's biography of Lloyd shows that one of Lloyd's great achievements as a captain was instilling a collective spirit to overcome the different island identities that had so often weakened earlier West Indian teams.

The repeated use of bouncers or short-pitched balls by the West Indian fast bowlers provoked the greatest criticism. Unless a batsman had quick reflexes, he could be hit by a bouncer. Within cricket the occasional bouncer was accepted as a legitimate dimension of fast bowling but the West Indies were accused of over-using bouncers on such a scale as to constitute physical intimidation and to cause fear of injury among batsmen. In 1984 the England opening batsmen Graeme Fowler was reputed to have said that 'the stumps never came into play at all' which presumably meant that all the balls he had received had been pitched short.[15] Graham Gooch wrote in 1985 that a number ten or eleven batsman who blocked half a dozen balls against the West Indies would be 'odds-on to get a bouncer whistling past his nose. Most will then freeze with terror, because they are not simply equipped to deal with it. If that is not intimidation, I don't know what is.'[16] When batting on a difficult pitch at the Kingston test in 1986 and only days after a ball from Malcolm Marshall had

15. McDonald, *Clive Lloyd,* p. 110.
16. Gooch, G. and Lee, A. (1985), *Out of the Wilderness,* London: Willow, p. 145.

broken Mike Gatting's nose, it occurred to the England batsman Allan Lamb, considered a courageous player of short-pitched fast bowling, 'that life, on occasions, [could] be more important than a cricket match.'[17] The Somerset batsman Peter Roebuck wrote that a 'barrage' of short-pitched fast bowling 'gradually exhausts a batsman's courage and resource and cheap wickets result.' When both sides used such tactics, a cricket match became 'not so much a duel of skill as trench warfare in which teams hammer away at each other until eventually one team weakens.'[18] During the final session of the third day of the England–West Indies test match at Old Trafford in 1976, the England openers Brian Close, then aged 45, and John Edrich, survived fearsome short-pitched fast bowling. Both were both hit several times and umpire Bill Alley warned Holding for intimidation after bowling three successive bouncers to Close. Bob Willis, the England fast bowler, called it 'the most sustained barrage of intimidation' and 'frightening to watch'. The English cricket administrator Gubby Allen, a former England fast bowler and captain who had played on the England 1932–3 bodyline tour of Australia but had refused to bowl bodyline and who had probably seen as much test cricket as any cricket administrator, called it 'the most ghastly exhibition of cricket' he had ever witnessed.[19]

The Indian opening batsman Sunil Gavaskar made one of the fiercest denunciations of the West Indian fast bowling tactics. In the test match at Kingston, Jamaica, between India and the West Indies in 1976, the Indian captain Bishan Bedi declared the Indian first innings closed when 306 runs had been scored but only six wickets had fallen. Three Indian batsmen had been injured facing bouncers and Bedi did not want to risk his bowlers being injured. Gavaskar thought that beamers, fast full tosses, bowled at him by Holding had been 'a strategy to intimidate us' and did not believe Holding's claim that he had bowled beamers because the ball had slipped from his fingers. In the second innings the Indian innings was terminated at 95 for five wickets, leaving the West Indies to score only twelve runs to win the match and the test series. Gavaskar claimed that this was not a declaration but that India had simply no other batsmen fit to bat. In his opinion 'the West Indians under Clive Lloyd reached a new low in a desperate effort to win by having all our eleven players hospitalised!' Because of injuries all seventeen members of the Indian touring party had been on the field of play at some time during the match. Of the West Indian spectators Gavaskar wrote that the 'only word I can think of to describe the behaviour of the crowd is "barbarian." Here was a man seriously injured, and these "barbarians" were thirsting for more blood, instead of expressing sympathy as any civilised and sporting crowd would have done.' Spectators encouraging Holding with cries of '"Kill him, Maan!", "Hit him Maan!", "Knock his head off Mike!"' proved for

17. Lamb, A. (1996), *My Autobiography,* London: Collins Willow, p.138.
18. *Cricketer International,* February 1984, p. 26.
19. *Cricketer International,* November 1978, p. 26.

Gavaskar that 'these people still belonged to the jungles and forests, instead of a civilised country.'[20]

Criticism of West Indian fast bowling was accompanied by complaints about slow over rates. Slowing down the over rate kept bowlers fresh to continue bowling fast and made it harder for batsmen to score quickly. In 1980 when the West Indians bowled only seventy-four overs on the first day of The Oval test, David Frith, editor of *Wisden Cricket Monthly,* complained that the 'heart beat of international cricket has slowed alarmingly this summer . . . the spectators had simply not had their money's worth' and argued that 'Once more cricket has to *legislate* itself back to full health.' The former England captain Ted Dexter explained that the very long run ups of the West Indian bowlers meant that they needed long periods of recuperation between overs to remain fresh and that slowing over rates was a means of achieving this.[21] In 1982 *Wisden* pointed out that over the past twelve years five fewer overs on average were bowled each hour in test cricket.[22] Slow over rates of the West Indian fast bowlers were also condemned for squeezing spin bowling out of test cricket. Increasing the number of overs to be bowled in one day was seen as a means of forcing captains to use spin bowlers because they bowled their overs more quickly than fast bowlers. In 1978 Gubby Allen argued that the over-reliance on fast bowling robbed cricket of variety and because of the declining use of spin bowlers batsmen needed to be good players of only fast bowling.[23] Spin was also seen as one of the more subtle art forms of cricket in contrast to the physical aggression and intimidation of fast bowling. Clive Lloyd admitted that the West Indies under his captaincy had turned to the four-man pace attack after losing a test match against India in Trinidad when the West Indian spinners had failed to prevent the Indian batsmen from scoring over 400 runs in the final innings of a test match. This was only the second instance in the history of test cricket where a side had scored over 400 in the fourth innings to win a test match. The West Indies, Lloyd said, had 'guys who bowled spin, not got people out', but he also mentioned that under his captaincy the West Indies had used fourteen spin bowlers.[24]

West Indian cricketers defended their use of a four-man pace attack and the slowing of over rates. Clive Lloyd, while acknowledging the pain of being hit by a cricket ball bowled at ninety miles per hour, said 'that's the game. It's tough. There's no rule against bowling fast. Batsmen must cope to survive.' His standard answer to

20. Gavaskar, S. (1980), *Sunny Days: An Autobiography,* Calcutta: Rupa, pp. 215–20.
21. *Wisden Cricket Monthly,* September 1980, pp. 34–5.
22. *Wisden Cricketers' Almanack 1982,* London: MacDonald Queen Anne, p. 88.
23. *Cricketer International,* November 1978, p. 29.
24. Steen, *Desmond Haynes,* pp. 21–2.

criticisms of the West Indian reliance on fast bowling was to say 'Fast bowling is a part of cricket. And nobody is going to change that now. And people can't start complaining when people bowl fast; that is not cricket.' Short-pitched bowling, in his view was 'part of the quickie's equipment. He can't be too regulated, or he would lose the surprise element. The umpire can't tell a fast bowler that there should be only one short ball an over, because after that the surprise element is lost. Complaints come from batsmen ill-equipped to play the stuff . . . We have fast bowlers who get people out. That's what the game is all about, and there's no reason why we should change because we keep beating teams.'[25] Lloyd denied the charge of barbarism made by Gavaskar in the Kingston test in 1976. He claimed that when Holding bowled round the wicket, he was not aiming at the Indians' bodies, but was trying to entice batsmen who were not getting into line to snick the ball to the wicket-keeper or slips. 'We had quick bowlers and their batsmen simply couldn't cope. But that's cricket. I can't say I was greatly upset. Because a wicket is quick, and batsmen get into difficulty, you can't bowl half-volleys, you still do your best to get them out. That's the game. If you can't play fast bowling you shouldn't be in the game at international level.'[26] Michael Holding argued that only incompetent batsmen would be hit by short-pitched fast bowling and that if there was a problem with such bowling it lay with 'the lack of technique of modern batsmen to cope with good, aggressive fast bowling' and that instead of calling for changes to limit the use of bouncers, others should have tried to develop techniques to cope with it. He believed that if spin bowlers were good enough, they would be selected to bowl in test cricket and asked why should a fast bowler be dropped to make way for a spin bowler who was less likely to take wickets.[27] Clive Lloyd maintained that obliging sides to bowl a minimum number of overs per day would force captains to use medium or slow bowlers which would spare some batsmen the ordeal of facing fast bowlers at the start of their innings. For Lloyd, 'Facing the quickies again, when you've got a hundred partnership say, is a very different proposition from facing them when you've just come in, still desperately trying to get a few.'[28]

West Indian players conceded that on occasions they had overused short-pitched fast bowling. In 1985 Michael Holding wrote that 'I freely admit that there may have been times in recent seasons when the West Indies fast bowlers have overdone the short-pitched bowling' but he added that in the test match at Old Trafford in 1976, the only test match in which he had been warned by an umpire for intimidatory bowling, the wicket had been so poor that balls lifted nastily when only just short of

25. McDonald, *Clive Lloyd,* pp. 107–8, 110.
26. McDonald, *Clive Lloyd,* pp. 85–6.
27. *Cricketer International,* August 1985, p. 15.
28. McDonald, *Clive Lloyd,* p. 111.

a length and that Brian Close had been hit because he was playing off the front foot. Holding felt that better prepared pitches would reduce injuries among batsmen.[29] After the 1976 Old Trafford match Lloyd said that 'Our fellows got carried away. They knew that they had only eighty minutes that night to make an impression and they went flat out, sacrificing accuracy for speed. They knew afterwards they had bowled badly.'[30] Whilst this was not exactly an admission that bouncers had been over used, bouncers were not used quite so much in the rest of the series, partly because bowling a fuller length brought more wickets.[31]

The Campaigns against Short-pitched Fast Bowling

Cricket administrators attempted to reduce the scale of short-pitched fast bowling and to increase the number of overs bowled per day. In 1976 the ICC agreed unanimously that the sides should attempt to bowl a minimum of 17.5 six-ball overs per hour in test matches.[32] A year later the ICC accepted a recommendation devised by Gubby Allen and Leslie Ames of England that a bowler would be allowed to bowl only two bouncers per over and not more than three in two consecutive overs and that by mutual agreement countries could introduce this as an experiment.[33] In 1982 the ICC deplored the excessive use of bouncers and all countries agreed to urge their teams to aim to bowl 16.5 overs per hour, but rejected proposals for a minimum of ninety-six overs per day in test matches, limiting a bowler's run up to twenty-five yards and for permitting only one bouncer per over.[34] It was decided in 1984 that the cricket board of the country where a test series was to be played could specify how many overs were to be bowled per day.[35] In 1991 the ICC decided that for a three-year experimental period only one short-pitched delivery could be permitted per over, a short-pitched delivery being defined as one that passed above a batsman's shoulder. Persistent infringements of this law could result in a bowler being cautioned and then being banned from bowling for the rest of the innings. In 1994 the law was revised to permit two bouncers per over.[36]

Attempts to restrict the numbers of bouncers per over and to quicken over rates were condemned by the West Indies and their supporters and also by the Pakistanis

29. *Cricketer International,* August 1985, p. 15.

30. Wilde, S. (1995), *Letting Rip: The Fast-Bowling Threat from Lillee to Waqar,* London Gollancz/ Witherby, p. 60.

31. McDonald, *Clive Lloyd,* p. 88.

32. *Cricketer International,* September 1976, p. 4.

33. *Wisden Cricketers' Almanack 1978,* p. 24, London: Sporting Handbooks, p. 1114.

34. *Wisden Cricketers' Almanack 1983,* London: MacDonald Queen Anne, p. 1294; *Wisden 1984,* p. 1251.

35. *Wisden Cricketers' Almanack 1985,* London: John Wisden, p. 1241.

36. Wilde, *Letting Rip,* p. 194–5.

who in the late 1980s and 1990s had developed a formidable pace attack. In 1990 Clive Lloyd wrote that restrictions on bouncers were 'nothing more than an attack on the West Indies' and 'an attempt to reduce the effectiveness of our pace attack'. Michael Holding asked if the cricketing public was so incensed about the West Indies' slow over rates, why did such large crowds watch their test matches, and argued that it was the quality of cricket, not the number of overs, that 'brings people piling through the turnstiles.'[37] Imran Khan, the Pakistani captain and fast bowler who had a key role in making the Pakistani team one of the strongest forces in test cricket, thought that the bouncer limitation was discrimination against fast bowlers, introduced by England and Australia with the support of Sri Lanka and India. 'It is harmful for cricket', he argued 'England and Australia have been through a phase where they were being thrashed by the West Indies. Instead of being fair about it, and trying to beat them on even terms, they are trying to handicap them. Good fast bowlers will always dominate, and there are periods in every country's history when they go through a dearth of good fast bowlers . . . The balance redresses itself in time.' Imran did not even think that the ruling was good for the technique of batsmen. Once batsmen knew that they could not receive a second bouncer in an over they would probably make the mistake of pre-empting shots by moving onto the front foot.[38] Wasim Akram suspected that the bouncer restriction had been brought in specifically to protect the England batsman Graeme Hick whose technique against short-pitched fast bowling was thought to be weak.[39]

Proposals by England's representatives at the ICC to restrict bouncers reflected an assumption that cricket should be conducted in accordance with white English traditions of how the game should be played and administered which to many West Indians and Asians were expressions of white supremacy. In 1991, *Caribbean Times,* published in England, asked whether there was 'a white supremacist plot to undermine Westindies long-standing status as kings of cricket.' After Chris Lane of *Wisden Cricket Monthly* had written that the West Indies were unpopular within 'the internal structure of the cricketing world', *Caribbean Times* felt that there was 'some justification then, for those in our community who detect an anti-Westindies conspiracy directed by white officials sitting at the top table of the game's anachronistic hierarchies.' To West Indian players and their supporters, campaigns to restrict the use of bouncers seemed part of an English attempt to undermine the strength of West Indian cricket and ensure that test cricket would be played in a style more likely to

37. *Cricket Life International,* August 1989, pp. 13–14.
38. Crace, J. (1992), *Wasim and Waqar: Imran's Inheritors,* London: Boxtree, p. 159.
39. Wilde, *Letting Rip,* p. 194.

produce English victories whilst attempts by English teams to emulate West Indian tactics and the much publicized efforts of English cricket to discover fast bowlers no doubt deepened West Indian suspicions of English motives. Even if it is accepted that England's representatives at the ICC were motivated by a disinterested concern that test cricket was becoming less attractive for players and spectators through the reliance on fast bowling leading to slow over rates and the disappearance of spin bowling, this could still have been seen as racist by blacks and Asians. Moreover trying to regulate West Indian fast bowling was criticizing an aspect of West Indian cricket that had always been dominated by African-Caribbeans. Since the First World War there had been great white and Asian batsmen and spin bowlers for the West Indies but no fast bowlers and except for a short period in the early 1950s, fast bowling had been the nucleus of West Indian bowling attacks. Given African-Caribbean awareness of the history of black exploitation by whites stretching over centuries, attempts by white English cricket administrators to regulate how cricket was played, and in particular to curtail an area of black strength and success, it is easy to see how such moves were seen by West Indians, and Pakistanis, as expressions of white arrogance. In 1995, Viv Richards wrote that some in cricket's establishment thought that the West Indies had 'been at the top for too long and they have attempted to devise all manner of means to curb our armoury with the absurd one-bouncer-an-over rule as well as over rates stipulations. There are many reasons for the legislation, and envy and racism are among them: believe it or not, there are people involved in cricket today, in the late twentieth century, who think we have no right to be competing on the same stage as them – *let alone beating them at their own game!* [40]

Suspicions among the supporters of the West Indies of racism within the ICC cannot be divorced from the animosities aroused by question of sporting links with South Africa. Chapter Four has shown how the English representatives at the ICC showed less enthusiasm for a full-blooded boycott of South Africa and had to be pressured into accepting a policy of automatic bans from test cricket for all who played, coached or administered cricket in South Africa. Even though England representatives condemned apartheid, they often gave the impression of being lukewarm about the boycott of South Africa, which many African-Caribbeans and Asians believed was one of the most effective methods of combating apartheid. In 1985 the cricket journalist E.M. Wellings wrote *Wisden Cricket Monthly* that the TCCB had become the rulers of English cricket in name only, with the power of decision resting with 'the coloured members of ICC, most particularly West Indies'. The TCCB, he argued, had banned the members of the Gooch rebel tour from test cricket for three years in order to 'please West Indies and the rest of them.' He compared the TCCB

40. Savidge and McLennan, *Real Quick,* p. 11.

with the Munich appeasers but added that they were 'not typical of Mrs. Thatcher's Britain'. He thought that the TCCB feared that the West Indies might cancel tests with England and wrote 'Well, let them. They will soon alter their tune, for they need us and our cricket much more than we need them. Indeed, if we invited South Africa to rejoin, we could also do without West Indies tests. We could also do without their players in our county sides, for some of the most disrupting influences in our game come from the Caribbean and should be returned there . . . While kow-towing to West Indies, the TCCB think nothing of breaking their word given in 1970 to South Africa.'[41] Such views were not the official voice of English cricket, but allowing Wellings to have a regular column in *Wisden Cricket Monthly,* one of the two leading cricket magazines sold in England, could well have been seen by African-Caribbeans as a racist bias against them in English cricket. Senior figures in English cricket rarely troubled to distance themselves in public from Wellings' views.

Some West Indians and Asians saw the calls for South Africa's readmission to the ICC in the early 1990s as intertwined with attempts to restrict short-pitched fast bowling. The ICC meeting that readmitted South Africa also decided to fine bowlers 5 per cent of their match fees for bowling overs too slowly. The West Indian representative Clyde Walcott had argued for a fine of 3 per cent and had felt that that the readmission of South Africa had been premature but 'again we were the lone voice'. The former West Indian fast bowler Andy Roberts was reported to have commented 'We have been the champions for too long and it upsets the white folks, because they are the ones bringing in all these rules. All the rules which have been introduced over the last 25–35 years have been set to combat the Westindies.' In his view the reason for the premature readmission of South Africa was that 'They need extra white people because with Australia, England and New Zealand, there is the Westindies, Pakistan, India and Sri Lanka, so they, need somebody else in there.' *Caribbean Times* journalist Nigel Carter wrote that as 'in the days of Empire, some in the ICC are attempting to ride roughshod over darker skinned peoples. They hope to force the decline of Westindies so they can take up the white man's burden and lord it over international cricket.'[42]

Asian Times in 1992 also believed that the England Australia representatives at the ICC were advocating rule changes to limit the efficacy of the West Indian and Pakistani fast bowlers because of their inability to develop comparably 'fearsome' fast bowlers or batsmen able to cope with 'demon bowlers.' One of its correspondents wrote that in 'the halcyon days of Empire any such bending of the rules would have been condemned as sacrilege . . . As chief custodians of the white man's burden lording it over international cricket, England also rode roughshod over darker skinned peoples' and had not called for restrictions on fast bowling when Trueman and Tyson

41. *Wisden Cricket Monthly,* March 1985, p. 7.
42. *Caribbean Times,* 23 July 1991.

were terrorizing the West Indies and Pakistan. The West Indies and Pakistan were urged to launch a bid for 'Black Power' at the ICC instead of seeming to attend to merely rubber stamp the ideas of England and Australia. The West Indian fast bowler Joel Garner argued that while 'rules are being challenged by other teams and countries, it appears as though we are only going along for the ride. The time is right to let our voices be heard.'[43] Condemnations of West Indian fast bowling as expressions of a white supremacist desire to retain control of international cricket were made in 1995 by Stephen Humbolt in *Caribbean Times,* who asked whether there was 'a White Man's Conspiracy at work in the Gentleman's Game.' He called on the Indian and Sri Lankan representatives not to support the attempts of England, Australia and New Zealand to restrict fast bowling. Because England and Australia were no longer producing fast bowlers 'in abundance, they seek to stifle' those from the West Indies and Pakistan, which 'smacks of a kind of racism'. In Humbolt's opinion, the 'top echelons of world cricket are held by the Westindies and Pakistan. Some in the inner sanctum in England and Australia hate this, and would do anything to see that it is not so.'[44]

Double Standards

Many African-Caribbeans saw criticisms of the all pace attack as an example of double standards and hypocrisy. Other countries had used short-pitched fast bowling and had bowlers who were more outspoken about trying to intimidate batsmen. The potential of short-pitched fast bowling had been demonstrated first by England against Australia in the bodyline series of 1932–3. In the 1950s the South African fast bowlers Heine and Adcock bowled fifty-three bouncers out of fifty-six balls in a test match against Australia and may have continued to do so had their captain not told them to stop.[45] Sunil Gavaskar thought that the bowling of five successive bouncers by the England bowler Chris Old was a blatant attempt to injure a star Indian spin bowler. In 1978 a ball from the England bowler Bob Willis hit the Pakistani nightwatchman Iqbal Qasim a nasty blow in the mouth. Willis, who later became an England captain, was reputed to have said that because breaking the jaw of the Australian batsman Rick McCosker had put him off his game for the rest of a match, he adopted a more detached approach so that injuries to batsmen could not again reduce the effectiveness of his bowling.[46] In 1980, when captaining Middlesex, Mike Brearley protested when an umpire tried to stop Wayne Daniel bowling bouncers to the Sussex tail-end batsman Tony Pigott. Earlier in the day Daniel had broken a

43. *Asian Times,* 28 July 1992.
44. *Caribbean Times,* 24 June 1995.
45. Benaud, R. (1998), *Anything But . . . An Autobiography,* London: Hodder & Stoughton, p. 142.
46. Wilde, *Letting Rip,* pp. 77–8.

bone in the hand of the Sussex opener Kepler Wessels.[47] In 1983 the Middlesex bowler Simon Hughes thought that ambitious county captains ordered their fast bowlers to 'Stick it up 'im . . . You can see he doesn't fancy it.'[48] Ian Botham was cautioned by an umpire for short-pitched fast bowling in the Nottingham test match against Australia in 1985.[49] In 1996 the England captain Michael Atherton urged Devon Malcolm to rough up the South African tail-end batsmen as the South Africans had done to England. After the match the England manager Raymond Illingworth was especially critical of Malcolm for not bowling more bouncers.[50]

Other countries had slowed down over rates. It has been alleged that at Headingley in 1953 England did this to prevent Australia from winning the test and so retain the Ashes and against Australia in 1954–5 the England captain Hutton was thought to have slowed the over rate to ensure that his fast bowlers Statham and Tyson remained fresh. In 1976 when the West Indies bowled only 13.91 overs per hour against England, England's rate of 14.44 was only slightly quicker.[51] In 1989–90 series, the West Indies bowled 11.93 overs per hour and England 11.95.[52]

Complaints about the West Indies' use of a four-man pace attack seemed hypocritical especially as other countries would have copied these tactics had they possessed bowlers of the same class. Ian Botham said 'Don't tell me if England had the fastest attack of four bowlers in the history of the game, as West Indies did, we or anybody else wouldn't use them in the same way. Of course we would. When the West Indies are winning, they bowl fourteen overs an hour, when they're losing they bowl eleven and I suppose you can't blame them. Test cricket is Test cricket.'[53] In 1984 Peter Roebuck, the Somerset captain, wrote that 'every international and first-class team would select four quick bowlers if they could, for the simple reason that this is the most effective way of winning cricket matches.'[54] After losing the 1976 series to the West Indies the England captain Tony Greig called for a fast bowler. In 1984 Ted Dexter began a search to unearth young English fast bowlers. Websters' Brewery provided £100,000 to help produce fast bowlers for England. By 1986 Dexter had looked at 4,000 potential bowlers though felt that only two might 'make good'.[55]

47. Khan, I. and Murphy, P. (1983), *Imran: The Autobiography of Imran Khan,* London: Pelham, pp. 138–9.

48. Hughes, S. (1997), *A Lot of Hard Yakka: Triumph and Torment: A County Cricketer's Life,* London: Headline, p. 104.

49. *Cricketer International,* September 1985, p. 3.

50. Illingworth, R. and Bannister, J. (1996), *One-man Committee: The Controversial Reign of the England Cricket Supremo,* London: Headline, pp. 250–1.

51. Wilde, *Letting Rip,* p. 58.

52. *Cricketer International,* June 1990, p. 3.

53. Quoted in Steen, *Desmond Haynes,* p. 25.

54. *Cricketer International,* February 1984, p. 23.

55. *Wisden Cricket Monthly,* October 1984, pp. 5, 7, July 1986, p. 43; Wilde, *Letting Rip,* p. 57.

West Indian bowlers admitted using bouncers to intimidate batsmen. Michael Holding, perhaps the fastest West Indian bowler, wrote that 'I never bowl bouncers without trying to intimidate batsman . . . I want him to be aware that if he gets on the front foot against me he might find himself in trouble – in other words he might get hurt. But that is quite a different thing from actually *wanting* or intending to hurt him.'[56] Intimidation, however, had long been a key element of fast bowling. Harold Larwood, the England fast bowler of the 1920s and 1930s and the main prong of the England bodyline attack against Australia in 1932–3, said that when a fast bowler drops 'one short everybody knows the ball is intended to intimidate, to unsettle, to test the batsman's combination of skill and nerve.'[57] In the mid 1970s the Australian fast bowlers Dennis Lillee and Jeff Thomson were more outspoken in public than any West Indian fast bowlers about their intention to intimidate batsmen. Lillee was reported to have said that he bowled bouncers 'to hit the batsman and thus intimidate him . . . I try to hit a batsman in the rib-cage . . . I want it to hurt, so that the batsman doesn't want to face me any more.' Thomson was supposed to have said that he enjoyed hitting a batsman more than getting him out and was not worried by seeing a batsman 'rolling around screaming and blood on the pitch'.[58] West Indian bowlers did not boast in public of an intention to hurt batsmen. When the West Indies used bouncers it was condemned as brutalizing cricket and robbing the game of its variety and subtlety, yet there was little outcry as other countries tried to emulate these West Indian tactics.

White cricket writers did not condemn the tactics of West Indian teams in such insulting terms as those of Sunil Gavaskar but occasional comments in *Wisden Cricket Monthly* in the early 1990s were phrased in a way that West Indians found offensive. In 1990 it printed a letter that argued that until 'We [i.e. England] can breed 7 ft. monsters willing to break bones and shatter faces, we cannot compete against these threatening West Indians. Even the umpires are scared that the devilish-looking Richards might put a voodoo sign on them!' In 1991, David Frith, editor of *Wisden Cricket Monthly,* argued that matches with the West Indies had become a manifestation of the racial tensions outside cricket, and instead of being occasions 'when cricketers of both sides should be teaching ordinary people how to co-exist and enjoy honourable sports combat, a damaging counter-image emerges' which undermined the capacity of sport to promote ethnic harmony.[59] Frith's comments were given great prominence in the *Daily Mirror,* which led Chris Lane, manager of *Wisden Cricket Monthly,* to claim that Frith had not called the West Indies racist and to

56. *Cricketer International,* August 1985, p. 15.
57. McDonald, *Clive Lloyd,* p. 110.
58. Wilde, *Letting Rip,* pp. 36–7.
59. *Wisden Cricket Monthly,* June 1991, p. 3.

accuse the *Daily Mirror* of sensationalizing and misrepresenting Frith. The West Indian batsman Desmond Haynes thought that the *Wisden Cricket Monthly* had 'been racist, but then the *Mirror* made it worse.'[60] To Nigel Carter writing in *Caribbean Times* Frith's comments were 'a wonderful example of how the neo-colonial mentality turns things on its head. Thus Westindies were not victims of the sledging, or defending themselves against racist intimidation from Australia's test team. According to Frith they were the source of racism.' The editor of *Caribbean Times* argued that those who thought like Frith and the *Daily Mirror* 'should just reconcile themselves to the fact that The Empire is striking back. They should sit up, sit back and enjoy the game.'[61] It is not clear how many whites in English cricket shared the views expressed in *Wisden Cricket Monthly* but it was one of the UK's leading cricket magazines. Given the legacy of slavery, the forms of oppression and exploitation which black African-Caribbeans had suffered from whites and the everyday instances of racism which those of African-Caribbean descent faced daily in Britain, it is not surprising that they saw the condemnation of the West Indies for using tactics which others used or tried to emulate as racist.

Spectators and Jungle Drumming

The criticisms that West Indian teams received in England were extended to condemn the behaviour of their supporters at matches in England. The test series against England in 1950, the first which the West Indies won against England in England, was also the first watched by relatively high numbers of African-Caribbeans following the beginning of migration to Britain in 1948. When the West Indies won at Lord's, their first test victory in England, West Indian supporters invaded the pitch immediately after the match in celebration. Such behaviour was welcomed rather than criticized by the English cricket establishment. *Wisden* even included a photograph of West Indian spectators with the heading 'Victory calypso' and a caption which said 'they invaded the ground, danced and sang calypsos.'

By the 1970s and 1980s many more African-Caribbeans were attending England-West Indies test matches in England and they brought Caribbean styles of spectating to cricket in England. The black West Indian style of watching cricket was far different from the English tradition with its emphasis on reserve, politeness, passivity and the avoidance of displays of undue passion, though it is not difficult to provide instances when white English cricket crowds have behaved very differently. For African-Caribbean spectators, watching cricket has been a means of participating in the match.

60. Steen, *Desmond Haynes,* p. 24.
61. *Caribbean Times,* 4 June 1991.

Richard Burton has argued that what 'gives West Indian cricket its unique Creole character is, precisely, the interplay of players, spectators and crowd.' Burton shows that in other forms of black West Indian culture, such as church services and carnivals, the distinction between performer and spectator has often been so blurred that spectating is participation, an essential part of the performance.[62] Burton has also demonstrated how traditions of spectating in the Caribbean have connections with cultural forms that asserted black identity and challenges to white privilege. After the abolition of slavery, carnival in Trinidad became a festival of black liberation. In Burton's view, the black stars of West Indian cricket are 'carnival kings and princes of the people, symbolic subverters and destroyers of a world where white is might and, as such, embodiments of a dream-world which, by identification and projection, every black west Indian, be he never so poor, is monarch for the day.' Burton also sees spectating as an extension of the black male cultural space of the street. The street culture with its emphasis on style, being cool, reputation, competition and aggression is projected into the cricket crowd behaviour of jesting, expansiveness, camaraderie, sometimes unruliness, and 'ostentatiously contemptuous defiance of the opposition'. For black West Indian spectators crowd noise creates a 'cathartic experience of controlled, directed violence', particularly so when supporting fast bowlers. The use of musical instruments by spectators, especially whistles and even more particularly drums, can be related to struggles for a black identity and for political equality. Brian Stoddart has shown that in nineteenth-century Barbados, African rhythms of music and instruments such as drums and whistles were 'essentially both a rejection of a white culture and the defence of a black one'.[63] African-Caribbean styles of cricket spectating were political in that they celebrated black identity and were part of the struggle to assert black control over cricket in the West Indies.

By the 1970s and 1980s many English whites were far more critical of the conduct of West Indian spectators than they had been in 1950. In 1976 an article in the *Cricketer* asked whether it was 'really beyond the wit of ground authorities to put a stop, by "conditions of entry", confiscation of instruments, or even mobilisation of public opinion, to the jungle drumming and other non-cricket noises that must surely exasperate thousands of paying spectators and hundreds of distant watchers? They might begin by calling for a couple of doctors to certify the man with the whistle.' The writer continued 'No racist prejudice here, by the way. There was a whole gaggle of white children at it with cans at Headingley on Saturday – in front

62. Burton, R.E.D. (1995)'Cricket, Carnival and Street Culture', in Beckles, H. McD. and Stoddart, B. (eds), *Liberation Cricket: West Indies Cricket Culture,* Manchester: Manchester University Press, pp. 91, 97.

63. B. Stoddart, 'Cricket, Social Formation and Cultural Continuity in Barbados: A Preliminary Ethnohistory', in Beckles, *Liberation Cricket*, p. 65.

of the scoreboard of course, to ensure maximum TV coverage for their moronic antics. And some of my best friends are white.'[64] The article was accompanied with a photograph showing a black spectator playing a drum. The caption to the photograph mentioned that 'the drumming and the can-clanging have become a major source of irritation during play.' Whilst *The Cricketer* may not have agreed with the views of its writer, it clearly did not consider that they were so offensive as to deny them publication though many West Indians may well have detected racist undertones in comments such as 'jungle drumming.' In 1987, after criticising Pakistani spectators for identifying with 'fanatical frenzy' with the Pakistan team, the editor of *Wisden Cricket Monthly* welcomed a ban on 'lethal flag-sticks and banners and noise-making instruments, which are such a nuisance and an incitement to crazy behaviour'. *Asian Times* saw attempts to control the behaviour of spectators supporting teams other than England as an establishment move to seize control of the game from 'the masses' and 'an "old farts" counter- revolution'.[65] The novelist Diran Adibayo thought that racism in cricket was expressed 'more subtly' than that in football, but that 'combined with snobbery, it can make grounds a very unwelcoming environment for black people'. By 1995 fluorescent signs at The Oval, a ground where traditionally large numbers of African-Caribbeans had watched West Indian test teams, stated that 'Alcoholic drinks, other than small amounts, whistles, drums, sirens and other instruments likely to cause unwanted noise MAY NOT be taken into the ground. Police and stewards may search spectators outside the ground and refuse entry to those carrying the above.'[66]

Supporting the West Indian teams in the 1970s and 1980s in a flamboyantly West Indian style can be interpreted as a product of the racism in British society. The West Indian cricket writer Clayton Goodwin pointed out that black frustrations over social and economic deprivation and 'restricted opportunity in housing, education and ambition' were 'almost tangible'. He wrote that 'the put-upon black people of Britain . . . feeling similar justifiable pride when Viv Richards and his team, who in other circumstances might be regarded as "second-class citizens" like themselves, have put one over on the heroes of their detractors.' For Goodwin it 'ill-behoves those brought up on the cream teas and manicured lawns of prep schools, or resident now in the stockbroker belt, to lecture on the form of loyalty to a specific society should take.'[67] The participatory nature of black West Indian cricket spectating meant that spectators could feel part of the world conquering West Indian team.

---

64. *Cricketer International,* September 1976, p. 17.
65. *Asian Times,* 19 August 1995.
66. *Asian Times,* 2 September 1995.
67. *Wisden Cricket Monthly,* August 1991, p. 8.

By the 1990s criticism of traditional Caribbean styles of cricket spectatorship seemed to have contributed to the decline in the numbers of black spectators watching test matches in England. By 1995 a writer in *Caribbean Times,* noting that far fewer black spectators were attending England-West Indies test matches in England, blamed this on higher ticket prices and the banning of whistles, horns, drums and bare torsos.[68] The recommendation of the English Cricket Board's Report *Going Forward Together,* published in 1999, that unless the attitude of the cricket establishment to banners, singing, musical instruments changed, those from the ethnic minorities would eventually transfer their 'inherent interest' in cricket to other sports seems to confirm that West Indian supporters had been offended by the criticisms of their behaviour.[69]

It is very probable that most whites who criticized the black West Indian style of cricket spectating did not imagine that their attitudes could be interpreted as belittling cultural forms with which African-Caribbeans had resisted white oppression and struggled for political recognition and equality. Their criticisms often stressed that irritation with the noise made by black spectators made watching cricket less pleasant. They also criticized the conduct of white Australian cricket crowds, especially the drinking and what seemed to be a bloodlust in support of Australian fast bowlers in the floodlit matches arranged by Kerry Packer. Their criticisms implied that traditional white English forms of spectator behaviour were the correct way to watch cricket and given the long history of white exploitation of blacks, such attitudes could easily have been interpreted by black West Indians as an expression, albeit an unconscious expression, of white supremacy. Some white critics of West Indian cricket crowd behaviour may have been stimulated by a dislike of coloured immigrants and fears that they would subvert what was imagined to be the traditional white British way of life, but such criticisms were hardly ever voiced in a cricketing context.

Denigrating Black West Indian Achievement

For many black West Indians cricket has long been a vital strand of their quest for political rights and equality with whites. C.L.R. James' writings argued that cricket in the Caribbean has always carried deep political and cultural significance. In 1963 James wrote that for a West Indian, consciousness of his history was 'a product of his cricket in a very definite sense. 'In Britain', he claimed

---

68. *Caribbean Times*, 16 September 1995.

69. *Clean Bowl Racism: 'Going Forward Together'*, (1999), London: ECB Racism Study Group, pp. 20–1.

Drake and Mighty Nelson, Shakespeare, the Charge of the Light Brigade, the success of parliamentary democracy, the few who did so much for so many, these constitute a continuous national tradition. Underdeveloped, newly independent countries have to go back many decades, sometimes centuries to find one. The West Indian people have none, at least none that they know about. To such people, Ramadhin and Valentine . . . the three Barbados batsmen whose names begin with W, the front page scoring of cricketers like Garfield Sobers and Rohan Kanhai fill gnawing gaps in their consciousness and in their needs.[70]

It has already mentioned how Michael Manley, Prime Minister of Jamaica from 1972 to 1980, has claimed that by demonstrating that blacks could be superior to whites, the batting of George Headley in test cricket between the wars boosted the self-belief of African-Caribbeans from the most deprived sections of West Indian society and so did much to promote the support for trade unionism, suffrage reform and Marcus Garvey's campaigns for black rights.[71] The appointment of Frank Worrell as captain of the West Indian team for a whole series in 1960, for which C.L.R. James had campaigned in the *Nation,* carried a symbolic importance for African-Caribbeans which went far beyond the cricket field. Growing black control over West Indian cricket was both a cause and a register of black political and social attainment in the Caribbean. Viv Richards, captain of the West Indies from 1985 until 1991, saw West Indian cricket achievement as promoting black liberation in general. In 1995 he wrote 'In my own way, I would like to think that I carried my bat for the liberation of African and other oppressed people everywhere.'[72] Hilary McD. Beckles, the African-Caribbean cricket historian, has written that when Richards batted at Lord's, he

intimidated, mocked and perhaps humiliated such gatherings. It was political; he said so, and I knew it. The score had to be settled . . . Each century, each double century, peeled away the optic scales accumulated over 400 years of inhuman subjection. The English were thrown into panic . . . because they sensed that with Richards it was more than sport; it was the business of history and politics – the struggle against injustice and inequality. We assisted them to understand those things by our unfettered spectator responses . . . I understood then the potence and social importance of strategic solidarity at the frontier.[73]

70. C.L.R. James, 'Cricket in West Indian Culture', *New Society,* 36, 6 June 1963.

71. For a discussion of Garvey's political philosophy and activities, see Jacques-Garvey, A. (1980), *Philosophy and Opinions of Marcus Garvey,* New York: Athenaeum, and Lewis, R., (1987), *Marcus Garvey: Anti-Colonial Champion,* London: Karia.

72. V. Richards, 'Foreword' in Beckles, *Liberation Cricket,* p. vii.

73. Beckles, H. McD. (1998), *The Development of West Indies Cricket: Volume 1: The Age of Nationalism,* London: Pluto, pp. 86–7.

The world leadership of cricket by the West Indies under Lloyd and Richards had carried black assertiveness and confidence to new heights, not only in the Caribbean but for those living in Britain.

In the last quarter of the twentieth century the economies of the Caribbean islands faced severe economic difficulties and the widespread poverty which accompanies underinvestment and debt repayment. The islands were among the poorest parts of the Western hemisphere. Yet in test cricket the West Indies were world leaders. As the West Indian cricket broadcaster and writer Tony Cozier said 'We are not under-developed or third world in cricket.'[74] For Viv Richards all Third World peoples could share in the West Indian domination of test cricket. He said that 'we in the third world who do not have a great deal to shout about in material terms, should take pride in what our people achieve . . . if you do well in one particular job, playing cricket or so, it's nice to let the brothers share in your achievement.' When the West Indies played in London before crowds including many of African-Caribbean descent, the players felt 'We must not let these people down.'[75] Domination of world cricket could be regarded all the more as an outstanding black achievement because it repre-sented black supremacy in a sport invented by English whites and which, by being conflated with notions of morality and selflessness, had been a key strand in the justifications for imperial power and control over those with other ethnic origins. The condemnation by so many whites in English cricket of the West Indian mastery of world cricket was a denigration of black attainment and a disparagement of one of the major grounds on which blacks had achieved political rights. Belittling cricket achievement seemed to negate black claims for equality with whites. For many African-Caribbeans in England the white response to the West Indian domination of world cricket confirmed the racist prejudices of white British society. As the editor of *Caribbean Times* wrote 'What is even more sinister is the attempt to rubbish the whole of the Caribbean through carping and slighting at one of the areas where our people have excelled against the odds . . . More than any others we have had to come up the hard way – and having battled heroically until we reached the top, it is hurtful and, intemperate and malicious for others to accuse us of vengeful violence and other unsubstantiated transgressions against the good name of the game.'[76]

74. Savidge and McLennan, *Real Quick,* p. 181.
75. McDonald, T. (1984), *Viv Richards: The Authorised Biography,* London: Pelham, p. 99.
76. *Caribbean Times,* 4 June 1991.

–6–

'Pak Off the Cheats'

Fierce competitiveness and ill feeling have often characterized international cricket but in the 1980s and 1990s test matches between England and Pakistan in particular were surrounded with bitterness, suspicion and recrimination. In 1996 the former England player Derek Pringle wrote of 'Pakistan as the side most likely to get the blood bubbling' and of England–Pakistan matches being 'filled with acrimony as old prejudices surface'.[1] To many Pakistanis the tensions of England-Pakistan cricket stemmed from assumptions of moral superiority among the white English and seemed to be a continuation of racist attitudes that had sustained the Raj.

Since the start of test cricket between England and Pakistan in the 1950s, Pakistan teams had felt slighted by English cricket. Mihir Bose, the Indian-born sports writer, has argued that the half-hearted praise from English cricket for Pakistan squaring the test series on their first tour of England in 1954, and especially as no other country had won a test match on its first tour of England, convinced Pakistanis that the 'audacity of a former colony, brown at that, to achieve a test victory was too much for the white sahibs. Ever since . . . Pakistanis have always felt that whatever they do they will never be able to win the unqualified approval of the English.' Each subsequent tour reinforced national stereotypes.[2] In 1956 the England A party touring Pakistan threw a bucket of water over the Pakistan umpire Idris Beg. Some accounts mentioned that they sprayed him with a hose pipe and more recently it has been said that he was 'captured, debagged and dunked in a swimming pool',[3] which perhaps illustrates how subsequent ill-feeling between Pakistan and England teams has caused the offensiveness of the incident to become magnified in the folk memory of Pakistan cricket followers. Although the England players had meant this as a joke, or at least claimed that it was meant as a joke, the sense of outrage in Pakistan led Lord Alexander, president of the MCC, to offer to terminate the tour. The appointment of Donald Carr, who had been captain of the A party in 1956, as manager of the MCC tour of Pakistan in 1973, was seen as offensive by many Pakistanis. In 1974 inadequate covering of the wicket at Lord's had caused Pakistan to bat on a

1. *Independent,* 24 July 1996.
2. Bose, M. (1996), *The Sporting Alien: English Sport's Lost Camelot,* London and Edinburgh: Mainstream, p. 198.
3. *London Review of Books,* 15 July, p. 30.

pitch so helpful to bowlers that the last seven wickets of the Pakistan second innings fell for only thirty-four runs, leaving England to score only sixty runs to win though further rain caused the match to be drawn. Pakistani players and supporters believed that a wrong decision by an English umpire had prevented Pakistan from winning the 1982 test series in England. Tony Lewis, a former England captain, cricket journalist and broadcaster, MCC committee member from 1992 until 1998 and MCC president from 1998 to 2000, observed that in 1992 Pakistan had come to England 'with all the sensitivity of the small nation wounded by repeated taunts of sharp practice. It was inevitable that they would arm themselves with a list of past injustices: that is what proud nations do.'[4]

Animosities between England and Pakistan were most intense during the England tour of Pakistan in 1987 and the Pakistan tour of England in 1992. In 1987 the belief of the England players and tour management that Pakistani umpires were systematically cheating to ensure that Pakistan won the series erupted into an ugly confrontation between the England captain Mike Gatting and umpire Shakoor Rana just before the close of the second day of the second test match at Faisalabad. Rana was reported to have called Gatting a 'f***, cheating c***' whilst Gatting replied that Rana was a 'shit awful umpire'. The next day there was no play because Rana refused to take the field until Gatting apologized to him. This was the only occasion in test cricket when a day's play had been lost because of an umpire's refusal to take the field. The England players gave Gatting their full support and threatened a strike. Play resumed on the following day when Gatting, after being ordered by the TCCB, sent a written apology to Rana. This was written on a scrap of paper and could be described as a most cursory apology. There are suggestions that the British government had pressurized the TCCB to ensure that the match was restarted. The 1992 series in England was marred by the response of the Pakistani players to a caution issued by the England umpire Roy Palmer at the Old Trafford test to the Pakistani bowler Aqib Javed, which appeared to many British journalists as unseemly as the Gatting-Shakoor Rana confrontation in Faisalabad. At the Headingley test even English observers felt that mistakes by the English umpires had a key role in England's victory but Pakistani players saw this as cheating by the English umpires. Throughout the summer there were English suspicions that the Pakistan fast bowlers Wasim Akram and Waqar Younis were achieving reverse swing by illicit tampering with the ball. Just after the final limited overs international at Lord's the England batsman Allan Lamb wrote in the *Daily Mirror* that the Pakistani bowlers had been cheating all summer by illegally gouging one side of the ball. Lamb's allegations led to two libel cases – the first between Lamb and Sarfraz Nawaz and the second between Imran Khan and Lamb and Ian Botham.

---

4. *Sunday Telegraph*, 30 August 1992.

English Perceptions of Pakistan Cricket

Personal animosities among players provoked ill feeling between England and Pakistan teams. Many in English cricket admired Imran Khan and thought that relations between England and Pakistani teams were better when he was captain. Tony Lewis was reported to have said in 1987 that 'Imran kept matters very much under control when he was captain. He is better educated than some, but now we are down with the alley cats.'[5] In 1992 Christopher Martin-Jenkins, editor of the *Cricketer,* wrote in the *Daily Telegraph* that whilst Imran had 'never been backward when it came to criticising umpires', he feared Imran's 'calming influence' would be missed.[6] But not all in English cricket shared this view of Imran. Ian Botham and Imran Khan respected each other's playing abilities but Botham felt sufficiently incensed by comments made about him by Imran in an Indian magazine that he sued Imran for libel. Javed Miandad, captain of Pakistan for the 1987 series in Pakistan and for the tour of England in 1992, and Haseeb Ahsan, manager of Pakistan in 1987, attracted bitter antagonism in English cricket. Miandad admitted to being an intensely competitive cricketer. In 1992 he was reported to have said 'Of course I am a fighter. I adore to fight all the time . . . It doesn't worry me that I've been branded the wild man of cricket. I'll tell your test stars Ian Botham and David Gower they're lousy cricketers if it helps Pakistan grind England's noses in the dirt. Cricket is a game of psychological warfare and there is a lot of bad-mouthing out there. I admit I am one of the worst. I hate people getting runs against Pakistan and I'll do anything – yes, anything – to stop them.' The Pakistan fast bowler Wasim Akram who played in 1987 series thought that it suited Miandad to have England furious about the Pakistan umpires in 1987 because this reduced the effectiveness of England as a team.[7] The former England cricketer Colin Milburn called Miandad the Colonel Gadaffi of cricket.[8] Tony Lewis said that Miandad and Haseeb Ahsan would 'take Pakistan cricket to further depths . . . they will certainly smile and shake your hand but that is all part of their duplicity. I think Miandad is a terrible ringleader. If people think Mike Gatting is cheating then Miandad is unbelievable. He gets up to every trick in the book.'[9] In 1987 Mike Selvey, the former England player and *Guardian* cricket journalist, claimed that Haseeb Ahsan had been responsible for Miandad's selection as captain and described them 'as "thick" as in thieves'.[10] In 1988 the cricket fanzine *Sticky Wicket,* published in England, produced a satirical article about Ahsan,

5. *Daily Mirror,* 15 December 1987.

6. *Daily Telegraph,* 24 August 1992.

7. Wasim Akram, (1998), *Wasim: The Autobiography of Wasim Akram,* London: Judy Piatkus, p. 42.

8. *Sun,* 22 July 1992.

9. *Sun,* 15 December 1987.

10. *Guardian,* 22 December 1987.

mentioning that he had written *I Was Sent Home for Having a Bent Arm* (Moron Publications), *Chip on the Shoulder* (Banana Republic Enterprises) and *I Was Javed's Dad,* (Devious & Co.) and attributing to him such quotations as 'Javed Miandad can do anything include dispute decisions, hang around & talk it over with the opposition, threaten Dennis Lillee. He is from a minority, an oppressed species . . . a group that no one likes. It is only fair that he has some advantages.'[11] Such comments were more a symptom than a cause of the ill-feeling between England and Pakistan. It is unlikely that Miandad was more competitive or indulged in sledging more often than Australia's Chappell brothers but they did not attract such vituperative comments in English cricket.

English cricket saw Pakistan cricket as riddled with cheating. There was a long-held belief that Pakistani umpires, with the encouragement of Pakistan captains and officials favoured Pakistan teams on a scale that constituted cheating. The conviction that Pakistan players and officials colluded with umpires to cheat was found even at the summit of English cricket. In an interview published in 1990 Raman Subba Row, chairman of the TCCB, said of 1987 that 'the cheating was aided and abetted by the Pakistani officials – oh, absolutely, absolutely! There is no doubt. It was a carefully conceived plan.'[12] Although the TCCB ordered Gatting to apologize to Shakoor Rana, the decision of Subba Row and Alan Smith, the chief executive of the TCCB, to award each of the England players a bonus of £1,000 could have meant they thought that the umpires had been cheating though this may have been a tactic to persuade the players to call off their threatened strike. The England players seem to have arrived in Pakistan expecting that the Pakistani umpires would be biased against them. After the first test that England lost by an innings, Gatting was reputed to have said 'We knew roughly what to expect but never imagined that it would be quite so blatant. They were desperate to win a Test match, but if I was them I wouldn't be very happy about the way they did it.' 'The bad decisions went against us by 10–1' Gatting added, 'I've never seen it so blatant over here. To put an inexperienced umpire into the first Test on a turning pitch, and even without first informing us, smacks of something.'[13]

The cricket journalists from England covering the 1987 tour seem to have thought that the Pakistan umpiring was so biased as to be cheating or bordering on cheating. John Woodcock of *The Times* was probably the journalist most reluctant to condemn the Pakistan umpiring but just after the tour he wrote there were two ways of looking at umpiring in Pakistan – the Tom Graveney way which believed that Pakistan had been cheating for thirty-five years and the Tony Lewis way which believed that

---

11. *Sticky Wicket,* April/May 1988, p. 3.

12. Bose, M. (1990), *Cricket Voices: Interviews with Mihir Bose,* London: Kingswood, p. 23.

13. *Wisden Cricketers' Almanack 1989,* London: John Wisden, p. 910; *Guardian,* 30 November 1987.

Pakistani umpires were unsatisfactory but unbiased. Having toured Pakistan more than any other British cricket journalist, Woodcock had always preferred the Lewis view because it was 'infinitely more restful' but after Faisalabad he was doing so with less confidence, especially as 'it was hard not to think of Shakoor Rana as a puppet, put in to pick a quarrel with the England side that had accused the umpires of cheating in Lahore'[14] where the first test had been played. In the *Guardian* Mike Selvey wrote that Miandad and Haseeb Ahsan had 'concocted a lethal cocktail out of Qadir's genius, turning pitches and sympathetic umpiring. Shakeel Khan and Shakoor Rana [the umpires] were a disgrace.'[15] The *Cricketer* and *Wisden Cricket Monthly* each assumed that the Pakistani umpiring had been questionable. Christopher Martin-Jenkins, editor of the *Cricketer,* wrote that 'In the case of Shakeel Khan and Shakoor Rana, the England team had reason to view them with suspicion and there were enough poor decisions in the event to suggest that the suspicion was well-founded.'[16] In the February issue of *Wisden Cricket Monthly,* whose front page photograph showed Shakoor Rana wearing a Pakistan test cap, the editor David Frith wrote that those who 'had no true idea of the conspiratorial nature of umpiring there now have no excuse for not being fully appraised.' He called 'Miandad the captain; the umpires are the lance-corporals.'[17]

Prominent figures from English cricket who had not been in Pakistan accepted that the Pakistani umpires had been cheating and that this was only to have been expected. Tom Graveney told the *Daily Mirror* that 'When you go to the sub-continent you know for sure that two things will happen. You will suffer Delhi belly – and you will get done by the umpires.' In his opinion, 'Claims of cheating by Pakistani players are nothing new. They have been doing it since 1951 when I first toured there. But it has got worse and worse and the time has come to call a halt. Enough is enough . . . It's important we don't sink to the Pakistani level.'[18] Ian Botham said 'I've seen some of the decisions on TV and quite honestly you wouldn't believe them on the village green, let alone Test cricket. I wouldn't think Gatt would react the way he did unless he had a genuine axe to grind. The players have my sympathy. I have played there and know what can happen.'[19]

There was a widespread conviction in English cricket that the Pakistan umpires with the connivance of Pakistan officials had been cheating in 1987, but the conduct of Gatting and his players was criticized. Even those who had no doubt that Gatting had been provoked beyond endurance took the line that Gatting had been wrong to

14. *The Times,* 10, 23 December 1987.
15. *Guardian,* 22 December 1987.
16. *Cricketer International,* January 1988, p. 3.
17. *Wisden Cricket Monthly,* January 1988, p. 3, February 1988, p. 3.
18. *Daily Mirror,* 10 December 1987.
19. *Daily Mirror,* 10 December 1987.

lose his temper with Shakoor Rana. When the England party arrived home Gatting, while still indignant about being sworn at by Shakoor Rana, admitted that perhaps he had been unwise to be come involved with the umpire[20] and in 1988 conceded that arguing with umpires on a cricket pitch 'wasn't the right thing to do'.[21] Even some of the journalists who sympathised with Gatting in Faisalabad criticized the behaviour of the England players in the final test at Karachi. The former England batsman Colin Milburn thought that there had been 'blatant provocation' in the first two tests but that in the third test at Karachi the England players 'seemed hell bent on aggro . . . The events at Faisalabad . . . seemed to have drained them of any self-discipline.'[22] John Woodcock thought that had Gatting's display of disagreement with the rejection of an England appeal for a catch at the wicket occurred at Lord's, the England captain would have been 'for the high jump' and added that if 'this goes on, there will be no reason for Pakistan ever again to take the slightest notice of what England say about how the game should be played.'[23] The *Daily Mail* wrote of 'England's disgrace', 'acts of downright petulance' and 'churlish behaviour' and of Gatting challenging the umpire's authority 'with ill-mannered arm-waving over one rejected appeal' and with showing 'incredulity when given out leg before'.[24]

The 1992 series showed again the depth of the assumption in English cricket that Pakistani teams were habitual cheats. Pakistan won this series largely because England batsmen could not cope with the reverse swing of the fast bowlers Wasim Akram and Waqar Younis. There were suspicions in English cricket that the Pakistani bowlers had been able to achieve reverse swing by illicitly roughing and gouging one side of a ball with their nails or possible something like a bottle top. In 1991 an editorial in the *Cricketer* mentioned reverse swing being talked about in England 'behind closed doors in county dressing rooms' and that the method of obtaining reverse swing was 'widely believed to have emanated from Pakistan, but is certainly not confined to that country.'[25] During the third test at Old Trafford in 1992 Mike Langley wrote in the *Daily Mirror* of 'England's ineradicable curiosity about how Pakistani bowlers can swing a worn ball on days when new ones don't deviate.'[26] During the lunch interval of the final limited-overs international at Lord's in August umpires John Hampshire and Ken Palmer changed the ball being used by the Pakistan bowlers but the match referee Deryck Murray, a former West Indian test cricketer,

---

20. *The Times,* 23 December 1987.

21. Gatting, M. and Patmore, A. (1988), *Leading from the Front,* London: Macdonald Queen Anne, p. 184.

22. *Sun,* 23 December 1987.

23. *The Times,* 21 December 1987.

24. *Daily Mail,* 21 December 1987.

25. *Cricketer International,* January 1991, p. 3.

26. *Daily Mirror,* 8 July 1992.

refused to say why the ball had been changed. The Pakistan manger Intikhab claimed that it been changed not because it had been tampered with but because it had gone soft. Matters came to a head when Allan Lamb, the white South African-born England batsman, gave an interview to Colin Price printed in the *Daily Mirror* under the massive headline HOW PAKISTAN CHEAT AT CRICKET. Wasim and Waqar, Lamb claimed, 'have been getting away with murder all summer' and that 'it was a well-known fact among the players all over the country' that the Pakistanis were tampering with the ball. He explained that the Pakistan bowlers scuffed one side of the ball and disguised this with sweat, a trick which Safraz Nawaz, another Pakistani fast bowler, had shown him some years earlier when they both played for Northamptonshire. 'It's got to be stopped', Lamb continued, 'and the great shame is that Wasim and Waqar are truly great bowlers, but there will forever be a stain on their achievements . . . I've watched all the matches closely and been totally pissed off by what I saw.' Lamb seemed to imply that the ball was changed at Lord's because Pakistani players had deliberately scoured one side of it.[27] In September 1992 Lamb was fined £5,000 by the TCCB for disregarding its regulation prohibiting players from making unauthorized public statements, a sum equal to that imposed on Gatting for making unauthorized statements about his row with Shakoor Rana in 1988. Lamb was also fined and banned from two matches by Northamptonshire, his county club. In November, after an appeal from Lamb, the Cricket Council reduced the TCCB fine to £4,000 with half of this to be suspended for two years. Lamb's solicitor had said that Lamb had not been paid for the *Mirror* articles, but added that 'any money which did accrue' would be paid to the Cystic Fibrosis Trust.[28]

Many in English cricket saw Lamb's accusations as confirmation of the Pakistani tendency to cheat. Mike Selvey wrote in the *Guardian* that from 'the moment the tourists arrived here there seems to have been a determination in some quarters to hang the "cheats" label on them.'[29] A *Daily Mirror* headline on 27 August referred to '"Cheat" bowlers'. In the *Daily Mirror*, C. Price and F. Wiechula wrote that Lamb was 'slowly being spit-roasted for his bravery in simply telling *Daily Mirror* readers the truth – that Pakistan tampered with the ball.'[30] In November 1993, just after Safraz Nawaz had withdrawn his libel action against Lamb for suggesting that he had shown Lamb how to obtain reverse swing by illicitly roughing up one side of a ball, Ian Botham, who, along with the England batsman Robin Smith, had been prepared to give evidence on Lamb's behalf, was reported to have asked the TCCB

27. *Daily Mirror,* 26 August 1992.
28. *The Times,* 24 September, 21 November 1992.
29. *Guardian,* 27 August 1992.
30. *Daily Mirror,* 28 August 1992.

'Once and for all why don't you tell the world officially what the Pakistanis were up to in the summer of 1992? . . . Everyone raved about their bowlers. But the ball-tampering activities were flushed out by Lambie's revelations, and now in the High Court – so possibly those games will be seen in a different light.'[31] Jack Russell, on the other hand, who played in three tests against Pakistan in 1992, could not recall talk in the England dressing room about Pakistani ball tampering.[32]

The widespread suspicions that cheating was endemic in Pakistan cricket were linked to dissatisfaction with cricket authorities' conduct in 1987 and 1992. English cricket journalists in 1987 were almost unanimous in arguing that the TCCB should have given Gatting more support. *The Times* discussed in great detail the manoeuvring which led the TCCB to order Gatting to apologize to Shakoor Rana but avoided direct comment on the desirability of this although the argument of David Miller, its chief sports correspondent, that abandoning the tour would show to the Pakistani authorities that England were not prepared to play 'under such conditions of moral duress' can be taken as a rejection of the TCCB line that the tour had to be completed.[33] Mike Selvey wrote in the *Guardian* 'That Gatting was grossly wronged is not in doubt. First he was insulted by an untrustworthy umpire and then let down by the TCCB.'[34] Martin Johnson of the *Independent* described ordering Gatting to apologise as 'pathetic, even by the Test and County Cricket Board's own remarkable standards . . . The shabbiest figures are the TCCB's chairman, Raman Subba Row, the chairman of their overseas tours committee Doug Insole, and their secretary Alan Smith.' When firm action was called for – and few here doubt that it should have been cancellation of the tour – they sold their team and management down the river.'[35] The *Daily Express* carried a front page headline GATTING'S HUMILIATION. The page one Opinion column of the *Sun* proclaimed that 'What the country wants and the Sun demands – is TOTAL support from the Government' and complained that 'the spineless bunch on the Test and Cricket Board would betray our team.'[36] The *Daily Mirror* article about Gatting being forced to apologize had the headline NO BALLS and a *Mirror* editorial stressed that the TCCB had 'bought peace of a kind, but it is peace without honour, a soiled compromise that will not, and does not, deserve to last.'[37]

In 1992 the ICC rather than the TCCB was criticized for not taking a stronger line with the supposed cheating by Pakistan, though it is probable that many followers

31. *Daily Mirror,* 19 November 1993.

32. Russell, J. (1997), *Unleashed,* London: Collins Willow, p. 128.

33. *The Times,* 10 December 1987.

34. *Guardian,* 22 December 1987.

35. Green A. (ed.) (1997), *Can't Bat, Can't Bowl, Can't Field: The Best Cricket Writings of Martin Johnson,* London: Collins Willow, pp. 116–17.

36. *Sun,* 12 December 1987.

37. *Daily Mirror,* 12 December 1987.

of cricket in England may not have not have been aware of the difference between the ICC and the TCCB, especially as Sir Colin Cowdrey, very much an establishment figure of English cricket, was chairman of the ICC and the ICC offices were at Lord's. Almost all the British press condemned the ICC decision not to reveal why the ball had been changed in the Lord's one-day international but often placed this in a context that included disparaging comments about Pakistanis. Some sections of the press suspected that the ICC was afraid of offending the Pakistani tourists. The *Daily Mirror* thought that Lamb would be fined in order to 'appease those prickly Pakistanis'.[38] The Conservative government, it was rumoured, had wanted the matter handled 'delicately so as not to upset the Pakistani community in this country.' In the *Daily Mail* it was argued that Lamb's interview had appeared when the TCCB was hoping that the heat would die down and was anxious to repair the damage done by the Shakoor Rana-Gatting affair.[39] Pat Sheehan and John Etheridge in the *Sun* wrote that the ICC 'are scared stiff of officially accusing the volatile Pakistanis of cheating because it could provoke a furious reaction. The ICC are even worried that the world champions might leave before their tour is over.'[40] When the ICC announced that the umpires' report on the state of the ball would not be made public, a *Sun* headline read:

INDECISIVE
COWARDLY
CLOWNS

and John Etheridge wrote that 'the pathetic failure of the ICC has left everyone in limbo. What a load of BALLS.'[41] Mike Langley of the *Daily Mirror* wrote that 'Gouging the ball is now a lesser crime in cricket than rocking the boat,' and that Allan Lamb 'has done for England what our bluff John Bulls once did so readily for themselves . . . Mince no words. Tell the truth – and damn the consequences.'[42] By not explaining why the ball had been changed the ICC neither confirmed nor denied Lamb's allegations, but an argument put forward by Christopher Martin-Jenkins in the *Daily Telegraph* may explain why the ICC made no comment. According to the rules of international limited-overs cricket, a ball changed for ball tampering could be replaced only by one in an inferior condition, but a ball that had merely gone out of shape had to replaced by one with the same degree of wear. The ball used at Lord's had been replaced by one in the same condition, which should have meant

38. *Daily Mirror,* 27 August 1992.
39. *Daily Mail,* 27 August 1992.
40. *Sun,* 25 August 1992.
41. *Sun,* 29 August 1992.
42. *Daily Mirror,* 27 August 1992.

that the ball had not been tampered with. Martin-Jenkins thought that the umpires may not have been familiar with the intricacies of these rules and a public statement that the ball had been changed because of tampering but not replaced by one in an inferior condition could have led to the ICC becoming embroiled in an expensive legal action.[43] At the Sarfraz's libel action in 1993, Don Oslear, the third umpire for the Lord's limited overs match, stated that the ball had been changed because it had been tampered with.[44]

Reasonably firm evidence suggests that Pakistan players and umpires could have cheated in the 1980s and 1990s. In 1987 Haseeb Ahsan's comments that cheating 'had become a technique for all cricket teams, that they must pressurize the umpire to the extent that they get one or two wrong decisions in favour of the bowler', were widely taken in England as proof of concerted Pakistani cheating, but his further comment that 'everybody is doing it. It has now become absolutely necessary in professional cricket today'[45] was a more or less accurate description of how test cricket was being played. In his sympathetic study of Wasim Akram and Waqar Younis, John Crace wrote that 'All Pakistan umpires unofficially admit that that Imran has been the one captain who has never asked them to help him out' and that on one occasion Pakistani umpires had walked into the Pakistani dressing room to ask Imran for their instructions.[46] The fact that Imran Khan wrote a foreword to this book seems to confirm Crace's account. Two Pakistan umpires had resigned in 1980. One claimed that the Umpires' Association was not sufficiently independent of the Pakistan Board and the other mentioned that attempts to persuade him to take a nationalist line when umpiring.[47] In 1989 the Pakistan cricket journalist Nasir Abbas Mirza wrote that test matches in Pakistan were won not so much on the field as by 'clandestine planning in offices'. He alleged that Pakistani umpires were at the mercy of BCCP officials and an umpire 'had no choice but to acquiesce in the unreasonable demands of the Board and the captain, which, depending on the man, may vary from asking for an LBW to outright victory.' As many umpires had relatively humble backgrounds, being 'in the BCCP's good books assures an opportunity for recognition and rubbing shoulders with the likes of Imran Khan and Viv Richards.'[48] At the end of 1987 statistics showed that batsmen of visiting teams were more likely to be given out LBW by Pakistani umpires than were Pakistani batsmen though Indian umpires gave an even greater proportion of LBW decisions against visiting teams.[49] Following the Pakistan-New Zealand test series 1990–1 Mudassar Nazar,

43. *Daily Telegraph,* 29 August 1992.
44. Oslear, D. and Bannister, J. (1996), *Tampering with Cricket,* London: CollinsWillow, p. 37.
45. Quoted in Gatting and Patmore, *Leading from the Front,* p. 179.
46. Crace, J. (1992), *Wasim and Waqar: Imran's Inheritors,* London: Boxtree, pp. 15–16.
47. *Cricketer International,* October 1987, pp. 18–19.
48. *Cricketer International,* June 1989, p. 21.
49. *Guardian,* 23 December 1987.

the Pakistan B team coach, was reported to have said that the 'outlawed practice of roughing up one side of the ball to enhance swing must be eradicated in Pakistan. It's got to stop.'[50] During the Sarfraz-Lamb trial Christopher Cowdrey produced video recordings which showed fifty-three instances of Pakistan bowlers interfering with the condition of the ball in 1992. In 1996 the former umpire Don Oslear wrote that in 1993 Waqar Younis said to him 'Apart from my action two days ago, I have not tampered with a ball *for some time*' which would seem to be an admission of ball tampering by Waqar.[51] It is possible, of course, that an expectation of cheating by umpires led to genuine mistakes being seen as cheating. As Derek Pringle wrote, 'once a feud is set up it is not easily defused, as it gets passed from one dressing room generation to the next, snowballing in significance until the original germ – a dodgy decision or two – becomes mutated to the broad swathes of prejudice such as "PAKI CHEAT!" so beloved of headline-makers, and now sadly part of the lingua franca wherever English is spoken.'[52] Even if it is accepted that Pakistan umpires may have cheated at times, this does not mean that they did so on the scale imagined by their critics.

The Pakistani Perspective

Pakistani players, officials and supporters resented English accusations of cheating and saw these as expressions of white English racism. To them it seemed that English cricket was only too eager to condemn Pakistanis as cheats whilst similar behaviour by England was overlooked or seen as no more than an understandable and forgivable human error. In 1992 the Pakistani players were awarded a bonus because they had had to put up with what they thought was 'a vicious English media which accused them of cheating almost every day.'[53] Many Pakistanis felt that whenever England lost, the automatic response from English cricket was to attribute this to Pakistani cheating. In 1987 Omar Kureishi, a Pakistani cricket journalist, wrote in *Dawn,* the English-language newspaper published in Karachi, that he had reached 'the conclusion that there is no way an English team can be beaten fair and square. They are invincible. If, perchance, they should lose (which is pretty frequently these days), it is always because they have been robbed. When they are abroad, it is easy to explain their failure on umpiring.'[54] *Asian Times,* the English language newspaper published in England for Asian communities, argued that the response of the British sporting press to the Shakoor Rana-Gatting confrontation expressed an underlying belief that

50. Crace, *Wasim and Waqar*, p. 86.
51. Oslear and Bannister, *Tampering,* pp. 37, 88.
52. *Independent,* 24 July 1996.
53. *Sunday Telegraph,* 30 August 1992.
54. *Dawn,* 13 November 1987.

'if Third World people can play the Britishers' own game better than the Britishers then they must obviously be cheating.' Sigbhat Kadri, spokesperson for the Standing Conference of Pakistani Organisations in the United Kingdom, was reported as saying that 'the moment that England find itself in difficulty it starts to find excuses by blaming umpires . . . I think what it is, is that the English are always being defeated by the black countries . . . they are no longer masters of sport, so they say they have been cheated.'[55] In 1994 when the *Daily Mirror* was claiming that Imran Khan had admitted using a bottle top on one occasion to doctor a cricket ball, an article in *Eastern Eye,* another English language newspaper published in Britain for an Asian readership, claimed that

> The issue is no longer about ball-doctoring or cheating . . . There is no sense of justice or honour in the British press's crusade to rid the world of 'Paki cheats' . . . **There is only one over-riding and uncontrollable emotion that is fuelling this relentless attack – Jealousy.**
>
> The only crime that Pakistan's cricketers are guilty of is that of being simply better than England . . .
>
> The whole sorry saga highlights the fact that England cannot accept that teams from the Sub-Continent are better than them.'[56]

Some whites in England also suspected that much of the white English outrage at supposed Pakistani cheating was related to beliefs that England would not have lost but for Pakistani cheating. In *The Times* Simon Barnes wrote that 'naturally we expect the descendants of Kipling's wily Pathan to cheat in some wonderfully ingenious way. Ball-doctoring has been portrayed as some kind of Eastern mystery, a Pakistani equivalent of the Indian rope trick . . . the English prefer to reduce the greatest bowlers in the world to gullygully men: sleight-of-hand conjurors, wily oriental gentlemen. England were not defeated, England were *tricked.*'[57]

To Pakistan cricketers and their supporters it seemed that English cricket applied double standards to umpires in England and Pakistan and that this reflected a deeply ingrained prejudice against Pakistanis and a conviction of English superiority. Whites in England saw Pakistani umpires as cheats who deliberately favoured Pakistan teams whilst English umpires were regarded as the 'best umpires in the world'. When English umpires gave wrong decisions which favoured England, English cricket observers saw this as human frailty. From the late 1980s the Pakistan cricket authorities, encouraged by Imran Khan, had called for test matches to be umpired by neutral umpires. Imran Khan agreed that English umpires were consistently better

55. *Asian Times,* 18/24 December 1987.
56. *Eastern Eye,* 17 May 1994.
57. *Times,* 29 August 1992.

than Pakistani umpires but that felt that not all of them were 'good' and mentioned encountering biased and incompetent umpiring throughout the world.[58] At meetings of the ICC, the TCCB representatives opposed the introduction of neutral umpires arguing that no sponsor had been found to meet its costs, but also because it believed that, as English umpires were the best in the world, neutral umpires were not needed at test matches played in England. In 1985 John Woodcock, then editor of *Wisden,* wrote that if neutral umpires were introduced into test cricket, 'England would never play under the best umpires which are their own, and that would hardly be satisfactory. They could meet Australia at Lord's with an Indian standing at one end and a Pakistani at the other.'[59] In *Dawn* Omar Kureishi asked 'Why is it that their umpires are guilty, at worst of human error, while our umpires cheat? Are we to accept that the English umpires are paragons of virtue while our umpires have flawed characters?'[60] Farooq Mazhar wrote in the *Pakistan Times,* published in Islamabad, that the English treated calls for neutral umpires 'as an insult to the integrity of their men in white.'[61]

To many Pakistanis it seemed that the Pakistani umpiring in 1987 had not been so biased as the English party and press alleged. The Pakistani view was that in the first test at Lahore the inability of English batsmen to distinguish between Qadir's googly and his flipper had led to so many of them being given out LBW.[62] The Pakistani press also accused the England players of trying to pressurise the Pakistani umpires with 'loud, concerted and pre-meditated appeals', a tactic which the England players accused the Pakistan team of practising.[63] England players were criticised for not showing more respect to the Pakistan umpires. In *Dawn*, Ali Kabir pointed out that when the English umpire Dickie Bird had given Imran Khan out wrongly in the World Cup semi-final, 'the whole nation took it in their stride of sportsmanship.'[64] In the *Pakistan Times* Abdul Haye wrote that no Pakistan captain had ever behaved in such an 'uncouth manner' towards as umpire as Gatting had done towards Shakoor Rana and that no Pakistan team had 'never squealed like Mike Gatting and his men are doing.'[65] In Pakistan the bonus paid to the England party in 1987 seemed a reward for offensive behaviour. In 1992 some Pakistanis felt that the Pakistani players had over reacted in the confrontation with umpire Roy Palmer in the Old Trafford test match. In 1998 Wasim Akram described Palmer as acting 'discourteously' but felt that he could not 'excuse the way he was harangued by our bowler and captain.'[66]

58. Crace, *Wasim and Waqar,* p. 15.
59. *Wisden Cricketers' Almanack 1985,* London: John Wisden, p. 54.
60. *Dawn,* 14 December 1987.
61. *Pakistan Times,* 27 November 1987.
62. *Dawn,* 29 November 1987; *Pakistan Times,* 3 December 1987.
63. *Dawn,* 27 November 1987.
64. *Dawn,* 20 November 1987.
65. *Pakistan Times,* 15 December 1987.
66. Akram, *Wasim,* pp. 91–2.

Suspicions between the two sides and their followers, however, had reached such a point that a Pakistan cricket journalist wrote that the English press was exaggerating the incident and trying to put the entire blame on the Pakistanis 'as if Roy Palmer is Jesus Christ. In fact he is the author of the drama, the villain of the piece.'[67] Dr H.K. Baloch wrote that English cricket was still seeking to avenge Faisalabad and that by making the mistake of speaking to umpire Palmer instead of calming Aqib Javed, Miandad played into the hands of those 'waiting to crucify' him.[68]

Pakistan players and officials were convinced that some English umpires were so biased against them as to constitute deliberate cheating. The English journalist Matthew Engel wrote in 1992 that generations of Pakistani cricketers had become 'terminally convinced rightly or wrongly, that English umpires are against them. It may be that there is an element of self-fulfilling prophesy in their attitude.' In 1996 he wrote that 'there really is a culture of anti-Pakistani feeling among English umpires. The best of them will hide it well, and try hard not to let it influence their judgements, even subconsciously. But many believe the Pakistanis have, more than anyone else, broken the laws about ball-tampering; that many of their players appeal aggressively and argumentatively; and that successive captains have allowed these habits to foster.'[69] In 1987 the Pakistan manager Haseeb Ahsan said 'We now feel that English umpires are no longer the best in the world.'[70] David Constant was the English umpire who provoked the strongest responses from Pakistan players in the 1980s. In 1982 the TCCB had accepted a request from the Indian tourists for Constant not to umpire their matches with England, but the Pakistani party, which was also playing test matches against England in 1982, felt slighted when the TCCB refused its request for Constant to be excluded from the umpires for the Pakistan tests. In the 1982 test at Headingley the Pakistanis felt that mistakes by Constant had prevented Pakistan from winning their first test series in England. Despite Pakistan reservations, Constant was again appointed an umpire for the 1987 Pakistan tests in England and during the Lord's test A.C. Smith, chief executive of the TCCB, released to the press a statement from all first-class umpires in England supporting their colleagues on the test panel.[71] In the final test Constant cautioned the Pakistan spinner Abdul Qadir for running in the pitch. Omar Kureishi wrote that Constant had done this only when it looked as if Pakistan could win the match and even though the bowler was wearing shoes with rubber spikes. In Kureishi's view the English press suggested that Qadir had 'all but dug up the pitch with a shovel.'[72] Kureishi also recalled that Constant had ticked off the Pakistani all-rounder

67. *Pakistan Times*, 11 July 1992.
68. *Dawn*, 22 July 1992.
69. *Dawn*, 11 July 1992; *Dawn Magazine*, 7 August 1996.
70. Green, *Can't Bat*, p. 109.
71. *Wisden Cricketers' Almanack 1988*, London: John Wisden, p. 42.
72. *Dawn*, 13 November 1987.

Mudasser Nazar in the 'most brusque and off-hand way.' Imran Khan thought Constant 'a rude man'.[73] English cricket observers thought that the appointment of relatively inexperienced umpires for the first test and not informing the England party of who the umpires would be in Pakistan in 1987 stemmed from Pakistani resentment at the appointment of Constant as an umpire for the 1987 series in England. In an interview published in 1990, Subba Row said that he thought that 'England walked into a trap' in Pakistan in 1987 and that the TCCB had made a mistake in declining Haseeb's request for Constant not to be an umpire. 'I don't think', he continued, 'we tackled that one very well. Objections by touring teams to umpires must be taken much more seriously than they are at present. There has to be a very, very good reason for such objections not to be accepted.'[74] Haseeb Ahsan said that during the Pakistan tour of England in 1987 'English umpires had tried to demoralise the Pakistan team and rob them of their credit due.'[75]

Pakistani complaints about English umpires were even stronger in 1992. The Pakistan tour manager Intikhab felt that his team was being treated unfairly. 'We have come here,' he said, 'to play cricket in the right spirit, but there has been pressure on our players . . . The umpires are looking at the ball very frequently when we are fielding. When England are fielding this is not happening. There is no consistency and that is unfair.' Imran Khan mentioned that at the Old Trafford, the England fast bowler Devon Malcolm had been allowed to bowl bouncers at the Pakistan tail tail-enders but when Aqib Javed had bowled short-pitched deliveries at Malcolm, 'the home umpires had jumped to his rescue' and so provoked the confrontation between Miandad and umpire Roy Palmer.[76] When England won the fourth test at Headingley, a match which England had to win to have any chance of winning the series, even some English observers felt that mistakes by the English umpires Mervyn Kitchen and Ken Palmer had helped England to win. Geoffrey Boycott thought that Gooch should have been given out three times in his second innings and that Miandad was right to feel cheated. Peter Ball of *The Times,* thought that the umpiring at Headingley did nothing to 'substantiate the professed belief that English umpires are uniquely competent'[77] whilst in the *Guardian* Mike Selvey wrote that it was wide of the mark to suggest that the umpires had been 'intentionally biased – all right, cheats', but pondered about the 'furore that would have ensued had this match been played in Karachi and the roles reversed.'[78] Scyld Berry wrote in the *Independent on Sunday* that

73. *Sun,* 8 December 1987.
74. Bose, *Cricket Voices,* pp. 22–3.
75. *Dawn,* 29 November 1987.
76. *Daily Telegraph,* 31 August 1992.
77. *Sun,* 28 July 1992; *Times,* 28 July 1992.
78. *Guardian,* 28 July 1992.

There was a smell during the fourth Test I had never detected before in a Test in England. There was something in addition to the inevitable, unconscious, bias which umpires have towards home teams and in particular home captains. Tight-lipped and highly formal, the umpiring at Headingley generated the impression that, come what may, judgements were not going to be delivered in Pakistan's favour until England were safely established in both their innings.[79]

In an Indian newspaper the former Indian test match batsman Sunil Gavaskar claimed that England had 'sneaked' a win at Headingley with the umpires' help.[80] The Pakistan vice-captain Salim Malik told a Pakistan cricket magazine that the umpiring at Headingley

crossed . . . all limits. The umpires were determined to engineer a win for England. For this they were prepared to go any distance . . . This was my third tour of England but I have never seen so much cheating there before. I have no hesitation in saying that a planned cheating programme was executed to frustrate us.[81]

In 1992 the Pakistani tourists complained that accusations of ball tampering were further examples of the bias and prejudice which they encountered in England. The Pakistani fast bowler Aqib Javed offered to pay £1,000 if Devon Malcolm could make a scuffed ball swing.[82] Immediately after Lamb made his accusations of ball tampering, Wasim and Waqar issued a statement that they were 'amazed that a fellow professional has stooped so low as to make such unfounded comments. We can only guess at Allan Lamb's motives . . . but we hope they are nothing so base as money or, even worse, our nationality.'[83] Whilst the Sarfraz-Lamb libel trial in 1993 revealed that the ball in the Lord's one-day international had been changed because it had been tampered with illegally, this did not prove that the Pakistani bowlers had been tampering with balls illicitly in other matches, though this is what Allan Lamb had alleged in his article for the *Daily Mirror.*

Even if is accepted that Pakistani players had practised ball tampering during and before the 1992 tour of England, they had strong grounds for seeing accusations of ball tampering as prejudice and the application of double standards against them. In 1992, Tony Lewis wrote that 'Fools are they who talk only of Pakistan duplicity.'[84] English county sides gouged cricket balls and allowed Pakistani bowlers to tamper

79. Quoted in Licudi, A. and Raja, W. (1997), *Cornered Tigers: A History of Pakistan's Test Cricket,* St John's: Hansib Caribbean, p. 48.

80. *Daily Telegraph,* 24 August 1992.

81. *Eastern Eye,* 27 October 1992.

82. *Daily Mirror,* 28 August 1992.

83. *Daily Mirror,* 27 August 1992.

84. *Sunday Telegraph,* 19 July 1992.

balls when playing for them. In 1992 the Surrey club was fined £1,000 for tampering with the ball in a match against Leicestershire. Waqar, a Surrey player, had not played in this match because he was playing for the Pakistan touring team. The Surrey club had also been warned about ball tampering in 1990 and 1991. Waqar had not played for Surrey in the 1990 match but in the 1991 game had a bowling spell when he took five wickets for eight runs with an old ball. Mickey Stewart, the manager of the England team, was a former Surrey player and in the 1992 match in which Surrey were found to have tampered with the ball, his son Alec, the England player, had captained the Surrey team.[85] Don Oslear suspected that in 1993 Lancashire and Surrey had tampered with balls when Wasim and Waqar had been playing for them.[86]

Other forms of ball tampering, such as lifting the seam or using lip salve or other substances to keep the shine on a ball had long been part of cricket. Simon Barnes of *The Times* wrote 'everybody knows that ball-doctoring is as much a part of English cricket as the tea interval' and Fred Trueman said that bowlers ' have been messing up the ball as long as I've been around, and from what I hear, a lot longer.' David Lloyd, who had been a test batsman and a county umpire, and who became the England coach in 1996, called the 'whole thing a hoot. People have been picking the seam for years. I've done it myself' and was reported to have said that one English umpire had been 'the doyen of seam picking in his day'.[87] Derek Pringle, who admitted using lip salve, wrote in 1996 that polishing cricket balls with illicit substances and lifting the seam were 'accepted by both professional players and the umpires.'[88] The West Indian fast bowler Michael Holding wrote that tampering with the ball was 'common practice for as long as I played.'[89] Geoffrey Boycott, who had felt that Wasim and Waqar were often much maligned in 1992 and such good bowlers that they could have bowled out England with oranges, compared ball tampering with speeding by motorists, irresistible and what everybody did at some time. For him, ball tampering was 'technically a breach of the rule but cheating – no it's too emotive a word.'[90] David Gower thought it debatable whether seam lifting was a 'habitual practice' in English cricket, but whilst 'not condoned' was 'accepted'.[91] Although the Pakistanis did not admit to scouring one side of the ball, it is easy to see how they saw it as hypocrisy and prejudice to condemn only one form of ball tampering.

85. *Times,* 25 September 1992.

86. Oslear and Bannister, *Tampering,* pp. 86–8.

87. *Times,* 27, 29 August 1992; *Daily Telegraph,* 27 August 1992.

88. *Independent,* 1 August 1996.

89. Holding, M. and Cozier, T. (1993),*Whispering Death: The Life and Times of Michael Holding,* London: Deutsch, 1993, p. 151.

90. *Independent,* 27 July 1996.

91. *Dawn,* 24 July 1996.

Pakistani players and officials resented that ball tampering by England did not provoke howls of protest about cheating. During the England tour of India in 1976–7 laboratory tests showed that England players had used Vaseline to give their bowlers an advantage. Bishen Bedi, the Indian captain, said that despite using 'unfair means', the England team 'got the fullest backing from its establishment!' Bedi, who also played county cricket, felt that in English cricket using lip ice or candle grease was called a 'professional trick'.[92] England playing against the West Indies in 1991 had been the only team to have had a ball changed because of illegal tampering, though this had gone largely unnoticed,[93] but the Pakistanis were aware that the umpire concerned, John Holder, was not included on the panel of test umpires in 1992. The incident in 1994 when the England captain Michael Atherton was found to have rubbed dirt on a ball in a test match against South Africa and about which he initially misled the match referee yet was allowed to remain England captain, was seen by Pakistanis as a further instance of English cheating being treated differently from that of Pakistanis. The front page of *Eastern Eye* carried a picture of Atherton rubbing dirt on the ball with the headline 'GOTCHA!' Its writer Nadeem Khan claimed that 'This is the moment that every Asian cricket fan has been waiting for . . . For far too long the issue of cheating has been confined to jibes at Pakistan . . . WHO ARE THE CHEATS NOW?'[94] Retired English cricketers and journalists called for Atherton to be dismissed as England captain but the incident was portrayed as an exceptional occurrence rather than evidence of a general tendency of English cricketers to cheat. The newspaper *Today* commented that 'had a Pakistani [been] captured on film doing what Atherton was doing, or an Indian who then withheld part of the truth from the match referee, or a West Indian who then admitted such a lack of frankness, we would never hear the end of it.'[95]

Some critics of Pakistan cricket thought that Pakistani protests at the prejudice against them was a tactic, perhaps even a smoke screen, to disguise the extent of cheating and corruption in Pakistan cricket and yet further evidence of Pakistani duplicity. Instead of being welcomed as an attempt to improve the quality of test umpires and an indication of Pakistani good faith, Pakistani calls for the appointment of neutral umpires were resisted by English cricket on the grounds of expense and because it was felt that would be an affront to the integrity and competence of English umpires. Tony Lewis even wrote that Imran Khan's campaign for neutral umpires

92. *Wisden Cricket Monthly,* May 1988, p. 11.

93. Illingworth, R. and Bannister, J. (1996), *One-man Committee: The Controversial Reign of England's Cricket Supremo,* London: Headline, p. 85.

94. *Eastern Eye,* 2 August 1994.

95. Quoted in Illingworth and Bannister, *One-man Committee*, p. 96.

had led the West Indians to believe that he would be satisfied with no umpires other than neutral umpires and that he was passing on 'his lack of respect for them to the whole team'.[96] Moreover, as the West Indies captain Viv Richards commented in 1989 'tit for tat accusations' about umpiring had become prevalent in international cricket.[97] Complaints about umpires favouring the home team in test cricket were nothing new. Michael Holding's beliefs in the impartiality of umpires were shattered when he toured Australia with the West Indians in 1975–6 where he was 'astonished by the abominable, biased umpiring'. In 1980 he thought that decisions given in New Zealand against the West Indies were 'downright biased', a result of 'poor overall standards' but also of players putting pressure on umpires with concerted appeals.[98] By 1989 the Pakistani Fareshteh A. Gati wrote that the 'West Indies grumbled in Australia, Australia grumbled in Pakistan, Pakistan complained in England and New Zealand, New Zealand whinged in India, India griped in England, England whined in New Zealand and Sri Lanka always comes in for stick from everyone.' He argued that as touring sides complained so often about biased home umpires, singling out Pakistani umpires rather than those of other countries made it seem to the supporters of Pakistan that 'there is a tacit understanding amongst the others to undermine the cricketing achievements of Pakistan and also of India. And what better way of doing it than by belittling their test victories.'[99]

Stereotyping Pakistanis

The England–Pakistan confrontations of 1987 and 1992 were often reported by the British press, and particularly the tabloid press, in language which played on jokey but offensive stereotypes of Pakistan and Pakistanis. The insulting term 'Paki' was not used but puns of 'Pak' and 'Pack' were common. Immediately after the Gatting-Shakoor Rana confrontation, the *Sun* had a front page headline PAK YER BAGS and after the Lord's limited over match in 1992 a *Sun* headline read PAK OFF THE CHEATS FOR FIVE YEARS.[100] The Pakistan manager Haseeb Ahsan was described as 'the Crackpot of Karachi'. Readers were offered the chance to win a '*Sun* Fun Dartboard – Stick On the Cheat of Pakistan!' which had an image of

96. *Cricketer Life International,* October 1989.
97. *Asian Times,* 12 May 1989.
98. Holding and Cozier, *Whispering Death,* p. 24–7, 200.
99. *Cricket Life International,* October 1989, p. 26.
100. *Sun,* 28 August 1992.

Shakoor Rana on them so that 'as well as getting a double top, you can hit him right between the eyes.'[101] In 1992, the *Daily Mirror* called the Pakistani team as 'Javed's Brat Pack' and described Javed Miandad as looking like a 'wild man with a face you might spot crouched behind rocks in an ambush along the Khyber . . . Friends say Javed is amusing, generous, devout and a wow at creating curries. Unfortunately these aspects of his character are rarely glimpsed on the field – except for his taste for stirring.' He was accused of 'arousing the always excitable Pakistani supporters'. Mike Langley recalled the Pakistani resentment over Ian Botham's comment in 1982 that Pakistan was the sort of place to send one's mother-in-law to and wrote 'I thought they'd laugh their curly slippers off and retort: "Well, what about Scunthorpe?" Laugh? Not them, they're too prickly and nationalistic . . . Pakistanis being even hotter on apologies than they are on vindaloos.'[102] A letter from Basharat Tufail to the *Guardian* in 1992 shows how some of Pakistani descent living in England, viewed the tabloid reporting of England–Pakistan cricket. He wrote that 'What we read and hear through the tabloid media is something much more sinister, an absolute hatred of Pakistan and fervent attempts by these reporters to misuse their platform of communication to spread their contempt for a team which has done nothing other than win the World Cup and continues to get better, much to their undisguised disgust.'[103]

Offensive comments about Pakistan cricketers and umpires were not restricted to the tabloid press. In 1992 Simon Heffer wrote in the *Sunday Telegraph* about how the cheating tactics of the Pakistan teams were making them the pariahs of cricket, an article that led to a libel case settled out of court in 1993 when the newspaper agreed to pay an undisclosed sum to charities nominated by the BCCP. Heffer claimed that 'No team has ever more merited the opprobrium of the international cricket community than our current visitors.' Pakistani teams did not allow sportsmanship to impede their need to win at all cost and their umpires had no reservations about ensuring unfair play. He thought that Miandad's 'ethical deficiencies make him the last man to captain his country, even if it is only Pakistan.' Heffer maintained that cricket in Pakistan had become politicized and that its cricket board had 'a corrupt view of the game.' Fair play, he thought, was probably only seen in Pakistan cricket stadia when they were used for public floggings.[104] Heffer's article had been prompted by the Pakistani behaviour towards umpire Palmer at the Old Trafford test. Heffer did not mention ball tampering.

101. *Sun,* 10, 16, 21 December 1987.
102. *Daily Mirror,* 8 July 1992.
103. *Guardian,* 25 July 1992.
104. *Sunday Telegraph,* 12 July 1992.

Few of those from English cricket who believed that cheating was endemic in Pakistan cricket attempted to explain why this was so. Much ignorance has always surrounded Pakistan cricket in England. Little has been written about the history of how cricket has been controlled and organized in Pakistan. Richard Cashman has made perceptive exploratory forays into the subject but his writings, excellent as they are, indicate how much is still to be learned about Pakistan cricket. The *Cricketer* has regular columns on Pakistan cricket that have charted the changes in the personnel of those running Pakistan cricket and demonstrated the tortuous nature of Pakistan cricket politics but these have not usually placed Pakistan cricket in its broader socio-political and cultural context. Broadsheet newspapers in Britain have occasionally commented on how politicians in Pakistan have tried to exploit the popularity of cricket in their country. Amit Roy and Kamran Khan wrote in 1988 how General Zia, the president of Pakistan, had a genuine love for the game and felt that Pakistan success in international cricket would show that his regime was not 'all bad'. The *Observer* claimed in the same year that Zia had been breathing down the necks of the Pakistan Board, who in turn were breathing down the umpires' necks and that this had contributed to the Shakoor Rana-Gatting confrontation.[105] Such articles were rare. Instead of trying to explain the character of Pakistan cricket and its political context, the more common response of the cricket press in England was that Pakistanis could be expected to cheat, that Pakistanis being Pakistanis would cheat. To Pakistanis this must have looked like national stereotyping, an expression of white English prejudice against Pakistanis.

Scyld Berry was one English cricket writer who tried to provide more than a superficial analysis of what he called the 'institutionalized bias' of Pakistani umpires. In *Cricket Odyssey,* his book on England's cricket in 1987–8, he attributed this to 'a government [in Pakistan] which is making the country rotten to the core' and claimed that after the blow to Pakistan national pride of failing to win the World Cup and then losing the one day internationals to England, General Zia had made it clear he was expecting improved results in the test series against England. But Berry also saw the changing moralities of cricket as a cause of friction between England and Pakistani cricketers. He asked how cricket's sportsmanship, a product of nineteenth century liberalism, could be transplanted to 'the brownness of Sind without growing pains?', a perspective which some might see as unduly Western-centric. In recent decades, Berry argued, gamesmanship had spread to county cricket, though not to the same extent as in test cricket. Whilst the 'old code of [cricket] ethics were out-dated for modern professionals, and nobody knew where to stand', the England party had imagined that they 'guarded the Holy Grail, the

---

105. *Sunday Times,* 12, 19 June 1988; *Observer,* 12 June 1988.

true spirit of the game as it should be played' and that 'Like missionaries, they would show the Pakistanis how cricket ought to be played, at the risk of confrontation if needs be.' Such an attitude had led England players to overlook how differences between their gamesmanship and that of Pakistani players were only a matter of degree.[106]

The Dislike of Touring Pakistan

The conviction that Pakistani players and umpires were cheats can be related to an assumption among so many English players and journalists that the 'otherness' of Pakistan showed the moral inferiority of Pakistan and Pakistanis. The reactions of England teams touring Pakistan often indicated an inability to see Pakistan in other than English terms. Tony Lewis wrote of a 'blind belief that what the English professional does is always right', which, as with Gatting, could cause English touring parties to become locked into a 'fortress mentality'. He believed that many England cricketers often forgot that it was a privilege to be touring another country and that 'orderly English professionals as soon as they are overseas . . . perform like overheated sergeants of the old Empire, loose (sic) patience and start a slanging match between "them" and "us."'[107]

Tours of Pakistan were perhaps more of an ordeal than tours to other countries playing test cricket. Political riots interrupted matches on six of England's eight tours to Pakistan. The climate, food, stomach upsets and Islamic prohibitions on the public sale and consumption of alcohol have not recommended the country to English cricketers. Most of the time England parties have been accommodated in five star hotels though some hotels in the more remote parts of Pakistan were not what international cricketers expected. Jack Russell recalled that on the 1987 tour of Pakistan, the England players for a match at Sahiwal were accommodated at the Montgomery Biscuit Factory. The town had only one phone and there was no television at the Biscuit Factory. 'The real fun,' Russell wrote, 'came at night-time, when the mosquitoes gathered, looking for vulnerable areas of pink English flesh. There were no mosquito nets . . . I went to bed fully clothed, with socks and a tracksuit on, wearing my wicket-keeper's inner gloves, and my face and hair covered with repellent gel.'[108] The *Guardian* cricket journalist Matthew Engel, who became editor of *Wisden* in 1992, suspected that in 1996, like many Westerners, England cricketers

---

106. Berry, S. (1988), *A Cricket Odyssey: England on Tour 1987–88,* London: Pavilion, pp. 109, 120, 148, 160.

107. *Sunday Telegraph,* 19 July, 30 August 1992.

108. Russell, *Unleashed,* p. 71.

did not find Islam an 'instantly attractive religion' and that although there were no bars, the ease with which drinks could be obtained made the restrictions on alcohol seem a 'national hypocrisy'.[109] Ian Botham was probably not alone in thinking that Pakistan was 'the kind of place to send your mother-in-law for a month, all expenses paid'.[110] In 1995 on an Indian television chat show Botham described India as 'a wonderful country full of wonderful people' but called Pakistan the worst country he had toured, disliking in particular 'Pakistan's prohibition, uncouth player behaviour, the food, the weather and the volatile political situation.'[111] According to Derek Pringle few players 'ever attempted to embrace or understand the culture they were plonked in the middle of, preferring instead to cocoon themselves with videotapes and an array of familiar comestibles.'[112] The poverty of Pakistan and its problems of an underdeveloped economy seem to have been scarcely considered by English players and cricket journalists. Pakistan was condemned for being different so from England.

Pakistan players and officials found the attitudes of English players to accommodation in Pakistan offensive. The Pakistan captain Wasim Akram wrote that except for some of more isolated venues on the 1987 tour, the England players

> were staying in five-star hotels, as good as anywhere on the international circuit . . . Visiting cricketers are treated like VIPs in our country. There's no hanging around at customs or passport control, they are garlanded with flowers as soon as they arrive, and whisked straight to their hotels without delay . . . Compare our two tours to England in 1987 and 1992 . . . it took us six hours to get out of Heathrow airport after we had been comprehensively searched for drugs . . . It was not a pleasant experience after such a long, tiring flight from Pakistan and didn't exactly make us feel we were welcome in the United Kingdom. In Pakistan the atmosphere is totally different, the welcome is warm and genuine.[113]

Similar reservations about Pakistan surfaced when the ICC decided that the 1987 World Cup would be played in India and Pakistan. In the *Cricketer*, Christopher Martin-Jenkins called the decision 'hasty, if not an ill-considered, decision'. He quoted the president of the Jamshedpur Cricket Association as asking 'How can a country which cannot transport the baggage of cricketers from one town to another stage the World Cup?' Martin-Jenkins thought that 'it cannot be done without a great deal of meticulous planning and a much more detailed exploration of those plans at the next meeting of the ICC is essential.' He hoped that the delegates of

109. *Dawn,* 7 August 1997.
110. Botham, I. (1995), *Botham: My Autobiography,* London: CollinsWillow, p. 211.
111. *Eastern Eye,* 6 October 1995.
112. *Independent,* 24 July 1996.
113. Akram, *Wasim,* p. 45.

India and Pakistan would not be too proud to reconsider their decision.[114] After the World Cup, however, Martin-Jenkins admitted to being 'agreeably surprised' by the organisation of the World Cup. 'The players', he wrote, 'were cosseted as never before and from the grounds, if not from all the hotels, journalists found telephones and telexes which really worked, thus removing the main problems of working in this part of the world.'[115] Apprehensions about holding the World Cup in Asia may not have been consciously racist, but they could easily have been seen by Indians and Pakistanis as condescending and belittling, a reflection of an assumption of English superiority.

Insults from Spectators

Pakistan touring teams and individual Pakistanis playing county cricket have been the target of abuse from spectators. At Worcester in 1986 Imran Khan's 'parentage and colour were the subject of barracking in words and song' while he batted for Sussex.[116] Though this may have been connected with Imran having left Worcestershire to play for Sussex, these hecklers chose to express their offensiveness through racist insults. Racist abuse was especially fierce at Headingley. Sidney Fielden, chairman of Yorkshire CCC public relations committee said in an interview published in 1990 that Yorkshire had a minority of racist spectators 'who think that because a player is black they must give him stick.'[117] During the 1992 test at Headingley a pig's head was thrown into the part of the seating where Pakistan supporters were congregated. In 1996 a third of the seats had been removed from the western terrace at Headingley for the England–Pakistan match but *Asian Times* reported that racist chants were still 'prevalent and unabated' and spilled over into fighting.[118] Chris Searle, founder of the Devon Malcolm cricket centre in Sheffield, wrote of white spectators screaming 'Stab the Pakis', the shameful behaviour of hundreds of young Englishmen and of the 'customary racist partiality of the police and the private security firms' and of the failure of England players to try to influence the crowd. Searle felt that the conduct of the spectators was more than 'yobbery' but that there had been had 'racist overtones right over length and breadth of the Western Terrace that Saturday afternoon – loud, clear and squalid' as if 'the pus of four centuries of Empire was pulsing out.'[119] On occasions Pakistan resentment at racist chanting and the depth of their commitment to the Pakistan team led to fighting with white spectators. At Trent Bridge in 1987 the throat of a Pakistan supporter

114. *Cricketer International,* December 1984, p. 5.
115. *Cricketer International,* December 1987, p. 3.
116. *The Times,* 15 August 1986.
117. Bose, *Cricket Voices,* p. 251.
118. *Asian Times,* 22 August 1996.
119. *Observer,* 18 August 1996.

was slashed.[120] In 1992 Pakistan supporters attacked the cars of Ian Botham and Mike Gatting after matches. Pakistanis have not been the only victims of racist abuse at cricket grounds in England. West Indians and Indians have also suffered.

Some cricket observers in England criticized the commitment of Pakistani support for their team. In 1987, the editor of *Wisden Cricket Monthly* wrote that at the one-day international at Edgbaston 'hordes of Pakistan "supporters" came not merely to watch the cricket but to identify – with a fanatical frenzy and to the embarrassment of Imran and his players – with "their team." Our enquiries have revealed that hundreds of them gained entry without paying, and that a battle plan was actually drawn up among them.' The editorial welcomed the TCCB's decision to ban 'lethal flag-stakes and banners and the noise-making instruments which are such a nuisance and incitement to crazy behaviour' and mentioned that whites with 'shaven heads and large boots' had been 'lurking in anticipation of confrontation.'[121] In 1990 the former Conservative Party chairman, Norman Tebbit, asked whether Asians living in Britain could pass his cricket test. He asked 'Which side do they cheer for? Were they still harking back to where they came from or where they were?' His comments seemed to suggest that support for India or Pakistan at test matches in England implied a refusal to integrate into British society.[122] Tebbit's remarks caused great offence to Asians living in England and many saw them as racist. As one cricket enthusiast of Pakistani descent argued, Scots who lived in England were not criticized for supporting Scotland in football matches with England. It can also be argued that the racism which those of Pakistani descent confront so often in England encourages them to assert their Pakistani identities

Friction at the ICC

Firm evidence about the politics of international cricket is frustratingly sparse. The press are not admitted to meetings of the ICC and reports of ICC meetings usually do little more than list the resolutions passed. Memoirs of those who were members of the ICC reveal little about its internal politics. Sketchy evidence, and it has to be stressed that it is sketchy, suggests that relations in the ICC between the England and Pakistan representatives were often acrimonious in 1980s and 1990s. It was assumed by Pakistan, and also by India and the West Indies, that the TCCB representatives imagined that they had the right to control cricket as they had for much of the twentieth century. England's role at the ICC seems to have been interpreted as a hangover of an English sense of innate superiority that had helped to uphold the Raj, and created an impression that countries whose cricket had become as strong

120. Licudi and Raja, *Cornered Tigers*, p. 40.
121. *Wisden Cricket Monthly*, July 1987, p. 3.
122. *The Times*, 21 April 1990.

or stronger than England's were not treated as equals. At the ICC the attitude of England representatives towards the isolation of apartheid South Africa appeared less enthusiastic than that of India, Pakistan and the West Indies. In 1993 English influence at the ICC was reduced when England and Australia agreed to relinquish their veto over proposals and the MCC ceased to administer the ICC though the ICC headquarters remained at Lord's. In the same year Sir Clyde Walcott of the West Indies became the first chairman of the ICC who was not white.

How far this less influential role in the ICC was forced on the TCCB and the MCC or resulted from a recognition of changing relationships in international cricket is not clear. Pakistan representatives, however, do seem to have objected to England's privileged position at the ICC. A.H. Kardar, the first captain of the Pakistan test team and president of Pakistan's Board of Control from 1972 until 1977, tried to 'break the post-imperial dominance of Lord's' but his 'prickly brilliance', and tendency to 'be dictatorial and quickly angered'[123] may well have been resented by the English cricket establishment. In 1992, Shahid Rafi, the Pakistan representative on the ICC, claimed that it was Pakistan which had initiated discussion at the ICC of the England-Australia veto, which he saw as 'undemocratic and creates a gap between the two and the six.'[124] At the ICC Pakistan representatives took the lead in calling for the appointment of neutral umpires in test matches, a policy that the TCCB long opposed.

How senior figures in the England cricket establishment regarded Pakistan criticism of the veto is uncertain, but other prominent personalities from English cricket harboured suspicions that Pakistan and the other non-white test-playing countries were trying to boost their influence in international cricket at England's expense. In the *Cricketer* in 1981 Robin Marlar, the former captain of Sussex who became the county's president in 1997, wrote of the granting of full membership of the ICC and test match status to Sri Lanka that 'the worst feature of this debate has been the racial element, no more buried and equally dangerous as the iceberg underwater. With Sri Lanka a Full Member, the predominantly white members might be outvoted four to three and thus thrown back on the interest vested in the foundation members [the England-Australia veto], an interest which is politically bankrupt in a world which counts votes and pulls down privilege.'[125] An editorial in *Wisden Cricket Monthly* in 1986 asked whether there was a 'Lahore/Karachi aim to centre world cricket power there?'[126] In 1987, Raymond Illingworth, the former England captain, saw the Gatting-Shakoor Rana affair as part of

123. *Wisden Cricketers' Almanack 1997,* London: John Wisden, p. 1404; *Dawn Magazine,* 7 August 1996.

124. *Dawn,* 4 July 1992.

125. *Cricketer International,* August 1981, p. 12.

126. *Wisden Cricket Monthly,* February 1986, p. 3.

an international plot to deprive this country of its influence in world cricket – a political power game. Cricketwise, Pakistan has always been iffy, and Pakistanis, in the main, difficult. Now they're becoming downright Bolshie. Given a chance they would trample all over us . . . Out there I heard and read repeatedly of campaigns to take the International Cricket Conference permanently to the sub-continent and to blazes with England . . . We have spread the game and made allowances for eccentricities in other countries. But we have been weak . . . It's time we showed we won't tolerate being messed about.[127]

Others saw Pakistan as part of a coalition of non-white countries against England and the other white countries. In 1989, E. M. Wellings wrote in *Wisden Cricket Monthly* that at the ICC 'Collectively the coloured group has bedevilled the game. It is time for others to form a common front in defence of it.' He described that ICC as 'that shoddy body' which had 'been running further and further off the rails for many years' and advocated that England and Australia break away.[128]

By the early 1990s the cricket authorities in India and Pakistan had realized that the money which could be generated by cricket in their countries could enable them to challenge the established authority of international cricket. This become clear at the ICC meeting in 1993, which allocated the 1996 World Cup to India, Pakistan and Sri Lanka. The TCCB delegates believed that it was the turn of England to stage the 1996 competition, but after the test playing countries had voted five to four in favour of England, the votes of the associate members of the ICC resulted in the 1995–6 World Cup being awarded to India, Pakistan and Sri Lanka, largely, it was believed, because they had promised associate members a larger share of the competition revenues than had the TCCB. The meeting did agree that the 1998 World Cup would be held in England. Much bitterness surrounded the meeting. It lasted over twelve hours, and was described by Alan Smith, the England delegate, as 'a fractious and unpleasant meeting beset by procedural wrangling . . . There was no talk of anything like cricket. It was, by a long way, the worst meeting I have ever attended.'[129] *Wisden Cricket Monthly* reported that there had been 'a real chance' of the ICC breaking up over the issue. Richard Hutton, editor of the *Cricketer,* wrote of the cricket world being split into two camps –

the one having its axis in the Indian subcontinent, whose emissaries are suddenly able to summon a solidarity little in evidence in their other dealings with each other; and the other on the independent founder members of ICC – England and Australia – the latter's Antipodean partner New Zealand, and a West Indies eternally grateful for donations of freely convertible currency from its Occidental benefactors.[130]

127. *Daily Mirror,* 10 December 1987.
128. *Wisden Cricket Monthly,* July 1989, p. 27.
129. *Wisden Cricketers' Almanack 1994,* London: John Wisden, p. 26.
130. *Cricketer International,* March 1993, p. 2.

To the English cricket world, India was the chief villain of the piece, but appeared to be have the full support of Pakistan and Sri Lanka. The Indian representatives, it was thought, had managed to overturn the ICC rule that a decision could be binding only if supported by two thirds of the full members and including at least one of the founder members England and Australia. To Richard Hutton, the Indians 'appeared to have got the bit between their teeth, to bust apart what they see as a gentleman's club. Sensing that numbers are on their side they feel justified in attempting to swing the balance of power in their favour', comments that could be interpreted as meaning that England had a right to dominate world cricket. To Jack Bailey, the cricket journalist who had been secretary of the MCC and of the ICC from 1974 to 1987, this ICC meting was the 'outward and visible sign . . . that the playing of cricket as a game, so long the chief preoccupation of those gathered round the tables of the MCC Committee room at Lord's, and pursued invariably with an attitude of quiet and civilised deference, had been overtaken . . . All that cricket used to stand for was thrown out of the window.'[131] The decision of the England delegation to accept that the 1995–6 World Cup would be played in the Subcontinent, was presented as a high-principled concession to retain the unity of international cricket. Lieutenant-Colonel John Stephenson, secretary of the MCC from 1987 until 1993, described the England decision as 'a most magnanimous, gentlemanly and wonderful gesture made for the good of international cricket.'[132]

Asian and neutral observers took a very different view of English responses to the World Cup decision. The American-born journalist Mike Marqusee, whose writings on English cricket have been praised for cutting through so much of the insularity of English cricket literature, wrote of the English cricket establishment's belief that the India, Pakistan and Sri Lanka boards had 'bribed' the associate members by offering them 'a greater slice of the World Cup pie' than England and of Christopher Martin-Jenkins calling the decision a triumph for money and politics over cricket.[133] England offered each Associate country £60,000 whereas the Asian group offered £100,000. In Marqusee's opinion, Sir Colin Cowdrey, the ICC chairman, instead of acting as impartial chairman, had 'batted for England'. According to the Mihir Bose, the English delegates had assumed that the meeting would be 'yet another old boys' gathering' with the Associate members continuing to be treated as 'much as the Soviet Union used to treat its Eastern European satellites'. The Asian group 'wheeled in politicians and lawyers and treated the event as if it were an American convention. They outflanked England.'[134] In the opinion of Bindra, an Indian delegate at the meeting and a former senior civil servant who had been

131. *Wisden Cricketers' Almanack 1994,* pp. 25–6.

132. *Wisden Cricket Monthly,* March 1993, p. 5.

133. Marqusee, M. (1997), *War Minus The Shooting: A Journey through South Asia during Cricket's World Cup,* London: Mandarin, pp. 16–17.

134. *Wisden Cricketers' Almanack 1997,* p. 21.

secretary to the Prime Minister of India, the ICC meeting showed that the TCCB had 'not got over their Raj hangover. They seem not to like their erstwhile colonial subjects coming to London and beating them at what they still consider their own game.' Almost identical words were used by Arif Ali Abassi of the Pakistan Board who spoke of 'the Raj hangover . . . They cannot accept the colonial beating them at their own game.' During the 1995–6 World Cup he said that 'the English have to show us that they can deliver, that they will expand the game as we have done' and pointed out that Pakistan proposals for a new constitution of the ICC, a global format for one day internationals, neutral test umpires and the development of the game in new regions had been crucial in modernising international cricket.[135]

The Asian group took the World Cup to new financial heights, and showed that they had realized the competition's financial potential far more than the England party. It was agreed that the hosts could keep all the profits after the expenses, including guaranteed fee of £250,000 to each competing country, had been paid. Through imaginative and aggressive marketing of the World Cup, the host countries were able to divide a profit of nearly $50,000,000.[136] Jagmohan Dalmiya, an Indian businessman, is usually credited with having masterminded the commercial exploitation of the Cup. Matthew Engel, editor of *Wisden,* believed that the attempt by Dalmiya to succeed Clyde Walcott as chairman of the ICC in 1996 had 'almost split asunder' the ICC, but there was little controversy in 1997, when he became the first president of the ICC for a three-year term.[137] The World Cup of 1999, held in England and organized by English cricket, did not appear as successful as that of 1995–6. Though Stephen Fay, a cricket writer and authority on banking, claimed that ticket sales were 'excellent' and that a 'respectable' television deal had been negotiated, the agency hired to find eight businesses willing to pay £2,000,000 each to be sponsors signed up only four.[138]

Perhaps because of England's failure to reach the final stages of the competition, the sporting public in Britain did not seem to regard the World Cup as the major sporting international sporting taking place in Britain in 1999. Manchester United's bid for the treble seemed to attract more public and media attention. It is doubtful whether the World Cup boosted interest in cricket in England. The World Cup, however, did awaken the England and Wales Cricket Board to the enthusiasm for cricket among Britain's Asian population. Indeed *Wisden* reported that they gave the competition its 'vibrancy' and showed that they were the one community in England who 'had absolutely not fallen out of love with cricket.' The Pakistan cheerleader Abul Jalil became the major personality of the World Cup.[139]

135. Marqusee, *War Minus The Shooting*, pp. 18–19, 82–3.
136. *Wisden Cricketers' Almanack 1997*, p. 22.
137. *Wisden Cricketers' Almanack 1998*, London: John Wisden, pp. 10, 1373.
138. *Wisden Cricketers' Almanack 2000*, London: John Wisden, p. 91.
139. *Wisden Cricketers' Almanack 2000*, p. 432.

Match Fixing

In the 1990s it was rumoured that international cricketers had been paid to fix matches and had accepted bribes from bookmakers to underperform, particularly in one-day internationals. Though accurate measurements of match fixing and bribery are not possible, it was generally supposed that betting on cricket seemed to be more wide-spread in Indian and Pakistan than elsewhere in the cricket world. Suspicions of bribery in international cricket became widespread first in 1994 when the Australian players Shane Warne, Mark Waugh and Tim May revealed that the Pakistani player Salim Malik had offered them money to throw a test match. Mihir Bose wrote in 1997 that 'the general feeling' was that 'betting and match-throwing were part of the subcontinent's cricket culture, and that nothing could be done about it.'[140] In England allegations of bribery and match rigging in international cricket seemed to concern Pakistani players more often than those of other countries, but this was not seen as exclusively a feature of Pakistan cricket. Accusations were levelled against players of other countries. The publication of a report by the Pakistan judge Malik Mohammad Qayyum in May 2000 concluded that the Pakistan test cricketers Salim Malik and Ata-ur-Rehman had been guilty of match fixing and recommended that they be banned from test cricket. The Qayyum enquiry could not find incontrovert-ible proof that six other Pakistani test players, including such big names as Wasim Akram, Waqar Younis and Inzaman-ul-Haq had attempted to fix international matches in 1990s but all were fined and told that they would be kept under investigation. There were suspicions that the cricket authorities in Pakistan had delayed publishing Qayyum's report, but the report and the punishments it recommended for leading Pakistani players showed that the Pakistan Board was attempting to deal with the issue of match fixing and bribery.

As firm evidence of bribery and match-fixing is so elusive, it is impossible to determine whether Pakistani players had been more deeply implicated than those of other countries. In 1998 the Australians Mark Waugh and Shane Warne eventually admitted to being paid by an Indian bookmaker for information about the state of the pitch in a limited-overs competition being played in Sri Lanka in 1994, but whilst agreeing that they had been 'naive and stupid', denied involvement in match fixing.[141] When the South African captain Hansie Cronje, who had often referred in public to his Christian principles, revealed in April 2000 that he had received payments from Asian bookmakers and when other South African players stated that he offered money

---

140. *Wisden Cricketers' Almanack 1999,* London: John Wisden, p. 23.

141. *Wisden Cricketers' Almanack 1999,* pp. 23–4. For a discussion of rumours surrounding bribery and bookmakers in Indian cricket, see Magazine, P. (2000), *Not Quite Cricket: The Explosive Story of How Bookmakers Influence The Game Today,* New Delhi: Penguin.

to them to underperform in matches, this came as such a shock to English cricket that it was argued that if Cronje had accepted bribes, anyone could have done so. There were unsubstantiated reports that prominent Indian players had received bribes. At the time of writing, June 2000, no England player has been accused in public of having accepted bribes but Chris Lewis informed the England and Wales Cricket Board in 1999 that an Indian sports entrepreneur had offered him £300,000 to persuade Alan Mullally and Alec Stewart to play badly in an England-New Zealand test match.[142] Lewis mentioned that when this offer was made to him, he was told that three England players had fixed matches, but he did not make their names public.[143]

The *Cricketer, Wisden Cricket Monthly* and the *Wisden* annual discussed allegations of match fixing and bribery, but until Cronje's admissions of involvement with Asian bookmakers, these matters did not provoke massive coverage by the sporting press in Britain. The far more detailed reporting of the Cronje affair by the press and television in Britain reflected no doubt the shock that someone such as Cronje could be involved with bribery but may also have reflected a feeling that another form of Pakistan cheating was not so very surprising or newsworthy. When the English sporting press reported rumours of Pakistani match fixing in the 1990s or on the Qayyum Commission in 2000, the tone of moral superiority that had surrounded much of the reporting of the 1987 and 1992 England–Pakistan test series was largely missing. This relatively limited press interest in allegations of bribery and match fixing by Pakistanis before the eruption of the Cronje affair may have been because Pakistanis had not usually been suspected of fixing matches involving England.

Sections of the English press in 2000 argued that the ICC ought to have taken a stronger line much sooner over allegations of match fixing. In the *Guardian* Matthew Engel wrote that the ICC had long had 'a reputation within the game for supine uselessness' and that since 1994 'at every point the response of cricket's administrators has been to minimise the problems of gambling-related bribes: always the bucket of water, never the fire engine.' Whilst acknowledging that the boards of control in the full member countries were reluctant to concede authority to the ICC, Engel suspected that the ICC president Jagmohan Dalmiya and the chief executive David Richards had known ' a good deal more than they were letting on . . . and were refusing to level with the public.'[144]

As the Cronje affair unravelled, blame for the bribery scandal became focused in particular on how the policies pursued by the ICC under the presidency of Jagmohan Dalmiya had been crucial in creating a climate in which match fixing could flourish.

142. *Observer,* 23 April 2000.
143. *Sunday Times,* 23 April 2000.
144. *Guardian,* 2 May 2000.

Reports suggested, but did not state in such bald terms, that the ICC was becoming mired in sleaze. It was mentioned that Inderjit Singh Bindra, Dalmiya's predecessor as president of the Board of Control for Cricket in India, and whose involvement with the building of a cricket stadium in India had been investigated by the Central Bureau of Investigation, had said that Dalmiya was 'in the grip of the mafia and sharks'.[145] Dalmiya was reported to be suing those alleging that he profited personally from contracts to televise a mini world cup competition in Bangladesh in 1999[146] and questions were raised about possible dealings between him, the ICC and the Asian businessman Mark Mascarenhas and his television company WorldTel, which broadcast the annual limited overs competitions held in Sharjah and Bangladesh. In the *Guardian* Vivek Chaudhary wrote that as president of the ICC Dalmiya had attempted to increase corporate involvement and sponsorship for cricket and 'generate new riches from television rights by increasing the number of one-day internationals'.[147] The increase in the number of one day international matches, growing from sixty-six in 1990 to 153 in 1999, especially when held in places where test cricket was not played, such as Sharjah, Bangladesh and Canada, were seen as a major factor in the rise of bribery. The cricket journalist and former England player Vic Marks wrote that 'it is crazy that countless one-day games with no inherent meaning take place worldwide each year.'[148] In the *Independent* Derek Pringle explained how the satellite televising of one day games, especially in the subcontinent, had brought the sport a financial windfall, but that administrators, 'sensing perhaps that the fatted calf would not last forever, have become greedy, creating more and more one day tournaments', which provided bookmakers with more opportunities for betting.[149] Rob Steen of the *Financial Times* argued that one way to reduce match fixing would be to cut the 'plethora' of one day competitions which attracted brimming crowds in Dubai, Dhaka and Nairobi but having 'no meaning beyond themselves . . . caring about failure can be tricky.'[150] The implication seemed to be that as such competitions meant so little to players, the temptation to accept bribes became greater. Steen also mentioned that the relatively low pay for international cricketers compared with other international sports could have added to the attractions of receiving bribes. Blaming match fixing on the increase in televised one-day matches was a condemnation of the ICC's policies associated with Dalmiya.

145. *Observer,* 23 April 2000; *Guardian,* 1 May 2000.
146. *Independent,* 3 May 2000.
147. *Guardian,* 1 May 2000.
148. *Observer,* 7 May 2000.
149. *Independent,* 2 May 2000.
150. *Financial Times,* 14 April 2000.

The criticisms levelled against Dalmiya emphasized the differences between Asian cricket culture and that in England. Vivek Chaudhary mentioned that Dalmiya's strongest supporters at the ICC were usually the delegates from India and Sri Lanka and claimed traditionalists saw Dalmiya as 'a maverick and unsafe pair of hands whose tenure has damaged test cricket and taken the game into dangerous, uncharted territory'. Mark Mascarenhas was reported to have said that there 'comes a point where any Asian businessman who exhibits the trappings of success is going to be under suspicion'.[151] In the *Observer* Kevin Mitchell pointed out 'younger Test nations' had turned to one-day cricket because tests with them had been considered 'unfashionable', 'not the stuff of traditional Test series, tours that had to be fitted in between the bigger ones against Australia or the West Indies.'[152] Frank Keating wrote that 'You desperately yearn for the days only a decade ago when the ICC was an almost unheard of adjunct of dear old MCC and its buffers . . . who would hold amiable meetings over pink gins about the value of leg-byes.' Since Dalmiya had been taken the 1995–6 World Cup to Asia, 'Doubtless to the joy of bookmakers. The game – and for sure the certainty of its morals and ethics and innate goodness – has never been the same.'[153] The expression of such a view by a sports writer who has so consistently opposed racism in British sport suggests a widespread suspicion in English cricket that international cricket had been morally cleaner when England was the dominant power in its control and administration.

Cricket and Pakistanis in England

Pakistan cricket journalists pointed out that English accusations of Pakistani cheating were most intense when Pakistan defeated England. Whilst they may not have been correct in assuming that the English could not abide being defeated by former colonies, complaints about cheating could be interpreted as belittling Pakistan achievement. For those of Pakistani descent in England it seemed that what should have been a source of legitimate pride was provoking denigration and confirming offensive stereotyping, casting aspersions on the honour of Pakistanis. Mihir Bose has argued that the accusation in 1992 that the successes of the Pakistan fast bowlers were due to illegal ball tampering, 'were a terrible blow to that most sensitive of Pakistani feelings: *izzat*, honour. Most crimes can be forgiven in Pakistan but to insult a man's *izzat*, something even the poorest will proudly hold, is worse than plunging a dagger to his heart.'[154]

151. *Guardian*, 1 May 2000.
152. Observer, 7 May 2000.
153. *Guardian*, 4 May 2000.
154. Bose, *Sporting Alien*, p. 198.

To Pakistanis the ill-feeling between England and Pakistan teams that became so pronounced in the late 1980s and early 1990s was part of long-held suspicions among Pakistanis of an English bias against them. Many Pakistanis felt that at the time of Partition Mountbatten and his advisers favoured Indian rather than Pakistan. The Pakistan scholar Akbar S. Ahmed has shown how fiercely resentment at the incorporation of Ferozepur, Gurdaspur, Kashmir and Calcutta into India has persisted in Pakistan. His description in an academic work published in 1997 of Mountbatten as the 'first Paki-basher' shows the intensity of the feeling among Pakistanis that Britain betrayed them over Partition.[155] Given the usually fraught state of relations between India and Pakistan, the frequent tendency of English cricket to favour India rather than Pakistan has added to Pakistani suspicions of prejudice against them. In 1987 the TCCB accepted India's request for David Constant not to umpire any of their tests against England but refused a similar request from Pakistan. In 2000, however, the Indian Jagmohan Dalmiya was the administrator blamed most often for creating conditions in which gambling-related bribery could grow.

The animosities in England–Pakistan cricket seem to have added a further layer to the prejudices which those of Pakistani descent face in England. In the 1990s the reporting of racial discrimination by Asians to community relations councils in towns with relatively large numbers of Asian inhabitants has increased, though this could reflect a greater willingness to report such incidents as much as a growth in ethnic animosity. Asians are thought to have increased competition for jobs even though unemployment is higher among Asians than for whites with similar education and qualifications. Whites often refer to all Asians, regardless of their ancestral origins, as 'Pakis', a term which those of Pakistani descent find offensive and which is often meant to cause offence. Ill feeling in cricket has also reflected and reinforced the tensions between whites and Pakistanis in Britain stemming from the rise of Islamophobia in the 1980s and 1990s. In part this was connected with suspicions among many whites in Britain and elsewhere in the West that Islamic fundamentalism encouraged international terrorism. In 1999 Faisal Bodi, editor of *Q-News* magazine, wrote that 'driven by the imperative of international influence, much of the West still chooses to misunderstand Islam and its followers as an alien and threatening force.'[156] Akbar Ahmed noted that an opinion poll had suggested that 80 per cent of the British public saw Islam as the 'next' major enemy after communism.[157] The fatwah against Salman Rushdie and incidents such as the public

155. Ahmed, Akbar S. (1997), *Jinnah, Pakistan and Islamic Identity: The Search for Saladin*, London: Routledge, Chapter 5.

156. *Guardian*, 18 November 1999.

157. Ahmed, Akbar S. (1992), *Postmodernism and Islam: Predicament and Promise*, London: Routledge, p. 37.

burning of his book *The Satanic Verses* fuelled animosity towards Islam and Muslims and to Pakistanis as one of the largest Muslim groups in Britain.[158] In white British popular culture the term 'Ayatollah' became used to denote a person in authority with an overbearing manner. Certainly many whites in Britain took an oversimplified view of Islam and ignored the varieties of Islam in their generalized animus against Muslims. In 1992 Imran Khan said that

> Pakistan cricketers touring England are treated somewhat like Islam in the West. Most of the time images of Islam in the West are depicted by terrorists, fanaticism, veiled women, brutal dictators and so on. Similarly our cricketers are looked upon as an indisciplined, unruly mob who put pressure on umpires, cheat, doctor cricket balls, whinge about umpiring decisions and are generally unsporting.[159]

Athar Ali, the London correspondent of *Dawn,* thought that in Pakistan it was believed that Pakistanis in England were picked on for religious reasons and that the extensive reporting in the Pakistan press of 'Paki-bashing' in England led Pakistan players and their supporters to expect unfair treatment in England.[160] The intensity of prejudice against Pakistanis in so many areas of English life led them to see the accusations of Pakistan cheating in cricket as what was to be expected, as further examples of 'Paki-bashing'.

---

158. For a discussion of how different groups of Muslims in Britain have viewed the Rushdie affair, see Mohood, Tariq (1992), 'British Asian Muslims and the Rushdie affair' in Donald, J. and Rattansi, A.T. (eds), *'Race', Culture and Difference,* London: Sage and Open University Press.

159. *Sun,* 8 July 1992.

160. *Dawn Magazine,* 7 August 1996.

−7−

Playing the Game: Race and Recreational Cricket

In the 1980s and 1990s Asian and black players have contributed much to first-class cricket in England. Eleven players of African-Caribbean descent have played for England and in 1999 Nasser Hussain, born in Madras, became captain of England. The performance of the England team, anything but impressive in the second half of the 1990s, would probably have been even worse but for Asian and black players. Asians and African-Caribbeans have also added much over the past three decades to recreational cricket in England and many now feel that England may only be able to become a force in test cricket again by exploiting the enthusiasm for cricket among the ethnic minorities and Asians in particular.

The Asian Presence in Club Cricket

The exact numbers of those from the ethnic minorities who play cricket regularly are not known but there is no doubt that they form a sizeable presence in English recreational cricket. In the later 1980s and 1990s the proportion of the Asian population who played was higher than that for blacks or whites. A survey published in 1994 of males from Greater Manchester, of whom for each ethnic group between two thirds and three quarters were aged between sixteen and twenty-six, showed that for every four of African-Caribbean descent who played cricket, four of East African Asian descent, eighteen of Indian descent, twelve of Pakistani descent and eight of white British descent played cricket.[1] Localized studies show that in areas with high numbers of ethnic minority players, teams with roughly equal numbers of white and coloured players have been rare. Asians have usually played for teams with only Asian players and African-Caribbeans for those with only black players though in the last few years long-established clubs playing at the higher levels of club cricket in areas with large ethnic minority populations have recruited highly talented ethnic minority players.

1. Verma, G.K. and Darby, D.S. (1994), *Winners and Losers: Ethnic Minorities in Sport and Recreation*, London: Falmer, p. 122.

In the 1990s the numbers of Asian teams playing cricket regularly have stayed the same or fallen slightly whereas the numbers of West Indian and white teams have fallen. Club titles and names of club officials suggest that of the 403 clubs from Middlesex affiliated in 1990 to the Club Cricket Conference, an organization for clubs and leagues primarily from south-east England, eleven were West Indian and sixty-three Asian. By 1999 the total number of affiliated clubs had dropped to 334, which included nine West Indian and sixty-five Asian clubs. Not all clubs from Middlesex, of course, were affiliated to the Club Cricket Conference, and club titles and names of officials may not always be an accurate guide to a club's ethnic composition. In 1990 half of the Leicester Mutual Sundays School League eighty teams had been Asian but in 1999 it had only thirty-two teams of which twenty-five were Asian. Its four West Indian teams had disbanded by 1999.[2] In 1990 there were two midweek evening leagues in Leicester – the Leicester Amateur Evening League and the Belgrave Evening Association. Each league had five divisions and a combined total of around 100 clubs of which over half were Asian. By 1998 the dwindling number of teams caused the leagues to amalgamate as the Belgrave Amateur Evening League. In 1999 this had twenty-eight teams of which seventeen were Asian. By 1999 its two West Indian clubs had disbanded. In the mid 1980s just over half of the sixty teams playing in the Birmingham Parks Association were Asian. By 1999 it had forty-four Asian and four white clubs.[3] In most towns with large numbers of Asian inhabitants, cricket clubs formed in the 1990s have usually been Asian clubs.

The higher numbers of Asian clubs have meant that there were leagues consisting exclusively, or almost exclusively, of Asian clubs, in the 1990s whilst leagues for West Indian clubs were rare. In 1990 the London-based Clive Lloyd Red Stripe League, a competition for West Indian teams, had ten clubs but by the late 1990s this was holding only a knock-out competition. One other West Indian cricket league in London was described in 1999 as 'on its last legs'. A Midlands cricket league had been started in the late 1980s with over twelve West Indian teams from Birmingham, Nottingham, Northampton and Sheffield, but this collapsed after two or three seasons. In north-west England the Pendle Cricket League had only Asian teams by the late 1990s and by 1998 the Bolton Metropolitan League had only Asian clubs whilst in 1996 twenty of the thirty-five teams in the Blackburn Midweek League were Asian. Neither Liverpool nor Manchester, nor any of what used to be textile towns in Lancashire, have West Indian cricket leagues. All clubs playing in the three divisions of the Middlesex Premier League, which despite its name is not the ECB designated premier county league for Middlesex, are Asian. In addition

2. Information supplied by Mr Howard Pollard, secretary of the Leicester and District Mutual Sunday Schools Cricket League, 17 March 2000.

3. Information supplied by Mr Mohammed Ashraf, secretary of the Arif Sports Birmingham Parks Association.

to the predominantly Asian Leicester Mutual Sunday Schools League and the Belgrave Amateur Evening League, eight of the ten clubs playing in the 3A Division of the Leicestershire League are Asian with one of the other two being the Caribbean Club.

Most Asian and black clubs belong to the lower levels of club cricket. In 1999 no Asian or Caribbean clubs played in the top two sections of the Everards County League in Leicestershire, the ECB designated county league, or in the two top divisions of the Leicestershire League. Lancashire's most prestigious leagues, the Lancashire League, the Central Lancashire League and the Bolton League, all centred on towns with high numbers of Asians, include no Asian clubs although they have a long tradition of employing Asian and West Indian professionals, and some clubs now have highly talented local amateur Asian players. The Liverpool Competition, which was designated the premier county league for Lancashire by the ECB, also includes no ethnic minority clubs, but by 1999 Bolton Indians and Deane and Derby were playing in the Manchester Association, one of the four senior feeder leagues for the county league. Lidget Green and Bowling Old Lane are predominantly Asian clubs which play in the Bradford League, often taken to be the leading cricket league in Yorkshire. In the 1980s the Manningham Mills Club of the Bradford League was also a predominantly Asian club but during the late 1990s it began to attract more white players.[4] In 1998 the West Indian Cavaliers Club from Nottingham won the championship of the Bassetlaw League, the leading cricket league in North Nottinghamshire, and have joined the newly created Nottinghamshire County League. The Spencer club, a predominantly African-Caribbean club from Wandsworth, plays in the premier section of the Surrey Championship and appears to be the only ethnic minority club to play in the leagues designated as having ECB premier county league status in Surrey, Middlesex, Kent and Hertfordshire.

The Quaid-e-Azam League may be the league in the North of England with the highest level of play. This league was established in 1981 by Pakistanis living in England.[5] Its title, meaning the father of the nation, is a tribute to Mohammed Ali Jinnah, the founder of Pakistan. Most of its clubs are from the Bradford-Leeds area but it also has clubs from around Manchester and Sheffield. Most of its matches are played on Sundays and the standard of its competition is partly so high because so many of its players are sufficiently talented to be employed as professionals by other clubs on Saturdays. It has enormous prestige among Pakistanis in England. The Pakistan High Commissioner has been the guest of honour at its annual prize-giving ceremony. As so few Asian clubs have their grounds and have to lease municipally owned pitches, which are often of a poor quality, Asian clubs have tended to be

---

4. I am grateful to Professor David McEvoy for providing me with details of the numbers of Asian clubs playing at the different levels of league cricket in Bradford.

5. *Guardian,* 1 June 1990.

concentrated at the lower levels of club cricket. ECB guidelines about the quality of grounds required at different grades of cricket may make it difficult for Asian clubs to rise far up the hierarchy of leagues. No club in the Quaid-e-Azam League has its own ground, but instead clubs hire the grounds of predominantly white clubs.

Most Asian clubs represent distinctive groups within the Asian population, which reflects the fragmented nature of Asian society in England but also relates to the tendency, found in other aspects of Asian society in England, to maintain ties with those of similar backgrounds. Usually kinship, clan identity, language, residential area, religion and ancestral villages or towns in Asia, very often related factors among Asians in England, are the basis on which most Asian cricket clubs have been formed in England. Some clubs are named after villages or regions in Asia, but it is equally easy to produce examples of Asian clubs whose titles are taken from districts of towns in England. Clubs with roughly equal numbers of Hindu and Muslim players are very rare, and most clubs are drawn from different groups within these religious affiliations. In Leicester, the English town with one of the greatest concentrations of Hindus, clubs were originally formed on the basis of caste, but this weakened in the 1990s[6] as residence in England, the effects of education in encouraging social contacts which cross caste boundaries, and higher levels of unemployment leading to the acceptance of jobs not traditionally connected with particular castes, have blunted the intensity of caste as a cause of social division among Hindus. In Bolton and Blackburn, Muslims of Indian and Pakistani descent have usually belonged to different clubs and often have clubs based on regions or towns in India or Pakistan. Muslims are often reticent about discussing with non-Muslims the traditions of Islam to which they subscribe or their mosque affiliations, but in 1993 one Muslim in Bolton claimed that mosque affiliation had no influence over the composition of Muslim cricket clubs, though another mentioned that all the players at his club attended the same mosque. At least two clubs had players who were all Baruchi Muslims.[7] In Bolton the Bolton Indians club has emerged as a club drawing players and support from across the local Hindu community and the Deane and Derby club became the leading Muslim club as it attracted support from different Muslim groups.[8] Yet such clubs have been unusual. In other towns Asian clubs have not been able, or perhaps have not tried, to gather support from almost all of the local Hindu or Muslim population.

In the 1970s and 1980s those from the different Caribbean islands often formed separate clubs. In 1990 there were clubs in Middlesex and Surrey that had originally been formed by those from Antigua, Dominica, Grenada, Guyana and Trinidad

---

6. Interview with Mr A Patel, secretary of Bharat CC, 13 March 2000.
7. Williams, J. (1994), 'South Asians and Cricket in Bolton', *Sports Historian,* 14 (May), pp. 60, 65.
8. Williams, 'South Asians and Cricket', pp. 57, 59.

though most of these had collapsed by the end of the 1990s. In Nottingham the Carib club was originally a club with mainly Jamaican players. There was also a St Kitts club in Nottingham. The West Indian Cavaliers club in Nottingham, one of the most successful African-Caribbean clubs in England, has players with ancestral roots in different parts of the Caribbean, but Tyron Browne, its secretary says that within the club there is often good-hearted banter between those with different island origins. Occasionally players with exaggerated ideas of their abilities have complained of not being selected for the first team on account of their island identity. Mr Browne also added that when an African-Caribbean team from different islands encountered discrimination from whites, a sense of black consciousness and solidarity overshadowed distinctive island identities.[9]

The growth in the number of Asian cricket clubs in the 1990s indicates the heterogeneity and perhaps growing fragmentation of Asian society in Britain, which can be related to the political tensions between India and Pakistan. In 1992, *Eastern Eye* claimed that 'Relations between Britain's Indian and Pakistani communities have reached an all time low. Tensions in the Sub-Continent have found their way to British shores.' In Blackburn animosity between youths of Indian and Pakistani descent resulted in a week of street fighting in which knives, petrol bombs and guns were used.[10] In 1992, fighting between the supporters of India and Pakistan caused the abandonment of a floodlit exhibition match between an Indian XI and a Pakistan XI played at Crystal Palace to raise funds for Imran Khan's cancer hospital.[11] When India defeated Pakistan in the Lombard World Challenge Under-15 World Cup, play was stopped by a pitch invasion and according to the *Guardian* the winning run was 'the signal for further mayhem, with rival factions clashing in front of the pavilion.'[12] Following the destruction of the Ayodha temple in India in 1992, sixteen temples and mosques were attacked in Britain.[13] A local government election in Bradford where the Conservative candidate belonged to the Jat clan and the Labour candidate to the Bains clan, was regarded as a contest between clans rather political parties. In a neighbouring ward, it was thought that a Labour majority was cut from 1,000 to 100 because Muslims voted for a Muslim Conservative rather than the Sikh Labour candidate.[14]

9. Interview with Mr Tyron Browne, secretary of West Indian Cavaliers CC, Nottingham, 18 March 2000.

10. *Eastern Eye*, 2 August 1992.

11. *The Times*, 29 July 1992.

12. *Guardian*, 21 August 1996.

13. *The Times*, 11, 12 December 1992.

14. Bradford Commission (1996), *The Bradford Commission Report. The Report of an Enquiry into Wider Implications of Public Disorders which Occurred on 9, 10 and 11 June, 1995*, London: HMSO, pp. 88–9.

Cricket playing among Asians expresses a determination to maintain Asian identities and culture in England. Cultural practices, such as wearing Asian dress and speaking Asian languages, are for many Asians linked with support for their religions and with maintaining social networks formed in Asia. Establishing clubs on distinctive groups in the Asian populations is part of this desire to uphold Asian values and identities in England. Interviews have shown that most Asians admit supporting India or Pakistan in test matches against England. English language Asian newspapers published in England such as *Asian Times* and *Eastern Eye* give extensive coverage to Indian, Pakistani and Sri Lankan test cricket, irrespective of the part of the world in which matches are being played. When Pakistan won the cricket World Cup in 1992, celebrations by those of Pakistani descent brought Bradford city centre to a standstill. One ethnic minority cricket development officer, who has played first-class cricket in India, has argued that the first generation of Asian immigrants to Britain, who by the 1990s had sons old enough to play adult cricket, came to Britain, often for economic advancement, but had little sympathy for British white culture and no desire to be absorbed by it. Encouraging their families to foster social ties with those of similar backgrounds, which includes playing cricket, was seen as a part of this resistance to white British culture.

Among Muslims it seems likely that the desire to retain social ties with those of similar backgrounds has been intensified by the growth of Islamophobia in Britain, which, in the 1990s, has been magnified by white revulsion over the fatwah against Salman Rushdie and the rise of Muslim fundamentalism in international politics. The report of the Runnymede Trust on Islamophobia, published in 1997, spoke of many hundreds of 'negative references' to Islam and that

Closed as distinct from open views of Islam . . . are routinely reflected and perpetuated in both broadsheets and tabloids, in both the local press and the national, in both considered statements and casual throwaway remarks, and in editorials, columns, articles, reader's letters, cartoons and headlines as well as in reported events. Closed views are also prevalent in the electronic media.

It regarded closed views of Muslims as seeing Islam as monolithic and failing to realise the diversity of Islamic religious traditions, as being inferior to the West and in particular 'barbaric, irrational, primitive, sexist' and 'violent, aggressive, threatening, supportive of terrorism'.[15]

Playing cricket as a means of retaining Asian identities and culture suggests why a higher proportion of Asians than African-Caribbeans play cricket in England. In very general terms it can be argued that the South Asian contribution to modern

15. Runnymede Trust (1997), *Islamophobia: A Challenge for All of Us: Report of the Runnymede Trust Commission on British Muslims and Islamophobia,* London: Runnymede Trust, pp. 5, 24.

Western popular culture has been limited. There has been a significant Asian impact on cooking and shop-keeping but the Asian influence on 'mainstream', and largely white, British clothes fashion, popular music, dance and television is far from great. Multiplex cinemas largely have ignored the products of Bollywood. Modern popular culture in Britain, especially among the young, has been much effected by American popular culture where the black presence has been especially pronounced in music, dance and clothes. Because of the strong black contribution to modern Western popular culture, those of African-Caribbean descent, while perhaps wishing to retain cultural values from the Caribbean, have been more involved with 'mainstream' British popular culture than Asians, though as Paul Gilroy has pointed out, black music and dance, while being part of and helping to shape Western popular culture can also challenge white supremacy.[16] In the 1990s the sport element in 'mainstream' British popular culture has been very much football and black acceptance, and involvement with 'mainstream' popular culture, is reflected in the very high numbers of blacks who play recreational football and who play as professionals. If it has not happened already, it seems likely that in the very near future an all-black team could represent a club playing in the Premiership or the Football League. The Asian presence in professional league football has been negligible. In part this reflects prejudice against Asians among white coaches and managers, but also it shows how Asian suspicion of 'mainstream' British culture has not caused them to take up football with the same enthusiasm as African-Caribbeans.

A study of boys sport at a multi-ethnic secondary school in the southern part of inner London in the early 1990s showed an assumption among Asian pupils that cricket was the first sporting preferences for Asians, basketball for blacks and football for whites.[17] The impression of one cricket development officer in the London area is that African-Caribbean teams now tend to have players who are aged over thirty and suggests that this could be because African-Caribbean clubs have not been so enthusiastic in promoting colts cricket, though reasons for this are unclear. Oral evidence from Lancashire suggests that a majority of Asians who play regularly were born and spent part of their formative years in Asia, but it would also seem that the number of Lancashire-born Asians who play is higher than the number of locally born African-Caribbeans who play. In the Leicester Belgrave Evening Association the average age of Asian players is thought to be around twenty, which could

---

16. Gilroy, P., 'Diaspora and the Detours of Identity', in Woodward, K. (ed.) (1997), *Identity and Difference,* London: Sage, p. 336.

17. Toms, M. and Fleming, S. (1995), '"Why Play Cricket . . . ?": A Preliminary Analysis', *Sports Historian,* 15 (May), p. 93; for a detailed analysis of the differing levels of involvement with sport and physical education among different groups of Asian pupils at a North London secondary school, see Fleming, S. (1995), *'Home and Away': Sport and South Asian Male Youth,* Avebury; Ashgate.

mean that most of them have been born in Britain. Asians have said that the success of India and Pakistan in international cricket in the 1990s helped to keep alive interest in cricket among Asians in England. Perhaps the West Indies' decline as a force in test cricket during the 1990s has contributed to young blacks being less interested in cricket. In the 1990s the numbers of blacks watching the West Indies at test matches in England seemed to fall, which was not the case with Asians when India or Pakistan played, though it has been suggested that the high cost of tickets and the prohibitions on traditional styles of African-Caribbean spectating may have led to fewer black spectators.

The Impact of Asian and Black Teams on Club Cricket

The 1990s have seen much concern about the decline of cricket playing in England. The restructuring of English cricket, which resulted in the creation of the England and Wales Cricket Board in January 1997 to provide a unified structure for professional and recreational cricket, stemmed from the belief that English test match cricket and the game at the grass roots level were interdependent. Both have to be healthy for the game to flourish. The Quick Cricket initiative to encourage cricket playing at primary schools and the appointment by the ECB of thirty-eight regional cricket development officers indicate the depth of concern over the future of recreational cricket. Lord McLaurin, chairman of the Tesco supermarket chain and the first chairman of the ECB, argued that given the increasing range of alternative leisure pursuits, it would be 'a very sizeable achievement' if cricket were to be as healthy in 2020 as it had been at the end of the twentieth century.[18] Localized data shows that as so many white and West Indian clubs have collapsed in the 1990s, the lower levels of recreational cricket by the end of the 1990s would have been in far more parlous condition but for the numbers of Asian clubs.

Despite the large number of Asian clubs, Asians have made a disproportionately small contribution to the administration of recreational cricket. Except for leagues with only Asian clubs, very few Asians have become involved with league administration. In 1999 the thirty-nine members of the Club Cricket Conference officers and executive council did not include one Asian name. For the 1999 season, only one Asian was among the seventeen officers of the Leicestershire League, even though eleven of its seventy-six clubs were Asian. The committee of the Leicester Mutual Sunday School League is unusual in that half of its members are Asians but special efforts had to be made to persuade them to serve on it. In 1999 more than 60 per cent of the teams in the Leicester Belgrave Evening Association were Asian but

---

18. *Wisden Cricketers' Almanack 1997,* London: John Wisden, p. 20.

only two of the twelve members of its committee and none of the six members of its management committee were Asian.[19] Mr A. Patel, the secretary of an Asian club and who has been involved with an Asian club for nearly a quarter of a century in Leicester, has said that Asians do not seem interested in league administration and could offer no explanation for this but does not think that there is any hostility from white committee members.[20] Indeed, predominantly white committees do urge Asians to serve on them. Mike Edwards, a former county cricketer employed by the ECB as cricket development officer, has said that ways need to be found to fast track those from the ethnic minorities into cricket administration. Rudra Singh, a former Indian test cricketer employed by the ECB as its cricket development officer in north-east and north-west Lancashire, has argued that a priority area for the promotion of cricket among ethnic minority groups must be their greater involvement with the administration and management of cricket.[21] Except for some very distinguished former players, such as Clive Lloyd who served on the Lancashire committee, very few Asians and African-Caribbeans have been elected onto the committees of first-class counties. Few seem to have become members of county clubs.

The contribution of Asians and African-Caribbeans to women's cricket has been limited. No evidence has been found of cricket clubs being formed in England for Asian or African-Caribbean women. No woman from the ethnic minorities has played for the England women's senior team, but is possible that the establishment at so many primary schools of Quick Cricket, a form of the game devised to introduce both sexes to cricket, may lead to more ethnic minority girls wanting to play the traditional game and some are already in the national junior squad. Support for men's cricket among Asian women has been far less than that among white women, though of course it can be argued that, given the time and money costs of playing cricket, the playing of cricket by men has often meant that family resources are directed to male rather than female interests. Very few Muslim women watch club cricket except from the privacy of cars. A Hindu male from Leicester has pointed out that more Hindu than Muslim women watch club cricket but not to the same extent as white women. At levels of cricket where the tea interval is still observed, and in many areas this is still strong at even the lower levels of club cricket, teas at white clubs are usually prepared and served by the wives and mothers of players. At Asian clubs teas are almost always served by men. The contention expressed in the early

19. Information supplied by members of the Leicester Mutual Sunday School League and the Leicester Belgrave Evening Association.

20. Interview with Mr A Patel.

21. I am grateful to Mr Singh for providing me with details of the presentations he makes to ethnic minority groups.

1980s that within South Asian culture, sport was a male cultural space into which women and adolescent girls rarely strayed,[22] would appear to be still the case. White women seem to be more involved with social fund-raising events than Asian women. Ethnic minority cricket has not provided opportunities for social contacts between women from different ethnic groups. In 1990, no Asian and no obviously West Indian clubs affiliated to the Club Cricket Conference had women secretaries or fixture secretaries. In 1999, only one of the sixty-five Asian clubs affiliated to the Club Cricket Conference had a woman secretary whereas six out of a sample of one hundred predominantly white Middlesex clubs had women secretaries.

Objective measures of whether ethnic minority players have raised the playing standard of club cricket are not possible. Clubs playing at the highest levels of league cricket in the North and Midlands have always engaged professionals and many of these have been, or became test-match cricketers, for the West Indies, India and Pakistan. In the 1990s clubs playing at a high level of league cricket but just below the highest tier began to employ professionals and many of these have been from Asia and the Caribbean but also Australia, New Zealand or South Africa. The presence of such professionals may well have raised the quality of cricket in such leagues, but matches can become contests between professionals with amateur players having little more than walk-on parts. Many talented Asians play at a level of club lower than what their talents merit and possibly this has improved playing standards at the more humble levels of cricket. It is no more easy to decide whether ethnic minority players have changed the style in which club cricket is played. A desire to imitate what are thought to be the strengths of test teams may influence how cricket is played by different ethnic groups, and it would be interesting to know whether Indian clubs use more spin bowlers and West Indians more fast bowlers. Watching Asian teams at the lower levels of club cricket in Lancashire suggests that the behaviour of Asian teams is very similar to white teams. Asian players from the batting side tend to applaud and cajole their batsmen much like white teams.

A frequent complaint from whites is that Asian teams are too competitive but such comments are often found in parts of the North where whites have traditionally taken pride in the fierce competitiveness of league cricket. *Anyone for Cricket?*, the report of research by Ian McDonald and Sharda Ugra into cricket cultures in Essex and East London, found that ethnic minority teams from East London played more

---

22. Leaman, O. (1984), *Sit on the Sidelines and Watch the Boys Play: Sex Differentiation in Physical Education,* York: Longman/School Council, p. 17. For further discussion of how ethnicity accentuates gender differences on sport participation among South Asians, see Carrington, B., Chivers, T. and Williams, T. (1987), 'Gender, Leisure and Sport: A Case-study of Young People of South Asian Descent', *Leisure Studies,* 6 (3).

competitively than white teams from the more rural parts of eastern and northern Essex, but a cricket development officer from the South East of England has said that white teams playing at the highest level of cricket in Essex play an equally competitive style of cricket.[23] Mr A. Patel of the Bharat club in Leicester claims that matches between matches between local Muslim and Hindu teams are contested far more fiercely than matches between Asian and white teams. In 1999 police were called to match between a Hindu and a Muslim side in Leicester when one player struck another with a bat but such incidents seem to be extremely rare. The aggression associated with Asian teams, and especially Muslim teams, may be related to the competitiveness of recreational cricket in Pakistan where street cricket is thought to have a combativeness not encountered in England.[24] Complaints about the excessive competitiveness of Asian teams, especially when made in localities where the competitiveness of league cricket has traditionally been a source of pride, seems to be a case of judging Asians by differing standards and a form of prejudice against them. But this may not always be the case. Because of their preference to play for Asian teams, many talented Asians play at a level far below what their abilities merit where pitches are often poor, yet they still play with the aggression and determination that has made them such good players. Whites, on the other hand, who are prepared to play with such poor facilities are rarely such good players and do not take cricket all that seriously. For them, playing cricket is having an afternoon or evening out with their mates, a bit of a laugh, not something to be taken too seriously. Such an attitude easily leads whites to see Asians as playing in far too competitive and combative style.[25] Talented white cricketers who want to improve their game tend to gravitate to clubs with better facilities.

Racism and Club Cricket

Interviews with Asians from Blackburn, Bolton, Bradford and Pendle in the North and from Leicester in the Midlands, and the data collected for the reports *Anyone for Cricket?*, *Crossing the Boundary* which looked racism in league cricket in the

23. McDonald, I. and Ugra, S. (1998), *Anyone for Cricket? Equal Opportunities and Changing Cricket Cultures in Essex and East London,* London: Roehampton Institute and University of East London, pp. 20–2. The material collected for the *Anyone for Cricket?* report is also discussed in McDonald, I. And Ugra, S. (1999), '"It's Just Not Cricket!" Ethnicity, Division and Imagining the Other in English Cricket', in Cohen, P. (ed.), *New Ethnicities, Old Racisms?,* London: Zed; interview with Mr Mike Edwards, Cricket Development Officer, Surrey Cricket Board, 3 March 2000.

24. See for instance the account of Pakistan street cricket by Hasnain Malik, educated at Oxford, in *Cricketer International,* January 1992, p. 25.

25. Interview with Mr Rudra Singh, 24 February 1999.

Leeds-Bradford area and *Clean Bowl Racism,* prepared by the ECB's Racism Study Group,[26] all show that Asians and blacks were convinced that there was discrimination against them in club cricket in 1990s. The ECB Racism Study Group was concerned with all forms of cricket and not merely club cricket and it also gathered information from sections of the population who were not especially interested in cricket. Fifty-seven per cent of those from the ethnic minorities who replied to its questionnaires believed that racism existed in cricket. Sixteen per cent of all of those taking part in the survey, who numbered over a thousand, had personal experience of racism in cricket, though this included all forms of the game, and attributed 53 per cent of this to white players, 39 per cent to spectators, 22 per cent to clubs, 9 per cent to officials and 11 per cent to umpires.[27]

Prejudice and discrimination against the ethnic minorities in club cricket have taken many forms. The secretary of the West Indian Cavaliers club from Nottingham recalls 'one or two instances' over twenty years ago of white opponents throwing bananas and making monkey noises but has seen nothing similar in recent years. *Crossing the Boundary* reported that 'Nearly all Asian and black players had experienced racism of one sort or another during their cricketing careers. Even those who at first responded that they had not experienced any racism later recounted experiences that suggested otherwise.' Many felt that racism was expressed in covert rather than more open ways. One black player said 'It may not always be right there in front of you but you know it's just lurking round the corner, you can tell by some people's attitude . . . There's not many people that come up and say they don't like you because of your colour or whatever. But you'll hear it going on behind your back.' Even whites admitted that there were occasional instances of racial comments being made.[28] An Asian respondent interviewed by the *Anyone for Cricket?* researchers thought that Asians had to face much racism in the lower leagues in Essex and spoke of 'a lot of racialism . . . abuses on the field . . . there is a lot of that for every Asian player. Lots of abuses, racially provoking players, making them lose their temper so they can get out, all silly things. If you complain, they totally ignore it. Nothing is done and if the white clubs make a complaint against you, always straightaway, they jump on you and take an action.'[29]

26. Williams, 'South Asians and Cricket'; *Anyone for Cricket?*; Long, J., Nesti, M., Carrington, B. and Gilson, N. (1997), *Crossing the Boundary: A Study of the Nature and Extent of Racism in Local League Cricket,* Leeds: Leeds Metropolitan University; ECB Racism Study Group (1999), *Clean Bowl Racism: 'Going Forward Together': A Report on Racial Equality in Cricket,* London: ECB Racism Study Group.

27. *Clean Bowl Racism,* p. 28.

28. *Crossing the Boundary,* pp. 17–18.

29. *Anyone for Cricket?,* p. 33.

Many whites have claimed that traditionally white clubs would welcome players of any colour, but Asians and African-Caribbeans have found that this is not always the case. Mr Tyron Browne has said that the West Indian Cavaliers Club in Nottingham became such a powerful side as African-Caribbean players joined it when some found that they were not being picked for the first teams of predominantly white clubs.[30] Asians in Bolton have said that they felt that the leading predominantly white clubs were interested only in Asians who were, or appeared to have the potential to become, outstanding players. The researchers for *Crossing the Boundary* were told 'It's very difficult for an Asian or West Indian lad, unless he's got a few mates with him, to go down to an all-white club. He's got to be really serious about playing to go and take all the shit so a lot of Asian lads will just not do it.'[31] Similar sentiments were expressed in Essex. It is possible, of course, that the discrimination which Asians may have experienced in other areas of life may have led them to assume that they would feel unwanted at predominantly white clubs. In his capacity as a cricket development officer among ethnic minorities in north-east and north-west Lancashire, the former Indian test match cricketer Rudra Singh argues that a traditional white view, at clubs relying heavily on bar receipts, was that ethnic minority players and their families contribute little to the profitability, viability and social life of a club. He thinks that whites and the ethnic minorities need to make everyone welcome and to accommodate to different cultures. Whilst those from the ethnic minorities often commented that white clubs were not sufficiently welcoming, Rudra Singh calls on non-whites to be less sensitive about issues that are not necessarily racist. He also felt that relations at clubs could be improved if more parents from the ethnic minorities would watch their children playing or being coached and be prepared to take more part in the running of clubs.[32]

Some Asians have seen a reluctance by white clubs to arrange fixtures with them as racial discrimination. The secretary of an Asian club in Essex said

I would telephone and say we are looking for an away game because we don't have a home ground. Afterwards, when they were trying to write down our name they would say, 'Punjab XI' and they would say: 'Actually we have an away fixture for ourselves at the moment' . . . So I instantly changed the name to Strikers XI and I started getting some fixtures in and started playing white teams. But when we would turn up, the face expressions we would get were like 'What's happening here?' I don't know whether it is an image of our culture or what.

30. Interview with Mr Tyron Browne.

31. *Crossing the Boundary*, p. 21.

32. I am grateful to Mr Singh for giving me copies of materials he uses in his talks at cricket clubs.

Another Asian club secretary said that if the secretary of a white club 'knows there is even an accent there they're not going to give you a fixture. As soon as they know it's an Asian side they will find an excuse saying "We are too strong" [or] "We haven't got a date free" – even though I find out later on that they have dates.' Muslim teams have found that in Essex fears that a Muslim team would not spend much in the club bar after a match has been used as an excuse to refuse them fixtures.[33]

In some locations the very low numbers of Asian clubs admitted to the higher levels of league cricket are seen as racial prejudice. This has been especially so among Asians in Bolton. Despite having spent £80,000 on making its ground one of the best in Bolton[34] and having won the Association's Second Division, the Deane and Derby club was not elected to the First Division of the Bolton and District Cricket Association in 1990 but two whites clubs from outside Bolton were admitted. This caused the Second Division clubs to sever their links with the Association and set up a new league, the Bolton Metropolitan League, though some whites from First Division clubs have said in private that the Second Division clubs were more or less invited to leave the Association. In 1993 ten of the sixteen teams in the Metropolitan League were Asian. In 1991 a banner with the words 'Apartheid here in Bolton. No politics in sport. All men are equal' was hoisted at a match between sides representing the Bolton League and the Bolton Association,[35] though how much support this commanded among Asians or whites in Bolton is not clear. In 1993 the Bolton Association again rejected an application from Deane and Derby to join its First Division, but accepted two white clubs. Said Patel, a Bolton Asian, was reported to have said that 'They're extending the boundaries from John-o-Groats to Land's End and there is no Asian club in between . . . I think the Bolton league [sic] is racist. They want no Black clubs in the competition.'[36] Subsequent applications by the Deane and Derby club and by Bolton Indians to join the senior division of the Bolton Association have been rejected. Members of both clubs have said that as Asians they feel that their commitment to Bolton has been spurned. When questioned white players and clubs officials have denied that racism has been a factor in the failure of the two Asian clubs to be admitted to the senior division of the Bolton Association, although some have admitted to not enjoying playing against Asian teams. There have been suggestions, but nothing firmer than suggestions, that some white clubs, have left leagues because of a dislike of playing against coloured clubs.

33. McDonald and Ugra, *Anyone for Cricket?*, p. 27.

34. *Bolton Evening News*, 29 June 1991.

35. *Bolton Evening News*, 15 July 1991.

36. *Eastern Eye*, 29 June 1993. Mr Patel was referring to the Bolton and District Cricket Association and not the Bolton League.

Three or four teams withdrew from the Nottingham Amateur League because it was thought they objected to it being dominated by the West Indian Cavaliers. By the late 1990s all the white clubs had withdrawn from the Bolton Metropolitan League. One reason for this was that dissatisfaction with municipal pitches, but one white player, who insisted that his comments should not be attributed to him, said that some of the Asian teams were 'too unsporting'. There had been resentment when it had been discovered that an Asian team representing the league in an inter-league competition had fielded unregistered players.

Comments such as 'Well, you know what they're like' and 'I don't want to sound a racist but' suggest that some whites are aware that they could be prejudiced against Asians. *Anyone for Cricket?* shows that in the Essex area the quality of Asian grounds has prevented Asian clubs from progressing to higher levels of club cricket.[37] The executive summary of the ECB's *Clean Bowl Racism* mentions that the poor quality of grounds had been used as an excuse to deny ethnic minority teams entry or promotion into leagues and so had to be 'seen as racism'. Its conclusion, however, reached after much deliberation, that 'the base line is that recent, newly formed clubs/teams, whether ethnic minority or white English, have little option but to play on the often inadequate local authority ("parks") grounds' suggests that it did not accept that excluding clubs from certain levels of cricket was always necessarily racist.[38]

Racism, Club Cricket and the First-class Game

Many from the ethnic minorities believe that opportunities for Asian and black cricketers born or raised in England to play first-class cricket have been restricted by a lack of interest among county clubs in ethnic minority cricket clubs. As cricket has been such a strong focus of Yorkshire identity and as so many Asians live and play cricket in Yorkshire, the failure of the Yorkshire club to select a local Asian or African-Caribbean for its first team has provoked much comment, particularly since Yorkshire's playing achievements in the 1980s and 1990s have not matched the club's traditions – it has won the county championship nearly twice as often as any other county but has not been the champion county since 1968. Many inside and outside Yorkshire have seen this failure to play a local Asian in the county first team as the result of an ingrained racism within the county club.

37. *Anyone for Cricket,* pp. 46–7.
38. *Clean Bowl Racism,* p. 8.

The stated policy of the Yorkshire club has always been that it would play any Asian whose ability was good enough for county cricket. In an interview published in 1990, Joe Lister, the Yorkshire CCC secretary, speaking when only those born in Yorkshire could play for the club, said that the county 'would play any cricketer provided he was born in Yorkshire', but he did not seem to believe that the Yorkshire Asian population was committed to the club. He claimed that when England played test matches at Headingley against the West Indies, India or Pakistan, 'the bulk of the West Indian supporters who come . . . come from Birmingham and London . . . The local Indians or Pakistanis don't come at all. I wouldn't know whose failing it is. We have some Indian and Pakistani members, but not many', though others may have argued that the local Asian population did not commit themselves to the club because they believed that it was not interested, or even hostile, to them. Lister conceded that reports of racist incidents at Headingley and Scarborough could have deterred Asians from attending matches. In 1990 the former Yorkshire and England batsman Geoffrey Boycott advocated the scrapping of Yorkshire's rule that only those born in the county could play for the club, a tradition that was then supported by Brian Close, chairman of the club's cricket committee. Boycott hoped that bringing in stars from Pakistan, India or the West Indies would encourage the emergence into the county team of black Yorkshiremen. He was reported to have said that supporters of the Yorkshire-born policy were 'like ostriches with their heads buried in the sand, living in the past on former glory . . . Brian Close and the rest of them think that cricket begins and ends in Yorkshire.'[39] Yet in his book *Boycott on Cricket,* published in 1990, Boycott, did not include the absence of local Asian players from the county team in his detailed analysis of the Yorkshire team's relatively poor playing record in the recent past.[40]

Sidney Fielden, chairman of the Yorkshire CCC public relations committee, was one member of the county committee who was concerned about the club's relationship with the local ethnic minorities. When the county cricket academy opened in 1989, he and its director Bob Appleyard sent literature about this to cricket organizations in Yorkshire in three languages. Fielden accepted that Yorkshire crowds did taunt black cricketers. In his view there was 'a minority which is racist and they seem to think that because a player is black they must give him stick.' When he took some coloured lads to a Yorkshire match, some committee members said 'Why doesn't Sid do that with white kids?' Fielden rejected the argument that coloured players received so much abuse because Yorkshire supporters believed that overseas

39. *Sunday Times,* 25 November 1990.
40. Boycott, G. (1991 reissue of the 1990 edition), *Boycott on Cricket,* London: Corgi.

test stars playing for other counties had caused Yorkshire to less successful. The most successful overseas cricketer in county cricket at that time, the white New Zealander Richard Hadlee, was not abused. Fielden believed that if Yorkshire played a Yorkshire-born coloured player much of the racist behaviour among Yorkshire spectators would disappear.[41]

Ralph Middlebrook, manager of the Yorkshire Cricket School and the cricket development officer for Leeds Leisure Services, seemed to be arguing in 1990 that it was the fault of Asians that none had played for Yorkshire. He claimed that no Yorkshire-born Asian had played for the county's first team because Asians preferred to play with teams from their own community. In his words they 'prefer to play with the Kegan valley cricket club or the Asian All-stars on park pitches on a Sunday or in minor league cricket . . . you only get better by playing with people as good as or better than you . . . Until Asians and West Indians from the county play in established leagues in sufficient numbers, we will not get one or two into the Yorkshire team.' He added that his efforts to persuade Asian youths to join clubs had not been successful. 'I bully them, cajole them and encourage them. And yet . . . I don't know what their parents say to them. But the boys do not have sufficient commitment. All too often they announce that an uncle, grandfather, or whoever, has just died and they can't play. Whether this is true or not true, I am not prepared to speculate. It just seems to happen rather a lot.'[42]

The unguarded comments by Brian Close, a former Yorkshire and England captain and the chairman of the county's cricket committee, in a television interview broadcast in 1990 about 'our boys', that is whites born in Yorkshire and 'Pakistanis who have only just come over here' provoked great offence among Asians in Yorkshire, although one sports journalist has contended that this led the county club and local Asian cricketers to consider how their relationship could be improved. In the early 1990s the club made greater efforts to develop links with local Asian cricketers. After sending letters in Urdu, Bengali and Gujerati to all of the 6,000 cricket clubs in Yorkshire inviting youngsters to the club's cricket academy for an appraisal of their ability, only fifteen who were not white turned up.[43] The club established an under-seventeen ethnic minority team and the Yorkshire Cricket Board set up an Ethnic Minority Forum. In November 1990 the rule that only those born in Yorkshire could play for the county was relaxed to allow those who had been raised but not born in Yorkshire to play for the club and for the 1992 season the Yorkshire-born

41. Bose, M. (1990), *Cricket Voices: Interviews with Mihir Bose,* London: Kingswood, pp. 42, 251.

42. Bose, *Cricket Voices,* pp. 153–4.

43. *Sunday Times,* 9 May 1990.

rule was scrapped totally. Though advocated as a means of allowing Yorkshire to compete on less unequal terms with other counties rather than the means of allowing more ethnic minority cricketers to play for the county, breaking one of the club's most cherished traditions did not lead to a local Asian or African-Caribbean playing for Yorkshire. Yorkshire engaged Sachin Tendulkar of India as its overseas professional in 1992 and Richie Richardson of the West Indies in 1993 and 1994 but their playing achievements did not cause Yorkshire to become a vastly stronger force in county cricket. In 1991 Adil Ditta, born in Middlesbrough of Pakistan of descent, was the first ethnic minority player to join Yorkshire's cricket academy and played for the county's second but not the first team before playing for Leicestershire's second team. In 1992 Ismail Dawood, born and educated in Yorkshire, was invited to join the Yorkshire academy, but did not play for either the Yorkshire first or second teams, although he was a member of the England under-nineteen team in 1993–4 and has played occasionally for the first teams of Northamptonshire and Glamorgan. By 1997 an employee of the club said that it was 'desperate to find a home-grown Asian who could make the grade'. In 1999 Yorkshire held trials for more than 200 youngsters of Pakistani origin whilst the captain of the Yorkshire under-thirteen team was Safraz Mohammed. In 1999 the county club had given scholarships at its academy to two fourteen-year-old local Asians and was closely watching three others.[44]

A common explanation among many whites in Yorkshire for the failure of a local Asian to play for the county's first team is that none has been good enough. In 1990 the *Sheffield Weekly Gazette* argued that 'There are no charges of racism to answer. Rather, there is some dismay at Headingley that no coloured player has yet proved good enough to graduate to county level.'[45] Bob Appleyard, the former Yorkshire and England player, felt that as Asians from Yorkshire were not playing for other counties this meant that there had been no local talented Asians for the county to overlook. One response to this point was that white Yorkshire-born cricketers who played for other counties had usually had some form of coaching from Yorkshire and that Asian and African-Caribbean cricketers in Yorkshire had been denied this.[46] Ralph Middlebrook's comments that only a very tiny number of white youths were good enough to play for the county could be read as meaning that Asians had exaggerated the abilities of local Asian cricketers.[47] Brian Clough, who first played

---

44. *Guardian*, 1 September, 1999; *Cricketer International*, August 1999, p. 4; [*Bradford Telegraph and Argus*] *Asian Eye*, 16 August 1999.

45. *Sheffield Weekly Gazette*, 20 July 1989, quoted in Searle, C. (1990), 'Race before Wicket: Cricket, Empire and the White Rose', *Race & Class*, 31, January–March, p. 46.

46. *Cricket Life International*, January 1990, p. 21.

47. Bose, *Cricket Voices*, pp. 155–6.

cricket in the Bradford League in 1944, is cricket chairman of the Bradford League club Bowling Old Lane, and as thirty Asians usually play each week for his club's three teams, it seems unlikely that he is prejudiced against Asians but he is perhaps in a position to assess the abilities of Asians playing in the Bradford League. He was outraged by the comments made by Imran Khan during the 1999 World Cup that one reason for England's poor performance was that racism caused Yorkshire to overlook talented local Asians. Clough said that

> There are a whole lot of Asian players playing in Yorkshire, so if they were good enough they would be getting in the county side. Why didn't Imran ask (former Bowling Old Lane player) Yousef Youhana or Ijaz Ahmed, two Pakistan players who have played in the Yorkshire leagues, whether they thought there were any good enough – I'm sure they would have said the same as me.[48]

Many Asians in Yorkshire take a different view and claim that discrimination in club and county cricket explains why no local Asian has played for the county first team. When the offer of the black West Indian Viv Richards to play for Yorkshire in 1989 was rejected on the grounds that he had not been born in Yorkshire, Afzal Raja, an Asian club cricketer in Yorkshire, thought that local Asians interpreted this as meaning that there was little chance of them playing for Yorkshire. In 1990 *Cricket Life International* mentioned that some Asians saw the policy of players having to be born in Yorkshire as 'camouflage' for 'what they felt was "nothing short of racism." Mohamed Iqbal from Bradford did not think that any promising Asian cricketers had been seen by the county. He said that 'every week Asian players are making runs and taking wickets and nothing happens. If Fred Bloggs scored a century or took eight for 20 I'm sure a 'phone call would have been made.' Other Asians recognized that white parents were often more eager than Asian parents for their sons to consider playing cricket as a career.[49] Even though young Asians were invited to the Yorkshire Cricket Academy and the Yorkshire Cricket Board had set up its Ethnic Minority Forum, Asians continued to believe that the county club was not particularly interested in recruiting Asian players. In 1997, *Crossing the Boundary* concluded that 'a sizeable minority of white players, and all ethnic minority players' believed that not enough was being done to identify and recruit ethnic minority players by Yorkshire. One black player reported 'I played for Yorkshire when I was 16 and can see exactly why there's no [Asian or black] players 'cause I didn't fit in at all. I felt like a complete outsider. I played for about two seasons and hated it, I really hated it. It's hard to explain, but you feel you're on a lower level. I wanted to play cricket at a high level and that put me off completely.'

---

48. *Asian Eye*, 13 September 1999.
49. *Cricket Life International*, January 1990, pp. 20–1.

Mohanlal Mistry, a Bradford Asian, said that if 'oil was found under the streets of Bradford companies like BP and Shell would be straight here to use that resource, but there are thousands of kids who are passionate about cricket and no-one is trying to tap into that.'[50]

Very few local Asians have been engaged by Lancashire. In the seasons 1996, 1997 and 1998 no local Asian played for the first team and one played in one second-team match for Lancashire. Employing such leading Asian test cricketers as overseas professionals like Farouk Engineer, Wazim Akram and Muttiah Muralitharan may have caused Asians to be less critical of the low number of local Asians who have played for the county. One white member of Lancashire has commented that when he collected contributions to Akram's benefit fund in Lancashire, many members seemed to begrudge making contributions and made disparaging remarks about Pakistanis and about Akram having been injured so often during his Lancashire career. In Leicestershire complaints from local Asians about the county overlooking Asian cricketers has led the county to arrange a two day cricket festival for Asian teams at the county ground in August 2000. Jack Birkenshaw, the Leicestershire coach, has contacted even the humblest leagues in the county and invited all who appear to be talented players, regardless of the level of cricket at which they are playing, to the county ground for assessments of their suitability for intensive training. Like the Yorkshire county club holding trials for 200 Asian young players in 1999, the competition organised by Leicestershire show how alienated local Asians have felt from the county club, but Asian discontent with the Leicestershire club rarely provoked comment in the national press. Whilst welcoming this initiative from Yorkshire, Taj Butt of the Quaid-e-Azam League has pointed out that 'there always seem to be lads who miss out for some reason and we would like to see a system where no one misses out. We would rather see these lads within the system rather than taking special measures to include them. In other words, we would rather see a system that includes these players to start with.'[51] Worries about the insecurities of professional cricket may have been a major cause for the low number of Asians raised in England who became county cricketers in the 1980s and 1990s. In the 1980s and 1990s only five players of Asian descent have played for England compared with eleven African-Caribbeans, but in 1991 those of Indian and Pakistani descent in England and Wales outnumbered African-Caribbeans by almost two to one and in the 1990s a higher proportion of Asians were playing recreational cricket.

50. *Asian Eye,* 12 July 1999.
51. *Asian Eye,* 18 August 1999.

The recommendation in the ECB report *Clean Bowl Racism* that county boards had an obligation to encourage ethnic minority clubs and leagues to become 'an integral part of the cricket family by embracing and accepting diverse cultures within their structure and environment' is an admission that ethnic minority cricket has often been sidelined by the mainstream cricket establishment, which has county cricket and the England team as its pinnacle.[52] In 1993 only ten Asians born or educated in England were on the books of the first-class counties, but by 1995 this figure had risen to twenty-one though in that year eight county clubs had none. In 1998, nineteen Asians qualified to play for England played in the county championship, which represented six per cent of all players qualified for England, a proportion higher than the Asian proportion of England's population, but probably less than the proportion of Asians playing cricket regularly in England. The attempts of the county clubs to forge closer links with their ethnic minority populations and to look more closely at the potential of talented ethnic minority cricketers has coincided with the ECB's declaration of an anti-racist policy. The report *Clean Bowl Racism* shows that the ECB recommended that the county boards ensure that ethnic minority clubs and leagues are integrated into the mainstream of English cricket, that all clubs affiliated to the ECB have written statements that they have an anti-racist open membership policy and are prepared to prohibit racially abusive comments and actions. Anti-racism training is provided for all ECB employees. The appointment of cricket development officers with ethnic minority backgrounds such as Cookie Patel in the Midlands and Rudra Singh in Lancashire show a determination to promote multi-ethnicity in cricket. The Lord's Taverners and the Cricket Foundation have each provided £60,000 for the promotion of four inner city/ethnic minority schemes to promote the playing of cricket.[53] Prohibitions on styles of spectator behaviour are to be lifted and the block booking of tickets for corporate hospitality groups are to be restricted in the hope of attracting more ethnic minority spectators to test cricket. Conversations with those from county clubs creates a strong impression that they are sincere in their attempts to forge links with local Asian cricketers. All of this can be seen as a recognition, though no doubt a belated recognition, of what the ethnic minorities, and Asians in particular, can do for cricket in England.

But these initiatives can be seen equally as a realization by the predominantly white cricket establishment that it ignored for too long the ethnic minority contribution to cricket and especially to recreational cricket. Until the late 1990s most county coaches and scouts argued that they could assess the potential of players to become a county player only if they played at the higher levels of club cricket. No doubt there was much to support this view, but it discriminated in effect against

52. *Clean Bowl Racism*, p. 49.
53. *Clean Bowl Racism*, pp. 12–13, 45–54.

players of great potential, and principally Asians, who played at the lower levels of club cricket. Asians may have exaggerated the numbers of Asians who had the ability to play first-class cricket, but there is no way of establishing how many were overlooked by county clubs. In the 1990s county clubs began to look more closely at players from all levels of recreational cricket, but it can be argued that this change of policy stems from the dire state of cricket, and especially the first-class game, in England. Growing awareness of the interdependence of all levels of cricket in England has led to the restructuring of cricket and prompted a concern that if England is to become a major power in test cricket again, cricket will need to tap all possible sources of playing talent and attract paying spectators from all groups. Whilst the cricket establishment has realized, some would say belatedly, that the present plight of English cricket results from a failure to include the ethnic minorities in the mainstream of cricket and so take advantage of their playing abilities, the overlooking of the ethnic minorities in the past suggests that the current change of heart has been produced by anxieties over the decline of the game among the white population in England. Had England still been a force in test cricket and cricket playing among whites been stronger, one wonders whether anti-racist initiatives would have been embraced with such enthusiasm.

Conclusion

Grounds for Optimism?

There are signs that at the start of the twenty-first century racial discrimination in cricket, whilst not absent, is weaker than ever before. The ECB is showing more readiness than its predecessors to admit and combat the existence of racism in the game. In 1999 the ECB appointed its Racism Study Group which produced the survey of racism in cricket *Clean Bowl Racism*. In order to drive racism from cricket *Clean Bowl Racism* recommended that all clubs affiliated to the ECB, regardless of the level at which they play, should have 'an active, open door membership policy' written into their constitutions and codes of conduct for all players, officials, members and supporters prohibiting racial abuse and racist conduct. First-class clubs were urged to ensure that racist literature is not distributed in or around their grounds and to provide stewards with training to act against racist chanting and abuse at international matches. The ECB and county boards are to encourage ethnic minority representation on their committees and in their administration. Cricket development officers from the ethnic minorities have been appointed by the ECB. The ECB has also set up a working party to ensure that these recommendations are implemented and to monitor their effects. The appointment of ethnic minority cricket development officers such as Rudra Singh and Cookie Patel and of development officers from the ethnic minorities such as Steve Sylvester in Hertfordshire, Garry Steer in Huntingdon-shire and Rupert Evans in Oxfordshire can be seen as further attempts by cricket in England to become less tainted by suspicions of racism.

It has already been shown that criticisms in England of the exuberant styles of cricket spectating at test matches in England by the supporters of the West Indies, India and Pakistan were intertwined with assumptions that white traditions of cricket spectating represented the correct method of watching cricket, assumptions that could be interpreted as expressions of white supremacy. A new attitude to the behaviour of cricket spectators was evident when the 1999 Cricket World Cup was played in England. The noisy and flamboyant behaviour of Indian and Pakistan supporters was praised and recognized as proof of the enthusiasm for cricket among Asians. It was even argued that such forms of cricket spectating could help to revive interest in international cricket in England and help to undermine impressions of cricket as a sport with an old-fashioned, somewhat fuddy-duddy air. Some even claimed that more excited spectators could help England to play better. The county clubs with grounds where test cricket is played have agreed to accept the *Clean Bowl Racism* recommendation that spectators be allowed to take musical instruments into selected parts of their grounds.

The appointment of Nasser Hussain, born in India but raised in England, as England captain is another indication that ethnic discrimination in cricket may be declining. Hardly any public complaints were made about England being captained by a player who is not white. In 1998 Adam Hollioake, of Samoan descent, captained the England one-day team. Many counties in the 1980s and 1990s have had Asian or black captains but Hussain at Essex, Mark Alleyne at Gloucestershire and Mark Ramprakash at Middlesex have been the only coloured captains who had not played first-class cricket overseas before taking up county cricket. Home developed African-Caribbean cricketers have not yet been canvassed widely as captains of England.

The greater sensitivity to ethnic issues in cricket can be related to the dismal performance of the England test match and one day international teams in the second half of the 1990s. In 1999 England lost the sixth successive Ashes test series, failed to progress beyond the first stage of the World Cup held in England, followed this by losing the home test series against New Zealand and then lost the series against South Africa in South Africa. This produced much heart-searching in English cricket. The restructuring of cricket in England resulting in the formation of the ECB and the establishment of the county cricket boards to forge closer links between club and county cricket, owed much to a growing realization of the interdependence of first-class and recreational cricket. The greater willingness of county clubs to look at the more talented cricketers playing at the lower levels of club stems from a feeling that if the England team is to become stronger, no cricket talent can be overlooked. Cynics may say that had England still been a major power in test cricket, the anti-racist initiatives in English cricket might have more half-hearted.

In the second half of the 1990s accusations of cheating by Pakistan did not figure as prominently as in the 1980s and early 1990s. The adoption in test cricket of neutral umpires, advocated first by Pakistan, has caused accusations of Pakistan umpires being cheats to disappear, though it must also be remembered that, at the time of writing, June 2000, England has not played a test series in Pakistan since the Gatting-Shakoor Rana confrontation. The issuing of the Qayyum report and the suspension of Pakistani cricketers from test cricket because of match fixing have not received coverage in the British press on the same scale as the allegations about ball tampering in 1992 and 1993, though this may have been because matches against England are not thought to have been fixed. Mastering the technique of reverse swing by the bowlers of most countries, including Darren Gough of England, has perhaps weakened suspicions that Pakistani bowlers achieved this by illegal methods. The 1996 Pakistan tour of England provoked little controversy perhaps because there was more recognition in England that Pakistan had a very fine side and it was no surprise when England lost the series. When, in July 2000, the Pakistani fast bowler

Waqar Younis became the first cricketer to receive a one-match ban from international cricket after the, match referee John Reid found that he tampered with the ball
in a one-day match between Pakistan and South Africa,[1] this caused comparatively
little adverse comment in England. The collapse of apartheid meant that playing in
South Africa or against South African teams was no longer entwined with the political
debates about how far an international boycott of South Africa was the most effective
method of combating apartheid.

Complaints about the West Indian fast bowlers were made less often in English
cricket by the 1990s, but this could have been because the West Indian pace attack
was not so formidable as in the 1970s and 1980s. Curtley Ambrose and Courtney
Walsh have been very great fast bowlers and have received effective support from
Ian Bishop but they have do not seem to have had quite the same combined menace
as the four-man pace attack of Clive Lloyd's West Indian team. Complaints about
West Indian bowling may also have not been so pronounced because the West Indian
side was less strong in test cricket in the 1990s than in the previous decade and a
half, but the decline of the West Indies as a force in test cricket seems to have been
due more to a weakening of batting than of bowling, which re-emphasizes the point
made by West Indians that criticisms of the four-man pace attack overlooked the
phenomenal all-round strength of their side.

Any decline of ethnic prejudice in cricket can be related to the determination
of coloured cricketers to register their opposition to racism in the 1990s. This was
shown most clearly by the response of the black England bowler Devon Malcolm
who decided to take legal action against *Wisden Cricket Monthly* for printing an
article, with the provocative tile 'Is It In The Blood?' by Robert Henderson in
1995 who questioned the loyalty to England of players not born in England.
Henderson called for England to select only players 'so imbued with a sense of
cultural belonging' who could give more than a call of duty in test cricket and
asked whether 'All the players whom I would describe as foreigners may well be
trying at a conscious level, but is that desire to succeed *instinctive,* a matter of
biology?'[2] In 1996 Henderson was reported to have said on a BBC Radio 5
programme that 'Part of being English is being white.'[3] Devon Malcolm and Phil
DeFreitas were each successful in their legal actions against the magazine. Although
David Graveney, secretary of the Cricketers' Association, had advised Malcolm
against taking legal action, Malcolm felt that the article 'attacked all black and

1. *Guardian,* 11 July 2000.
2. *Wisden Cricket Monthly,* July 1995, pp. 9–10.
3. *Asian Times,* 13 June 1996.

Asian cricketers in England, suggesting there was something biological which just might prevent them playing their hearts out for England.'[4] The determination of Malcolm and DeFreitas to take legal action made clear that coloured cricketers not only found such comments offensive but were prepared to act against them.

Whilst the publication of the Henderson article by one of England's premier cricket magazines can be seen as evidence of an insensitivity to racism within cricket, the reaction to it suggests that many white cricket enthusiasts found the article offensive. David Frith, editor of *Wisden Cricket Monthly,* admitted in the August issue of the magazine that many of Henderson's suppositions and perhaps his 'cold language' had 'caused outrage', which suggests that many had not agreed with Henderson's views, or at least with how they were expressed.[5] Matthew Engel, editor of *Wisden Cricketers' Almanack,* wrote that as the magazine and the *Almanack* shared the same ownership, the publication of the Henderson article had been a mistake and a 'peculiarly painful episode for us'. Describing the Henderson view as 'piffle', Engel did feel that it was a legitimate area of discussion to consider whether some players raised overseas felt sufficient commitment when playing for England but argued that this had nothing to do with race.[6] Following the adverse comments made about the Henderson article, few other articles of a similar tone have appeared in the cricket press, though this could perhaps be due to fears of provoking expensive libel cases. The Henderson article was the catalyst which led to the formation in 1995 of the Hit Racism for Six campaign, a pressure group of cricket enthusiasts who felt that the game was being besmirched by racism and in particular the tendency to pretend that racism was not a problem in cricket.[7]

The attempts to combat racism in the late 1990s can also be explained as part of white English adjustment to the post-colonial world, as a recognition that white supremacy can no longer be taken for granted or rather that non-whites will accept white supremacy. The changing climate of international cricket politics meant that in 1993 England and Australia renounced their powers to veto proposals at the ICC. The poor performance of the England team in the 1990s added to the difficulties of trying to maintain a dominant role for England in the management of international cricket. England has had only a minor role in the development of the Sharjah Tournament as a major international one-day tournament. Jagoman Dalmiya of India, rather than any England representative, is usually credited with the attempts to spread cricket

---

4. Malcolm, D. (1998), *You Guys Are History!,* London: CollinsWillow, pp. 139–45.

5. *Wisden Cricket Monthly,* August 1995, p. 5.

6. *Wisden Cricketers' Almanack 1996,* London: John Wisden, p. 11.

7. See, for instance, Roehampton Institute (n.d.), *Hit Racism for Six: Race and Cricket Today,* London: Centre for Sport Development Research, Roehampton Institute.

as a global international sport, though Chapter Six has shown how in England in 2000 Dalmiya's policy of increasing the number of one-day international competitions, which often seemed to lack importance for players, was seen as a major factor in causing players to accept bribes from Asian bookmakers. The World Cup of 1999, organized and played in England, appeared to be a damp squib compared with that of 1996 played in Asia. Having the ICC administration accommodated at Lord's recognises England's status as the cradle of cricket and of the MCC's former significance in cricket, but given the financial power of cricket in Asia, this looks more and more anachronistic. For a long time cricket seemed to be a survival of imperialist mentalities after the dismantling of empire. Even in the late 1980s and early 1990s Asian cricket administrators were talking of the Raj outlook in the England cricket establishment, by which they presumably meant an assumption that England should be the dominant partner in the management of international cricket. By the end of the twentieth century it was difficult for English cricket not to see that the world had moved on. In 1998 the Women's Cricket Association agreed to merge with the ECB and the MCC decided that women could become members, moves which can be said to reflect an awareness that cricket had to catch up with the times and jettison the impression of being one of the last bastions of old-fashioned reactionaries. In the same way, the greater sensitivity to racism can be seen as a realization that cricket has to come to terms with the post-colonial world in which tradition and whiteness are no longer the basis of authority.

Will Cricket Promote Ethnic Harmony?

Cricket, as a sport played at the international level and recreational level by three of the major ethnic groups in England, has the potential to promote ethnic understanding and harmony, but it is not easy to feel confident that cricket will do this in the early twenty-first century. Cricket's potential to improve racial relations is dependent on the extent of interest in cricket and this could well decline. The reforms in the structure of first-class and recreational cricket are based on the plausible assumption that a stronger England team would stimulate interest in cricket, but it is hard to be optimistic about England's prospects of becoming a major power in international cricket in the near future. Since 1993 all county championship matches have been scheduled for four days in the hope that this would make them a better training ground for test match cricketers, but this has not improved England's test cricket. Establishing premier county leagues in order to raise the standard of club cricket and so improve the supply of players for county clubs, has proved anything but straightforward. In some counties, such as Lancashire, leagues that were already playing cricket of a very high standard have refused to join the proposed hierarchy of leagues. Dividing the county championship into two divisions may make county cricket more competitive but having Saturday as the final day of the four-day county championship matches, the only one when many paying spectators would be able to attend, shows that the administrators of first-class cricket have accepted that county championship cricket will never again attract large numbers of spectators.

The future well-being of cricket depends largely on stimulating interest in the game among the young. The Quick Cricket initiative may be cultivating interest in the game among primary schoolchildren of both sexes and the organization of under-eleven, under-thirteen, under-fifteen and under-seventeen teams by many clubs may be helping to make up for the weak state of cricket at many state secondary schools. What would probably do most to create enthusiasm for cricket among the young would be the emergence of an England cricket super hero, another Ian Botham, who could be a role model, but football's dominance over English sporting culture makes this seem unlikely. Media coverage of football swamps all other sports and there seems little prospect of this being reversed. In 1999 Manchester United's successful quest for the Premiership, FA Cup and European Champions Cup treble pushed into the shadows the cricket world cup, a major international sporting event being held in Britain, although it could have been presented and marketed more effectively and may have attracted more attention had the England team done better. Holding international football competitions in the summer and the relatively late date for the final of the European club championship add to cricket's difficulties in challenging football for public interest. Ian Botham, the last super hero of England cricket, had to choose in his teens between a career in cricket or football. The glamour attached to football and the earnings of even run-of-the-mill first-class footballers, may well mean that the man who could have been the new Botham is now a profess-ional footballer. As the insecurities of professional cricket are as great as those of professional football, the likelihood is that the prospect of higher earnings have led several who could have been effective test cricketers to take up football instead.

The efforts of the ECB's cricket development officers and the determination of county clubs to look at promising cricketers from all levels of cricket could well mean that no, or at least fewer, talented players, and especially those of Asian descent, will be overlooked by county clubs. In the late 1990s it was argued that the Asian enthusiasm for cricket was the great hope of English cricket, but the Asian enthusi-asm for cricket may not last. The previous chapter showed that the playing of cricket among Asians is to a large degree an attempt to assert in England Asian identities reflecting differing languages, ancestral origins and religions. The strength of Asian recreational cricket registers Asian exclusion from 'mainstream' culture in England, although often this has been a self-willed exclusion. It seems likely that among young Asians, education, the workplace and exposure to the general pervasiveness of 'main-stream' popular culture could make maintaining distinctively Asian cultures more difficult. Oral evidence shows that cricket playing seems to be more popular among Asians born in Asia or East Africa than among those born in England. In Birmingham, a marked rise of interest in football among Asians has been noticed. Asian interest in cricket could decline if Asians accept more of 'mainstream' culture and feel less need to stress their Asian identities and traditions. Among African-Caribbeans, the growth of football has been accompanied by fewer playing cricket. Some may argue that the postmodern condition where mass culture and identities are being undermined by a multiplicity of choices over lifestyles and values means that a mainstream culture no longer exists, but accepting this view implies that postmodernism would corrode Asian identities and the desire to express them through playing cricket. If more Asians feel able to play cricket at clubs with good facilities and with predominantly white players and members, this could be seen as evidence of ethnic harmony, that whites and Asians in cricket are showing more respect for each other's cultural traditions. Yet a growth of ethnic harmony could mean that Asians feel less need to defend their cultural values through playing cricket. Ironically a rise in ethnic tolerance could weaken the Asian desire to play cricket whereas a rise in racism could strengthen the need that Asians have felt to reinforce their contacts with others of similar backgrounds and which has often been expressed through playing cricket.

The status of cricket as a sport in which teams representing major ethnic groups in Britain give it the potential for being a force for ethnic understanding, but there is no way of knowing for certain whether cricket will succeed in becoming a bastion of racial harmony. Cricket, like other sports, will never be able to isolate itself from racist pressures in society at large and developments overseas. Totally reliable measures of racism are not possible but there is much to suggest that it is far from absent in Britain. In March 2000 the white journalist Richard Ellis, whose wife is black, wrote

Liberal white Britons must face facts: despite smug boasts of 'aren't we a nice multicultural, all-get-on-together society', it just isn't so. Outside of small pockets, Britain is foul, racist, and deeply prejudiced . . . For every high-profile racist attack, there are a hundred others – some reported, some not. For every physical attack, there are a thousand verbal assaults. And underpinning it all is an insidious, systematic racism that subtly and not so subtly discriminates against black people from cradle to grave.[8]

A racial element can be detected in the debates about asylum seekers to Britain. During the 1999 World Cup spectators coming from Asia but not from Australia and New Zealand, had to prove to immigration officials that they were genuine cricket enthusiasts. Unemployment rates among the ethnic minorities are still higher than those among whites. The MacPherson report into the Stephen Lawrence affair confirmed suspicions of institutional racism in the police service. A sudden, sharp downturn in the economy and accompanying higher levels of unemployment could

8. *Observer*, 26 March 2000.

raise ethnic tension. Following the collapse of communism, many Western governments regard what they call Islamic fundamentalism as the main threat Western
world-wide political and cultural hegemony. An international crisis could make the
plight of Muslims in Britain, many of whom are of South Asian descent, even more
fraught. South Asians who are not Muslims could find prejudices mounting against
them too. Even though cricket would no doubt attempt to be an example of multi-
cultural and multi-ethnic co-operation, it would not be able to insulate itself from
rising levels of ethnic animosities and suspicions in other areas of society. Cricket
was for so long regarded as a mirror of English values, of what many whites imagined
was the best of English culture. Yet during the twentieth century cricket was also
pervaded with assumptions of white supremacy that led to racial prejudice and discrimination. At the end of the twentieth century, cricket in England was showing a
greater awareness of the need to combat racism but only time, and forces outside
the world of cricket, will tell whether cricket can become an effective force for the
attainment of ethnic harmony.

Bibliography

Manuscripts

Cricket Council File: Cancelled South African Cricket Tour to the UK – General File: England and Wales Cricket Board: Lord's Cricket Ground.

Cricket Council File: Lord Caccia's Visit to South Africa 1974 File: England and Wales Cricket Board: Lord's Cricket Ground.

Cricket Council File: South Africa (1) January 1978 – December 1980: England and Wales Cricket Board: Lord's Cricket Ground.

Cricket Council Minutes: England and Wales Cricket Board: Lord's Cricket Ground.

Foreign and Commonwealth Office: UK Policy on Apartheid in Sport: Basil D'Oliveira Affair: FCO 25/709: Public Record Office.

Foreign and Commonwealth Office: Repercussions of Apartheid Policy on Sport, 1 January 1968 – 31 December 1969: FCO 45/310; Public Record Office.

Foreign and Commonwealth Office: Repercussions of Apartheid Policy on Sport: FCO 45/311: Public Record Office.

Foreign and Commonwealth Office: Repercussions of Apartheid Policy on Sport: FCO 45/311: Public Record Office.

MCC Committee Minutes: MCC Library, Lord's Cricket Ground.

Interviews and Telephone Conversations

Mr J. Abrahams, National Cricket Coach, (Northern Region), 16 February 2000.

Mr Ali, Dyadra Dynamo CC, Bolton, 4 October 1993.

Mr and Mrs I. A., Muslims from Bolton, 5 October 1993.

Mr Mohammed Ashraf, secretary of the Arif Sports Birmingham Parks Cricket Association, 22 March 2000.

Mr S. Bulka, secretary of the Maccabi Association CC, London, 22 May 2000.

Mr T. Browne, secretary of the West Indian Cavaliers CC, Nottingham, 18 March 2000.

Mr Taj Butt, Recreational Development Officer, Bradford, 27 February 1997.

Mr Currier, secretary of the Ithica Sports Invitation Cricket League, Birmingham, 24 March 2000.

Mr C. Day, secretary of the Leicester Belgrave Evening League Umpires Section, 19 March 2000.

Mr G. Dawkes, retired county cricketer, 30 December 1997.

Mr M. Edwards, Cricket Development Officer, Surrey Cricket Board, 3 March 2000.

Mr F., a Muslim from Bolton, 4 September 1993.

Mr El Farooz, founder of Blackburn Unity CC, Blackburn, 19 July 1996.

Mr G., Red Rose CC, Bolton, 8 September 1993.

Mr M. Gordon, secretary of Belmont CC, 2 May 2000.

Mr Hanif Helifa, a Muslim from Bradford, 19 May 1999.

Ms M. Harvey, secretary of the Bradford Mutual Sunday School Cricket League, 3 March 1997.

Mr and Mrs K., Muslims from Bolton, 24 March 1993.

Mr R.K., Chach Association CC, Bradford, 5 March 1997.

Mr N. K., Kashmir CC, Bolton, 28 February 1993.

Mr L. Jarvis, chair of the Leicestershire Cricket Association, 19 March 2000.

Mr M., West Bolton CC, 8 September 1993.

Mr K.P., a Hindu from Bolton, 19 September, 1993.

Mr A. Patel, Bharat CC, 13 March 2000.

Mr P., Bolton Indians CC, 6 June 1999.

Mr H. Pollard, secretary of the Leicester Mutual Sunday School League, 17 March 2000.

Mr Q., a Muslim from Blackburn and official of the Pendle Cricket League, 8 July 1996.

Mr A.R., Deane and Derby CC, 2 March 1993.

Mr R., Pendle Cricket League, 11 July 1996.

Mr S., former white player in the Bolton Metropolitan League, 4 August 1998.

Mr Sanderson, secretary of the Belgrave Amateur Evening Cricket League, 20 March 2000.

Mr J. Shaw, secretary of Bolton Cosmopolitan Cricket League, 4 March 1993.

Mr Rudra Singh, Cricket Development Officer, (North-east and North-west Lancashire), 24 February 2000.

Newspapers and Periodicals

Asian Times
Belfast Telegraph
Bolton Evening News
[Bolton Evening News] Buff

Bradford Telegraph and Argus
[Bradford Telegraph and Argus] Asian Eye
Caribbean Times
Cricket
Cricket Life International
Cricketer
Cricketer International
Daily Express
Daily Herald
Daily Mail
Daily Mirror
Daily Telegraph
Dawn
Eastern Eye
Field
Financial Times
Guardian
Independent
Independent on Sunday
Jewish Chronicle
Lancashire Evening Telegraph
Leicester Mail
Leicester Mercury
[Leicester] Sporting Blue
London Review of Books
Manchester Guardian
Mirror
Muslim News
Nelson Leader
New Society
Observer
Pakistan Times
Sticky Wicket
Sun
Sunday Telegraph
Sunday Times
Times, The
Voice
Wisden Cricket Monthly

Books, Articles and Theses

Archer, R. and Bouillon, A. (1982), *The South African Game: Sport and Racism,* London: Zed.

Ahmed, A.S. (1992), *Postmodernism and Islam: Predicament and Promise,* London: Routledge.

Ahmed, A.S. (1997), *Jinnah, Pakistan and Islamic Identity: The Search for Saladin,* London: Routledge.

Akhtar, J. (ed.) (1996), *Pakistanis in Britain in the 1990s & Beyond Conference Report,* Birmingham: Pakistan Forum.

Akram, W. (1998), *Wasim: The Autobiography of Wasim Akram,* London: Judy Piatkus.

Anwar, M. (1996), *British Pakistanis: Demographic, Social and Economic Position,* Coventry: Centre for Research in Ethnic Relations, University of Warwick.

Arlott, J. (1967), *Cricket: The Great Ones: Studies of the Eight Finest Batsmen of Cricket History,* London: Pelham.

Aspinall, A.E. (1912), *The British West Indies: Their History, Resources and Progress,* London: Pitman.

Atherton, M. and Gibson, P. (1995), *A Test of Cricket: Know the Game,* London: Hodder & Stoughton.

Bailey, J. (1989), *Conflicts in Cricket,* London: Kingswood.

Bailey, P., Thorn, P. and Wynne-Thomas, P, P. (1984), *Who's Who of Cricketers,* London: Guild.

Bale, J. (1994), 'Cricket Landscapes and English Eternalism', Paper presented at the Eastern Historical Geography Association, Codrington College, Barbados.

Bale, J., and Maguire, J. (eds) (1994), *The Global Sports Arena: Athletic Talent Migration in an Interdependent World,* London: Cass.

Bannister, J. (1992), *Jack in the Box: A TV Commentator's Diary of England v West Indies,* London: Queen Anne.

Banton, M. (1987), *Racial Theories,* Cambridge: Cambridge University Press.

Banton, M. (1977), *The Idea of Racism,* London: Tavistock.

Bearshaw, B. (1990), *From the Stretford End: The Official History of Lancashire County Cricket Club,* London: Partridge.

Beckles, H. McD. (ed.) (1994), *An Area of Conquest: Popular Democracy and West Indies Cricket Supremacy,* Kingston: Ian Randle.

Beckles, H. McD. and Stoddart, B. (eds) (1995) *Liberation Cricket: West Indian Cricket Culture,* Manchester: Manchester University Press.

Benaud, R. (1998), *Anything But . . . An Autobiography,* London: Hodder and Stoughton.

Berry, S. (1982), *Cricket Wallah: With England in India 1981–2,* London: Hodder and Stoughton.

Berry, S. (1988), *A Cricket Odyssey: England on Tour 1987–88,* London: Pavilion, 1988.

Birbalsingh, F. and Shiwcharan, C. (1988), *Indo-Westindian Cricket,* London: Hansib.

Bird, D. and Lodge, K. (1997), *Dickie Bird: My Autobiography,* London: Hodder and Stoughton.

Birley, D. (1999), *A Social History of English Cricket,* London: Aurum.

Blofeld, H. (1970), *Cricket in Three Moods: Eighteen Months of Test Cricket and the Ways of Life behind It,* London: Hodder and Stoughton.

Blofeld, H. (1998), *Cakes and Bails: Henry Blofeld's Cricket Year,* London: Simon & Shuster.

Bogues, A. (1997), *Caliban's Freedom: The Early Political Thought of C.L.R. James,* London: Pluto.

Bolt, C. (1971), *Victorian Attitudes to Race,* London: Routledge & Kegan Paul.

Booth, D. (1998), *The Race Game: Sport and Politics in South Africa,* London: Cass.

Bose, M. (1990), *A History of Indian Cricket,* London: Deutsch.

Bose, M. (1986), *A Maidan View: The Magic of Indian Cricket,* London: Allen & Unwin.

Bose, M. (1990), *Cricket Voices: Interviews with Mihir Bose,* London: Kingswood, 1990.

Bose, M. (1994), *Sporting Colours: Sport and Politics in South Africa,* London: Robson.

Bose, M. (1996), *The Sporting Alien: English Sport's Lost Camelot,* London: Mainstream.

Botham, I. and Hayter, P. (1997), *The Botham Report,* London: CollinsWillow.

Boycott, G. (1991), *Boycott on Cricket,* London: Corgi.

Boyes, G. (1993), *The Imagined Village: Culture, Ideology and the English Folk Revival,* Manchester: Manchester University Press.

Bradford Commission (1996), *Bradford Commission Report. The Report of an Enquiry into Wider Implications of Public Disorders which Occurred on 9, 10 and 11 June, 1995,* London: HMSO.

Bulmer, M. and Solomos, J. (1999), *Racism,* Oxford: Oxford University Press.

Cardus, N. (1930), *Cricket,* London: Longmans Green.

Cardus, N. (1948 reprint of the 1934 edition), *Good Days,* London: Hart-Davis.

Carrington, B., Chivers, T. and Williams, T. (1987), 'Gender, Leisure and Sport: A Case-study of Young People of South Asian Descent', *Leisure Studies,* 6.

Cashman, R. (1980), *Patrons, Players and the Crowd: The Phenomenon of Indian Cricket,* New Delhi: Orient Longman.

Cashman, R. (1994), 'The Paradox of Pakistani Cricket: Some Initial Reflections', *Sports Historian,* 14 (May).

Cashmore, E. (1982), *Black Sportsmen,* London: Routledge & Kegan Paul.

Cashmore, E. (1990), *Making Sense of Sport,* London: Routledge.

Centre for Sport Development Research (n.d.), *Hit Racism for Six: Race and Cricket Today,* London: Centre for Sport Development Research, Roehampton Institute.

Choueiri, Y.M. (1997), *Islamic Fundamentalism,* London: Pinter.

Cohen, P. and Bains, H.S. (eds) (1988), *Multi-Racist Britain,* London: Macmillan.

Cohen, P. (ed.) (1999), *New Ethnicities, Old Racisms?,* London: Zed.

Collins, T. (1998), *Rugby's Great Split: Class, Culture and the Origins of Rugby League,* London: Cass.

Colls, R. and Dodds, P. (eds) (1986), *Englishness: Politics and Culture 1880–1920,* Beckenham: Croom Helm.

Constantine, L.N. (1933), *Cricket and I,* London: Allan.

Constantine, L. (1946), *Cricket in the Sun,* London: Stanley Paul.

Constantine, L. (1954), *Colour Bar,* London: Stanley Paul.

Crace, J. (1992), *Wasim and Waqar: Imran's Inheritors,* London: Boxtree.

Cronin, M. (1999), *Sport and Nationalism in Ireland: Gaelic Games, Soccer and Irish Identity since 1884,* Dublin: Four Courts.

Cronin, M. and Mayall, D. (eds) (1998), *Sporting Nationalisms: Identity, Ethnicity, Immigration and Assimilation,* London: Cass.

de Mello, A. (1959), *Portrait of Indian Sport,* London: Macmillan.

Daily Worker Cricket Handbook 1950, London: People's Press Printing Society.

Dale, T.F. (1899), 'Polo and Politics', *Blackwoods Magazine,* 165, June.

Dixey, R. (1982), 'Asian Women and Sport: The Bradford Experience', *British Journal of Physical Education,* 13 (4).

D'Oliveira, B. (1968), *D'Oliveira: An Autobiography,* London: Collins.

D'Oliveira, B. (1969), *The D'Oliveira Affair,* London: Collins.

Donald, J. and Rattansi, A. (1992), *'Race', Culture and Difference,* London: Sage and Open University.

Eager, P. and Ross, A. (1988), *West Indian Summer: The Test Series of 1988,* London: Hodder and Stoughton.

ECB Racism Study Group (1999), *Clean Bowl Racism: 'Going Forward Together': A Report on Racial Equality in Cricket,* London: ECB Racism Study Group.

Edwards, H.M., '"Friends for Life": English Cricket's Relationship with Apartheid South Africa during Her Period of Sporting Isolation', University of Southampton BA Dissertation.

Eley, S. and Griffiths (1991), P., *Padwick's Bibliography of Cricket, Volume II,* London: Library Association.

Entine, J. (1999), *Taboo: Why Black Athletes Dominate Sports and Why We Are Afraid to Talk about It,* New York: PublicAffairs.

Fleming, S. (1995), *"Home and Away": Sport and South Asian Male Youth,* Aldershot: Ashgate.

Foot, D. (1985), *Cricket's Unholy Trinity,* London: Stanley Paul.

Fryer, P. (1984), *Staying Power: The History of Black People in Britain,* London: Pluto.

Gardiner, A.G. (1913), *Pillars of Society,* London: Nisbet.

Garner, J. (1988), *'Big Bird' Flying High: The Autobiography of Joel Garner,* London: Barker.

Garvin, J.L. (1934), *The Life of Joseph Chamberlain, Volume 3, 1895–1900,* London: Macmillan.

Gatting, M. and Patmore, A. (1988), *Leading from the Front: The Autobiography of Mike Gatting,* London: Macdonald Queen Anne.

Gavaskar, S. (1980), *Sunny Days: An Autobiography,* Calcutta: Rupa.

Gilchrist, R. (1963), *Hit Me for Six,* London: Stanley Paul.

Giller, N. (1997), *Denis Compton,* London: Deutsch.

Gilroy, P. (1987), *'There Ain't No Black in the Union Jack': The Cultural Politics of Race and Nation,* London: Hutchinson.

Giuseppi, U. (1974), *A Look at Learie Constantine,* London: Nelson.

Gordon, H. (1939), *Background of Cricket,* London: Barker.

Gooch, G. and Keating, F. (1995), *Gooch: My Autobiography,* London: CollinsWillow.

Gooch, G. and Lee, A. (1985), *Out of the Wilderness,* London: Willow.

Grace, W.G. (1980 reprint of the 1899 edition), *'W.G.' Cricketing Reminiscences & Personal Recollections,* London: Hambledon.

Grant, J. (1980), *Jack Grant's Story,* London: Lutterworth.

Green, A. (1997), *'Can't Bat, Can't Bowl, Can't Field': The Best Cricket Writings of Martin Johnson,* London: CollinsWillow.

Greenidge, G. and Symes, P. (1980), *Gordon Greenidge: The Man in the Middle,* Newton Abbot: David & Charles.

Guha, R. (1992), *Wickets in the East: An Anecdotal History,* Delhi: Oxford University Press.

Guha, R. (1998), 'Cricket and Politics in Colonial India', *Past & Present,* 161, (November).

Halko, K.G. (1993), 'The Gujeratis of Bolton: The Leaders and The Led', Open University Ph.D. thesis.

Hain, P. (1971), *Don't Play with Apartheid: The Background to the Stop the Seventy Tour Campaign,* London: Allen & Unwin.

Hargreaves, J. (1994), *Sporting Females: Critical Issues in the History and Sociology of Women's Sports,* London: Routledge.

Hawke, Lord (1924), *Recollections & Reminiscences,* London: Williams & Norgate.

Haworth, D. (1986), *Figures in a Landscape: A Lancashire Childhood,* London: Methuen.

Headlam, C. (1903), *Ten Thousand Miles through India & Burma: An Account of the Oxford University Authentics' Cricket Tour with Mr. K.J. Key in the Year of the Durbar,* London: Dent.

Hignell, A. (1995), *The Skipper: A Biography of Wilf Wooller*, Royston: Limlow.

Hill, J. (1994), 'Reading the Stars: A Post-modernist Approach to Sports History', *Sports Historian*, 14 (May).

Hill, J. (1997), *Nelson: Politics, Economy and Community*, Edinburgh: Keele University Press.

Hill, J. and Williams, J., (eds) (1996), *Sport and Identity in the North of England*, Keele: Keele University Press.

Hobbs, J. (1931), *Playing for England! My Test-cricket Story*, London: Gollancz.

Hobbs, J.B. (1981 reprint of the 1935 edition), *My Life Story*, London: Hambledon.

Hobson, J.A. (1905), *Imperialism: A Study*, London: Allen & Unwin.

Holding, M. and Cozier, T. (1993), *Whispering Death: the Life and Times of Michael Holding*, London: Deutsch.

Hollis, C. (1969), 'Bowled Out', *Spectator*, 18 April.

Holt, R.J. (1989), *Sport and the British: A Modern History*, Oxford: Clarendon.

Holt, R.J. (1996), 'Cricket and Englishness: The Batsman as Hero', *International Journal of the History of Sport*, 13 (1), March.

Home, Lord (1976), *The Way the Wind Blows: An Autobiography*, London: Collins.

Hopps, D. (1996), *Free as a Bird: The Life and Times of Harold 'Dickie' Bird*, London: Robson.

Howat, G. (1975), *Learie Constantine*, London: Allen & Unwin.

Howell, D. (1990), *Made in Birmingham: The Memoirs of Denis Howell*, London: Macdonald Queen Anne.

Humphry, D. (1975), *The Cricket Conspiracy*, London: National Council for Civil Liberties.

Hughes, S. (1997), *A Lot of Hard Yakka*, London: Headline.

Illingworth, R. and Bannister, J. (1996), *One-man Committee: The Controversial Reign of the England Cricket Supremo*, London: Headline.

Jacques-Garvey, A. (1980), *Philosophy and Opinions of Marcus Garvey*, New York: Athenaeum.

James, C.L.R. (1963), *Beyond a Boundary*, London: Hutchinson.

James, C.L.R. (1963), 'Cricket in West Indian Culture', *New Society*, 36 (6 June).

Jarvie, G. (1985), *Class, Race and Sport in South Africa's Political Economy*, London: Routledge & Kegan Paul.

Jarvie, G. (ed.) (1991), *Sport, Racism and Ethnicity*, London: Falmer.

Jarvie, G. and Walker, G. (eds) (1994), *Scottish Sport in the Making of the Nation: Ninety Minute Patriots*, Leicester: Leicester University Press.

Keating, F. (1981), *Another Bloody Day In Paradise!*, London: Deutsch.

Khan, I. and Murphy, P. (1983), *Imran: The Autobiography of Imran Khan*, London: Pelham.

Lamb, A. (1996), *My Autobiography*, London: CollinsWillow.

Lambert, D. (1992), *The History of Leicestershire County Cricket Club*, London: Christopher Helm.

Lapchick, R.E. (1975), *The Politics of Race and International Sport: The Case of South Africa*, Westport: Greenwood.

Lawrence, B. (1995), *Master Class: The Life of George Headley*, Leicester: Polar.

Leaman, O. (1984), *Sit on the Sidelines and Watch the Boys Play: Sex Differentiation in Physical Education*, York: Longman/School Council.

Lee, A. (1996), *Raising the Stakes: The Modern Cricket Revolution*, London: Gollancz.

Lemmon, D. (1987), *Cricket Mercenaries: Overseas Players in English Cricket*, London: Pavilion.

Lewis, B. and Schnapper, D. (1994), *Muslims in Europe*, London: Pinter.

Lewis, R. (1987), *Marcus Garvey: Anti-Colonial Champion*, London: Karia.

Lewis, T. (1991), *Cricket in Many Lands*, London: Hodder and Stoughton.

Licudi, A. and Raja, W. (1997), *Cornered Tigers: A History of Pakistan's Test Cricket*, St. John's: Hansib.

Long, J., Nesti, M., Carrington, B. and Gilson, N. (1997), *Crossing the Boundary: A Study of the Nature and Extent of Racism in Local League Cricket*, Leeds: Leeds Metropolitan University.

Lyons, A. (1988), *Asian Women and Sport*, London: Sports Council.

MacClancy, J. (ed.) (1996), *Sport, Identity and Ethnicity*, Oxford: Berg.

McDonald, I. and Ugra, S. (1998), *Anyone for Cricket? Equal Opportunities and Changing Cricket Cultures in Essex and East London*, London: Roehampton Institute and the Centre for New Ethnicities Research, University of East London.

McDonald, T. (1984), *Viv Richards*, London: Pelham.

McDonald, T. (1985), *Clive Lloyd: The Authorised Biography*, London: Granada.

Magazine, P. (2000), *Not Quite Cricket: The Explosive Story of How Bookmakers Influence The Game Today*, New Delhi: Penguin.

Malcolm, D. (1998), *You Guys Are History!* London: CollinsWillow.

Malik, K. (1996), *The Meaning of Race: Race, History and Culture in Western Society*, London: Macmillan.

Mangan, J.A. (ed.) (1988), *Pleasure, Profit and Proselytism: British Culture and Sport at Home and Abroad, 1700–1914*, London: Cass.

Mangan, J.A. (ed.) (1992), *The Cultural Bond: Sport, Empire, Society*, London: Cass.

Mangan, J.A. (1998), *The Games Ethic and Imperialism: Aspects of the Diffusion of an Ideal*, London: Cass.

Manley, M. (1988), *A History of West Indies Cricket*, London: Guild.

Marqusee, M. (1994), *Anyone But England: Cricket and the National Malaise*, London: Verso.

Marqusee, M. (1997), *War Minus the Shooting: A Journey Through South Asia during Cricket's World Cup*, London: Mandarin.

Marshall, M. (1987), *Gentlemen & Players: Conversations with Cricketers*, London: Grafton.

Martin-Jenkins, C. (1994), *The Spirit of Cricket: A Personal Anthology*, London: Faber and Faber.

Mason, D. (1995), *Race and Ethnicity in Modern Britain*, Oxford: Oxford University Press.

Mason, P. (1971), *Patterns of Dominance*, London: Oxford University Press.

Mason, T. (1988), *Sport in Britain*, London: Faber and Faber.

Mason, T. (ed.) (1989), *Sport in Britain: A Social History*, Cambridge: Cambridge University Press.

May, P. and Melford, M. (1985), *A Game Enjoyed*, London: Stanley Paul.

Midwinter, E. (1992), *The Illustrated History of County Cricket*, London: Kingswood.

Miles, R. (1989), *Racism*, London: Routledge.

Moorhouse, G. (1984), *To The Frontier*, London: Hodder and Stoughton.

Mulvaney, D.J. (1967), *Cricket Walkabout: The Australian Aboriginal Cricketers on Tour 1867–8*, London: Melbourne University Press.

Murphy, P. (1989), *Declarations*, Letchworth: Ringpress.

Murray, B. (1985), *The Old Firm: Sectarianism, Sport and Society in Scotland*, Edinburgh, Donald.

Murray, B.K. (1999), 'The D'Oliveira Affair 1968/9: Thirty Years After', Paper presented to the Twelfth Bi-ennial Conference of the Australian Society for Sports History, Queenstown, New Zealand, 1–5 February.

Murray, G., Hirst, F.W. and Hammond, J.L. (1900), *Liberalism and the Empire: Three Essays*, London: Johnson.

Nauright, J. (1997), *Sport, Cultures and Identities in South Africa*, London: Leicester University Press.

Nelson Cricket Club (at Seedhill) 1878–1978 Centenary Brochure (n.p., n.d.).

Norrie, D. (1997), *Athers: The Authorised Biography of Michael Atherton*, London: Headline.

Odendaal, A. (ed.) (1977), *Cricket in Isolation: The Politics of Race and Cricket in South Africa*, Cape Town: Odendaal.

Oslear, D. and Bannister, J. (1996), *Tampering with Cricket*, London: CollinsWillow.

Padwick, E.W. (1984), *A Bibliography of Cricket*, London: Library Association and J.W. McKenzie.

Panyani, P. (ed.) (1996), *Racial Violence in Britain in the Nineteenth and Twentieth Centuries*, London: Leicester University Press.

Raiji, V. (1986), *India's Hambledon Men*, Bombay: Tyeby.

Raiji, V. (1963), *Ranji: The Legend and the Man*, Bombay: V. Raiji.

Reeve, D. (1996), *Winning Ways*, London: Boxtree, 1996.

Rich, P.B. (1986), *Race and Empire in British Politics*, Cambridge: Cambridge University Press.

Ross, A. (1983), *Ranji: Prince of Cricketers*, London: Collins.

Runnymede Trust (1997), *Islamophobia: A Challenge for Us All: Report of the Runnymede Trust Commission on British Muslims and Islamophobia,* London: Runnymede Trust.

Russell, D. (1996), 'Sport and Identity: The Case of Yorkshire County Cricket Club, 1890–1939', *20 Century British History,* 7 (2), 1996.

Russell, D. (1997), *Football and The English: A Social History of Association Football in England, 1863–1995,* Preston: Carnegie.

Russell, J. (1997), *Unleashed,* London: CollinsWillow.

Said, E. (1978), *Orientalism,* London: Routledge.

Sandiford, K.A.P. (1994), *Cricket and the Victorians,* Aldershot: Scolar.

Savidge, M. and McLellan, A. (1995), *Real Quick: A Celebration of the West Indies Pace Quartet,* London: Blandford.

Searle, C. (1990), 'Race before Wicket: Cricket, Empire and the White Rose', *Race & Class,* 31 (3), (January–March).

Searle, C. (1993), 'Cricket and the Mirror of Racism', *Race & Class,* 34 (3), January–March.

Sewell, E.H.D. (1931), *Cricket Up-to-date,* London: Murray.

Sewell, E.H.D. (1945), *An Outdoor Wallah,* London: Stanley Paul.

Shawcroft, J. (1989), *The Official History of Derbyshire County Cricket Club,* London: Christopher Helm.

Sheppard, D. (1964), *Parson's Pitch,* London: Hodder and Stoughton.

Sissons, R. and Stoddart, B. (1984), *Cricket and Empire: The 1932–33 Bodyline Tour of Australia,* London: Allen & Unwin.

Smith, D. and Williams, G. (1980), *Fields of Praise: The Official History of the Welsh Rugby Union 1881–1981,* Cardiff: University of Wales Press.

Snow, P. (1998), *The Years of Hope: Cambridge, Colonial Administration in the South Seas,* London: Radcliffe.

Sports Council (1980), *Sport in South Africa: Report of the Sports Council's Fact-finding Delegation,* London: Sports Council.

Standing, P.C. (1903), *Ranjitsinhji, Prince of Cricket,* Bristol: Arrowsmith.

Steen, R. (1988), *This Sporting Life: Cricket: Inside Tales from the Men Who Made the Game What It Is Today,* Newton Abbot: David & Charles.

Steen, R. (1993), *Desmond Haynes: Lion of Barbados,* London: Witherby.

Stoddart, B. and Sandiford, K.A.P. (eds) (1998), *The Imperial Game: Cricket, Culture and Society,* Manchester: Manchester University Press.

Stollmeyer, J. (1983), *Everything under the Sun: My Life in West Indies Cricket,* London: Stanley Paul.

Streeton, R. (1981), *P.G.H. Fender: A Biography,* London: Faber & Faber.

Sugden, J. and Bairner, A. (1993), *Sport, Sectarianism and Society in a Divided Ireland,* Leicester: Leicester University Press.

Swanton, E.W. (1985), *Gubby Allen: Man of Cricket,* London: Hutchinson/Stanley Paul.

Swanton, E.W., Plumptre, G. and Woodcock, J. (eds) (1986), *Barclays World of Cricket: The Game from A to Z,* London: Guild.

Tatz, C. (1996), *Obstacle Race: Aborigines in Sport,* Sydney: University of New South Wales Press.

Thompson, F. (1927), *Essays of To-day and Yesterday,* London: Harrap.

Toms, M. and Fleming, S. (1995), '"Why Play Cricket . . . ?": A Preliminary Analysis', *Sports Historian,* 15, (May).

Verma, G. and Darby, D. (1994), *Winners and Losers: Ethnic Minorities in Sport and Recreation,* London: Falmer.

Vasili, P.(1998), *The First Black Footballer: Arthur Wharton 1865–1930: An Absence of Memory,* London: Cass.

Walcott, C. and Scovell, B. (1999), *Sixty Years on the Back Foot: The Cricketing Life of Sir Clyde Walcott,* London: Gollancz.

Walton, J.L. (1899), 'Imperialism', *Contemporary Review,* LXXV.

Welldon, J.E.C. (1906), 'The Training of an English Gentleman in the Public Schools,' *Nineteenth Century,* 60, (September).

Wells, D. (1896), 'Great Britain and the United States: Their True Relations', *North American Review,* CCCCLXII, (April).

Whimpress, B. (1999), *Passport to Nowhere: Aborigines In Australian Cricket,* Sydney: Walla Walla.

Wild, N. (1974), *The Greatest Show on Earth,* Nelson: Hendon.

Wild, R. (1934), *The Biography of Colonel His Highness Shri Sir Ranjitsinhji Vibhaji, Maharaja Sam Saheb of Nawanagar, GCSI, GBE, KCIE,* London: Rich & Cowan.

Wilde, S. (1990), *Ranji: A Genius Rich and Strange,* London: Kingswood.

Wilde, S. (1995), *Letting Rip: The Fast-Bowling Threat from Lillee to Waqar,* London: Gollancz/Witherby.

Williams, J.A. (1992), 'Cricket and Society in Bolton between the Wars', Lancaster University Ph.D. thesis.

Williams, J. (1994), 'South Asians and Cricket in Bolton', *Sports Historian,* 14, (May).

Williams, J. (1999), *Cricket and England: A Cultural and Social History of the Inter-war Years,* London: Cass.

Williams, J. (2000), 'Asians, Cricket and Ethnic Relations in Northern England', *Sporting Traditions,* 16 (2).

Willis, B. and Murphy, P. (1981), *The Cricket Revolution: Test Cricket in the 1970s,* London: Sidgwick & Jackson.

Wolstenholme, G. (1992), *The West Indian Tour of England 1906,* published by the author.

Woodward, K. (ed.) (1997), *Identity and Difference,* London: Sage.

Woolnough, B. (1983), *Black Magic: England's Black Footballers,* London: Pelham.

Wynne-Thomas, P. (1997), *The History of Cricket: From the Weald to the World,* London: Stationery Office.

Yeboah, S.K. (1988), *The Ideology of Racism,* London: Hansib.

Index

Index